HARNESSING THE SKY

HARNESSING THE SKY

★ ★ ★

**Frederick "Trap" Trapnell, the U.S. Navy's
Aviation Pioneer, 1923–52**

*Paul –
Keep flying high!
Fritz*

Frederick M. Trapnell Jr. and Dana Trapnell Tibbitts

Dana Tibbitts

**Naval Institute Press
Annapolis, Maryland**

Naval Institute Press
291 Wood Road
Annapolis, MD 21402

Library of Congress Cataloging-in-Publication Data

Trapnell, Frederick M., Jr.
  Harnessing the sky : Frederick "Trap" Trapnell, the U.S. Navy's aviation pioneer,
1923–52 / Frederick M. Trapnell Jr. and Dana Trapnell Tibbitts.
    pages cm
  Includes bibliographical references and index.
  ISBN 978-1-61251-848-0 (alk. paper) — ISBN 978-1-61251-855-8 (ebook) 1. Trap-
nell, Frederick M., 1902–1975. 2. United States. Navy—Aviation—Biography. 3.
Test pilots—United States—Biography. 4. Fighter pilots—United States—Biogra-
phy. 5. Admirals—United States—Biography. 6. United States. Navy—Aviation—
History—20th century. 7. Airplanes, Military—United States—Flight testing—
History—20th century. 8. United States. Navy—Officers—Biography. 9. World War,
1939–1945—Aerial operations, American. I. Tibbitts, Dana Trapnell. II. Title. III.
Title: "Trap" Trapnell, the U.S. Navy's aviation pioneer, 1923–52. IV. Title: Frederick
"Trap" Trapnell, the U.S. Navy's aviation pioneer, 1923–52.
  V63.T76T73 2015
  359.9'4092—dc23
  [B]
                                                                        2015006810

∞ Print editions meet the requirements of ANSI/NISO z39.48-1992 (Permanence of
Paper).
Printed in the United States of America.

23 22 21 20 19 18 17 16 15   9 8 7 6 5 4 3 2 1
First printing

We dedicate this book to graduates of the U.S. Naval Test Pilot School

CONTENTS

ILLUSTRATIONS

PREFACE

Little has been written about the development of U.S. Navy flight testing through the 1930s and 1940s, or the men who formulated flight test standards for precision and accuracy that prevail today. Nor would this story be complete without a close look at the man whose leadership in flight testing paved the way for U.S. Navy air supremacy during World War II and for modern carrier aviation in the second half of the century.

Trap would undoubtedly have told his own tale in fewer words than this book offers. When asked for a personal biographical sketch for his inauguration as an honorary fellow of the Society of Experimental Test Pilots, he wrote with typical wry understatement:

> *I was born naked in 1902 in Elizabeth, New Jersey, and attended Pingry School in that town and the Naval Academy—from which I graduated without distinction in 1923. This led to serving 29 years in the United States Navy, 26 of which were in the semi-respectable status of a Naval Aviator. Practically all of my shore duty was in Flight Test where I became familiar with the lingo and some of the primitive procedures of the 30s and 40s. I commanded a couple of Patrol Squadrons and the carriers USS Breton and USS Coral Sea—without going aground—noticeably. So in 1951 I became a Rear Admiral. In 1952 the medicos caught up with me and grounded and retired me.*
>
> *Since 1953 I have been loosely associated with Grumman Aircraft and have resided in Long Island. I am very happy in my status as an Honorary Fellow of SETP, where I can harmlessly indulge my opposition to any further progress in any direction.*
>
> *Very sincerely,*
> *Frederick M. Trapnell*

These two paragraphs say as much about the man as he thought anyone needed to know. From the vantage point of nearly four decades since his passing, however, what was simply a way of life for this trail-blazing experimental test pilot has come into focus as a vital piece of our history, the story of a generation of early aviators that is poorly documented. We recount this history at the urging of those who mark Trap's legacy as paramount in a century of U.S. naval aviation.

Most of Trap's work was highly classified, and, like many of his generation, he was reticent to talk about himself or his work. He eschewed attention or approbation for milestones achieved in the line of duty and recoiled from self-promotion, drawing little gratification from the adulation of others. He loved what he did as its own reward and sought neither recognition nor celebrity.

We have relied on a surprisingly thin historical record to supplement personal recollections and anecdotal reports in capturing the lifework of this remarkable man. A single box of salvaged personal items including log books, letters, a lock of red-gold baby hair, and photographs reaching back more than one hundred years helped us reconstruct the life of a person who traveled light and shunned both clutter and sentimentality.

ACKNOWLEDGMENTS

We wish to thank the many people who helped us through the struggle to create this manuscript. We owe a debt of gratitude to Bill Allen of Allen Airways in San Diego and his wife Claudia, as well as to Dave Seeman, formerly of Grumman Aircraft, both of whom have been strong supporters of our effort from the outset. Dick Hallion and Ken Weir not only applied their aviation and flight-testing expertise to reviewing the manuscript but also gave us strong support for this project. Professional editors Tom Trapnell and Madeline Adams reviewed and helped us revise the manuscript.

We are indebted to the librarians and archivists who dug deep into their repositories for us and helped guide our many hours of research in their establishments: Janis Jorgensen of the Naval Institute, Joe Gordon of the Naval History and Heritage Command, Phil Edwards and Brian Nicklas of the Smithsonian Aviation Library, Charles Johnson and Nathaniel Patch at the National Archives, Paula Smith of the Society of Experimental Test Pilots, Peter Merlin of NASA Dryden, Hill Goodspeed at the National Naval Aviation Museum, and Richard Harris of the U.S. Naval Test Pilot School.

Two retired Navy rear admirals, Edward Feightner and Bill Harris, shared with us some interesting and relevant flying experiences, and former seaman Willie Lagarde, who served on the USS *Yorktown* with Trap, gave us much encouragement and a firsthand perspective of war at sea. Former Grumman flight test engineer John Torkelsen was an invaluable catalyst for telling Trap's story. Margaret Davis Martin and Pamela Hyland provided photos and some history of their respective fathers, Bill Davis and John Hyland. Finally we wish to thank our editors at the Naval Institute Press, particularly Tom Cutler, who persevered to make this book a reality.

We also want to thank others who contributed to the publication and promotion of this vital story: Mark and Kay Barchas, Robert and Patricia Booth, Bob and Diane Claypool, Doug and Laura Debs, Andy and Eleanor Doty, Carl and Franziska Dubac, Micki Farrell, Fred and Joy Frye, Lisa Horton, Louise W. King, Bud and Pat Lester, Gerald MacKay, Ron and Hilde Rundell, Elmo and Joan Sanders, Sande Stuart, Jim and Mary Jane Weisler, and John and Sara Wells.

Finally, we want recognize our respective spouses, Nomi Trapnell and Brett Tibbitts, for their unflagging effort and support through this five-year journey.

HARNESSING THE SKY

CHAPTER 1

★ ★ ★

DARK STORM EASTWARD

Naval Air Station Anacostia, D.C., November 15, 1940

From his second-story office window, Lt. Cdr. Frederick "Trap" Trapnell, senior flight test officer for the U.S. Navy, surveyed the airfield, brooding. The Navy was being sucked into a war for which it was totally unprepared.[1] American carriers harboring deck-loads of biplanes told the story: It would take years before the Navy could put fighters on its flight decks to match the Spitfires and Messerschmitts dueling over Great Britain. To make matters worse, planners now pegged September 1941—less than a year away—as the time by which U.S. military forces must be ready to go to war.[2]

Sending young Americans out in obsolescent aircraft against the superbly equipped and battle-hardened Luftwaffe verged on criminal. Trapnell was resolute: It would not happen on his watch.

Parked outside on the apron was Vought's XF4U-1 Corsair. Trap was to take it up this morning for an official speed test to demonstrate the prototype's ability to achieve the magic four hundred miles per hour.[3] While putting little stock in breaking speed records, he understood Rear Adm. John Towers' ambition as chief of the Bureau of Aeronautics to set the world record with one of his Navy fighters. It would mean prestige for the service and perhaps additional funding from Congress.

As Trap stepped out of the hangar, the early morning light caught the sleek profile of the Corsair, glinting off the inverted gull wings and smooth, silver-skinned fuselage that wrapped the most powerful airplane engine anywhere in service. Indeed this was an elegant, racy machine. Airplanes that fly good usually look good, he told himself; too bad the reverse wasn't true.[4]

He zipped his flight suit against the crisp bite of the winter morning and strode out to begin his preflight check. Walking around the machine, he noted the temporary changes made in preparation for today's speed run. The radio

1. Vought XF4U-1 Corsair fighter prototype, which Trap flew at
402 mph in an official Navy speed trial

Official U.S. Navy photo, Naval History and Heritage Command

mast and antenna had been removed, and the hand-holds at the wingtips and gun ports in the leading edge of the wing were covered with tape, all to minimize drag.[5]

The ground check complete, Trap clambered into the cockpit and was soon turning onto the takeoff runway, where he opened the throttle wide and released the brakes. This airplane wanted to go; acceleration pressed him into the seatback harder than any aircraft he'd ever flown.

Twenty minutes later he was at 22,500 feet, approaching a theodolite range set up by the National Advisory Committee for Aeronautics on the shore of the Chesapeake Bay to precisely measure the speed of airplanes in flight.[6] He could just pick out the range markers on the ground as he brought the Corsair around to line up for his first run, and then he opened the throttle wide. The airspeed meter told him the airplane was moving fast. The crew on the ground would be scrambling to calculate and cross-check their readings. As planned, he made four passes over the range, two in each direction to correct for windage.

Testing complete, he eased the throttle back to cruising power and headed for Anacostia. Achieving four hundred miles per hour would please the admiral, but Trap knew it would not make this Corsair a satisfactory fighter.[7]

Fighter planes were naval aviation's Achilles' heel. Outdated biplanes were slowly being replaced by the new Brewster and Grumman monoplane fighters just coming into service, but Trap was under no illusion: neither airplane stood a chance against the German Luftwaffe.

Any way Trap looked at it, the situation was grim. The Navy had just received brand new fighter prototypes from Bell Aircraft, Grumman, and Vought, but they were only prototypes, still years away from being ready for service. More alarming to Trap, testing had already demonstrated that, like the Corsair, none of these planes in their current configuration was acceptable as a Navy fighter; they were, however, the only prospects on the horizon.

Isolationists in Congress had prevailed for years to keep the United States out of "foreign entanglements," advocating a military policy that emphasized continental defense while relying on the Europeans to contain Hitler. As a result, military budgets had withered dangerously.[8]

But that tide had now turned. The fall of France in May had ended all hope of European containment. When 350,000 British soldiers rescued from Dunkirk left their equipment and weapons behind on French beaches, little remained to deter a German invasion of Britain. Against all odds, the British had managed to hold off the Luftwaffe in what Winston Churchill called the Battle of Britain; now, however, German bombers were routinely plastering English cities, their rampage broadcast in front-page photos showing London ablaze night after night. This very morning, headlines on Trap's desk decried the frightful destruction wrought just the previous evening by four hundred German bombers on the city of Coventry and its magnificent cathedral. The blitz was a no-holds-barred attempt to break the will of the British people, and Trap saw this cloud of destruction rising like a thunderhead on the eastern horizon.

The deluge of German troops, tanks, and airplanes flooding across Europe had swept aside isolationist arguments and sent military strategists scrambling to ready U.S. forces for war. Even now, they feverishly laid contingency plans for the inevitable. Keeping a wary eye on Japanese thrusts into China, the Navy had begun ratcheting up its rusty war machine in preparation for deploying across the Atlantic to face a German foe.

In a drive to get naval aviation forces up to par, the Bureau of Aeronautics had brought Trap back to Anacostia to shore up their test and development efforts. His job was to evaluate all new Navy airplanes, collaborate with manufacturers to fix their problems, and help the Navy secure a winning hand of warplanes. Navy brass was counting on this new senior flight test officer to pull a rabbit out of a hat and bring forth a superior fighter plane for what was shaping up to be a violent air war. But on this brisk November morning, the situation remained dire.

As he turned the Corsair in for landing approach over the Anacostia River, he caught sight of two sailboats below, racing in tight formation, sails taut with a brisk wind off the Potomac. An exhilarating morning to be out on the water, he thought. The Navy had become his life, but the sight of the sailboats transported him back to where his journey had begun.

CHAPTER 2

★ ★ ★

THE LAUNCHING, 1902–25

Frederick Trapnell's love affair with the sea began early. In one of his first letters, written with thick pencil and crude penmanship, the eight-year-old describes his harrowing trip down the New Jersey shoreline with young shipmate Tom. A sudden gale catches them by surprise, hurling their skiff onto the rocks and throwing young Fred overboard, where he wonders briefly if he might drown. But it would take more than a minor shipwreck to squelch this young sailor's passion for the exhilaration and rigors of the sea-going life.[1]

Fred's father, Benjamin, a successful corporate attorney in New York City, came from a prominent West Virginia family. After dropping out of the U.S. Naval Academy, he turned to law, building his reputation as a sharp-tongued and sometimes incendiary lawyer who served as U.S. attorney for West Virginia during President Cleveland's second term.[2] In 1899, he married Ada Probasco of Urbana, Ohio, and the couple settled in Elizabeth, New Jersey, raising four children in a comfortable home on Westminster Avenue. Their firstborn, Nicholas, was two years older than Frederick, who was born July 9, 1902. Wally and Evelyn arrived in 1903 and 1908 respectively.

Benjamin was tough on his boys and held them to rigorous standards of personal conduct, demanding the truth, the whole truth, and nothing but the truth. No quarter was given for economizing on facts or whining about circumstance. They were to solve their own problems without crying or complaint. A high premium was placed on their academic performance. While they enjoyed the privilege of certain comforts and educational opportunities, Benjamin permitted no arrogance or air of superiority. Rather, they were to respect their elders and learn from hard-working people in all walks of life.

Fred and Nicholas attended the Pingry School, whose program emphasized scholastics and moral instruction for boys. Moved ahead by one grade early on, Fred was the youngest in his class and less mature and physically developed than his peers, but he was smart enough to hold his own academically, and he always placed near the top of his class.

Following Pingry, the brothers enrolled at the Stevens School in Hoboken, the high school affiliate of the prestigious Stevens Institute of Technology, which Nicholas would later attend. In addition to rigorous preparation for college, Stevens' emphasis on science and mechanical engineering for a new generation made the school an ideal fit for the Trapnell boys.

Although a capable student, Fred tended toward shyness during his teenage years and loathed the braggadocio prevalent among his peers. He shunned competitive sports and the social circuit, preferring the camaraderie of his brothers and a few close friends. When not in school, he and Nicholas could be found at the docks, shipyard, marina, or over at the Reading Railroad yard.

Fred's interests inclined more toward ships and the sea, especially sailing vessels, but like his brother he was also drawn to the steam locomotives that traveled the tracks just blocks from their house. The allure of the occasional square-rigged ship or small fore-and-aft rigged schooners and racing yachts that slipped through the Verrazano Narrows, visible from their house, was more intriguing than the big steamships that regularly plied New York harbor. Fred learned to sail early and by the age of nine or ten became adept with his own skiff. Drawn by the salty tang of sea air, the wind in his sails, the rush of the water along the hull, and the spray breaking over the bow, he was never more in his element than out on the open sea.

Noting his middle son's affinity for nautical design and mechanics, Benjamin planned a day trip to the Brooklyn Navy Yard in the summer of 1914. Twelve-year-old Fred wrote a detailed account of their tour, which concluded, "I enjoyed the day more than any other day in my life." This excursion inspired Fred's dream to one day become a naval architect and design U.S. Navy ships.[3]

Fred became a familiar sight around a boat yard in Elizabethport on Newark Bay, where he studied the shapes of hulls and the effects of design and construction on their performance under sail. He learned the intricacies of ropes and fixtures, rigging and fittings. He queried sailors and riggers, observing their work with an eagle eye, trawling for the principles of seaworthy ships and the practices of the men who built them, revelations more enthralling to him than any schoolroom subject.

The Trapnell boys frequented the Reading Railroad shops, gravitating toward the railroad locomotives and engineers, switchmen and firemen, men keen to share their craft with avid youngsters and offering rides in the cab when schedules allowed. The sheer power of steam at work caught Fred's imagination. An engine able to generate enough power to move a mechanical colossus across entire continents was a thing of beauty and inspiration.

On slow afternoons, the brothers could be found at the locomotive shops, where huge overhead cranes trundled boilers, wheel sets, or entire locomotives from one workstation to another. The fitters and mechanics fielded their questions over the clang of rivet hammers and the hiss of welding torches. The blazing ring of fire used to heat steel tires so they could be mounted on drive wheels captured their attention, as did the massive sleeping engines, their steam and fire strangely still. For Fred, this was real life, far more compelling than anything at the local picture show.

THE BUDDING NAVAL ARCHITECT

Through his teenage years, Fred crewed frequently on larger sailboats, often in races, where he developed expertise in sail handling and the nuances of trimming sails and rigging to achieve peak performance. He became adept at sailing in heavy weather under shortened canvas, understanding that a key indicator of a boat's performance was how well she could sail toward the wind, to windward in sailor's parlance. Under this condition, air flowing over the sails generates lift in the upwind direction and, properly configured, the hull, keel, and rudder work against the sea to push a sailboat to windward. These hydrodynamic insights laid vital groundwork for his later instinctive grasp of aerodynamics.

Fred demonstrated exceptional talent as a pen-and-pencil artist from an early age; his sketches depicted ships and locomotives with striking accuracy, proportion, and attention to detail.[4] Not only did he become a skilled mechanical draftsman, but he also wrote well: clearly, descriptively, and to the point. Fred soon set his sights on attending the U.S. Naval Academy and becoming a naval architect.

Inspired by *Motor Boating* magazine's notice of a national open amateur competition for "My Ideal Auxiliary" in the summer of 1918, sixteen-year-old Fred put his concepts for a cruising sailboat on paper.[5] His entry prescribed a thirty-foot yawl and included the requisite outboard profile, arrangement plans, sections, construction details, lines, and a table of offsets—specifications expected from a professional yacht designer.[6] On February 4, 1919, Fred received a welcome letter with a $35 check from the *Motor Boating* editor in chief announcing, "You will probably be pleased to hear that we are planning to use your Ideal Auxiliary design in the March issue of *Motor Boating*."[7]

A few days later, he sat for the six-hour qualifying examination for appointment to the U.S. Naval Academy.

DONNING THE BLUE AND GOLD

Fred entered the Naval Academy in July of the same year, just two days prior to his seventeenth birthday. In keeping with school tradition, he was initially dubbed "Slim" and "Freddy." But the moniker that stuck through the rest of his life was "Trap."

The Naval Academy class yearbook of 1923, *The Lucky Bag*, commented on the "power of his ready smile." As early shyness gave way to settled confidence, Trap became more outgoing and developed an easy charm that opened the way to larger spheres of influence. As *The Lucky Bag* noted, his affability made an impression on more than just the midshipmen. "He's handsome, tall and gracefully thin, and has that romantic, wavy brown hair that sets hearts fluttering. But he's decently modest about it, so we grant it to him without malice."[8]

2. Trap as a midshipman, from
The Lucky Bag, 1923

*Official U.S. Navy photo, personal files of
Frederick Trapnell Jr.*

Though something of a slow starter with the female set, this changed as Trap outgrew his awkward adolescence and began to fill out the blue and gold uniform. He also forged friendships that would endure for the rest of his life, including those with classmates Arleigh Burke and George Anderson, both of whom went on to become chief of naval operations.

Despite rigorous scholastic preparation, Trap found the academics at the Academy challenging and the competition fierce. He also learned that to become a naval architect in the U.S. Navy required him to graduate in the top 5 percent of his class, a standard he was unable to achieve, so despite his instinctive grasp of ship engineering and steam power technology, this ambition was beyond his reach. Nonetheless he graduated in the upper third of his class.[9]

INTO THE FLEET

Upon graduation from the Naval Academy, Trap was commissioned an ensign on June 8, 1923, and reported on board the battleship USS *California*, flagship of the U.S. battle fleet, where he concentrated on becoming a first-rate line officer.[10]

He was assigned as division officer responsible for some thirty enlisted sailors. While not generally college educated, many were considerably older than he and had spent a number of years in the Navy. They reluctantly accepted this twenty-one-year-old kid fresh out of the Academy as their superior officer, although the more seasoned men fully expected to bear the brunt of the young man's immaturity and bravado. But something happened early in Trap's tenure that garnered their respect.

Battleships like *California* had a double hull below the water line to provide protection from torpedo strikes. Two thick layers of steel, separated by a sixteen-inch zone of airspace, surrounded the ship. Protecting the surfaces of this interhull zone required periodic cleaning and repainting of both sides of the narrow gap between hulls. Working in these dank, dark confines presented a psychological struggle; for anyone with the slightest claustrophobia, it could be terrifying.

A working party from Trap's division was assigned to repair and refinish a section of the interhull zone on *California*, which they accessed through a small hatch in the inner hull. The chief petty officer leading the party would make specific work assignments. In view of the unusual psychological stress associated with this task, a commissioned officer was also required to accompany the group. Though not expected to work, he would oversee the operation and preserve discipline. Ensign Trapnell was to be the overseeing officer.

While not subject to many fears, Trap was a man who thrived in wide open spaces. He had never faced prolonged physical confinement like the tight interval between hulls, nor did he relish the prospect; but he had to set an example. Furthermore, he thought it senseless to go in there simply to supervise, so he explained to the bewildered chief that he would carry a hammer and chisel and should be given a regular work-party assignment along with the others.

The men clambered through the hatch into the work area and squirmed like spelunkers through the dark between the steel faces. The chief had made assignments, and Trap set to work with his chisel, hoping to shake the crushing sense of entombment. The work party continued in two-hour shifts, taking short breaks out in the open where the men smoked silently before returning between hulls for another session. They worked with dogged determination, along with their new division officer, until the sweat soaked through their clothes.

Trap's first stint between hulls wasn't his last. He was back in those dark recesses more times than he cared to count. Nor did it get any easier. But it did earn him the respect of his crew. Word got around. This officer was in the hellhole chipping paint with the rest of his men.[11]

DIOMEDIA EXULANS

In June 1924, after a year as line officer on board *California*, Trap transferred to USS *Marblehead*, a brand new light cruiser, where he went to work getting her ready for sea trials. After her commissioning and shakedown cruise, she headed for the southern Pacific Ocean to visit Tahiti, Samoa, and Australia.[12] This cruise ignited Trap's interest in aviation.[13]

His fascination with flight harked back to early observations of the birds that accompanied his seaborne journeys, dipping, diving and riding the same currents that filled his mainsail. Just as he had pondered how the shapes of sails and hulls affected the movement of his ship through the water, Trap had also contemplated the aerodynamics of sustainable flight.

When *Marblehead* arrived in the southern oceans, Trap came across a creature he had only read about in books, the great wandering albatross, which bore the scientific name *Diomedia exulans*. His first encounter with *Diomedia* took his breath away as he suddenly became aware of a broad shadow cast across the deck before him. Looking up, he saw a graceful white winged silhouette against a deep blue sky, seeming to hang in midair, keeping abeam the ship's masthead in a nearly motionless shallow glide, effortlessly following the ship for what seemed like miles without so much as a flutter of its considerable wings.

Trap was spellbound. The mystery of the albatross' nearly motionless flight had puzzled sailors for centuries. *Diomedia* was the most exquisite thing he had ever seen, the perfect flying machine. Unlike a sailboat bound to the water surface, it floated freely in space. How would it feel to fly like that winged albatross? The vision of this remarkable seabird would haunt him for the rest of his life.[14]

THE AVIATION BUG

Trap's emerging interest in aviation was piqued by *Marblehead*'s aircraft. She carried two float planes, used primarily as scouts that flew well beyond the ship's field of vision to locate the enemy, extending the fleet's range of visibility and effective firepower. Each airplane was manned by a pilot and radio operator, launched by catapult amidships, and recovered from water landings by a crane. Trap paid close attention to these operations and queried the pilots at length. He was intrigued.

Airplanes had become a common sight in battle fleet operations. In 1924, USS *Langley*, carrying eight aircraft, joined the fleet as the Navy's first aircraft carrier.[15] By sheer numbers, her airplanes substantially expanded the fleet's scouting and spotting capabilities. Although interesting, this was hardly the sort of mission to inspire a career change for Trap. The Navy, however, was building two huge new aircraft carriers, USS *Saratoga* and USS *Lexington*. Talk among *Marblehead*'s aviators centered not only on these new ships but on their remarkable airplanes that could deliver a bomb or torpedo powerful enough to destroy a capital ship.[16]

As he considered the implications of this innovation, something stirred inside him. A carrier-based aircraft with a big bomb or torpedo would be a formidable weapon in its own right, one that could reach far beyond the range of even the biggest battleship guns. Such aircraft might not only revolutionize naval operations but might move aviation into a lead role as a new Navy striking force. The lure of this proposition proved irresistible. He applied for aviation duty.

CHAPTER 3

★ ★ ★

NAVAL AVIATION 1911–26, HISTORICAL INTERLUDE

Naval aviation had become a vital component of U.S. naval forces during the fifteen years prior to Trap's enrollment in flight school. Congress authorized the Navy to purchase its first airplane in 1911, a small amphibious seaplane designed and built by the Curtiss Aeroplane Company. Through World War I, naval aviation used only seaplanes, which were devoted primarily to patrol and bombing duties.

Prior to 1920, the Navy bureaucracy had given little thought to the airplane as a fighting weapon of war. Instead, doctrine held that the battleship, with its heavy-gun range of up to 30,000 yards, or seventeen miles, was the decisive armament in naval warfare. Other ships and capabilities, including airplanes, served an auxiliary role to support battleship ordnance.[1]

Airplanes enhanced battleship operations in two significant ways. The first was to surveil the open ocean looking for the enemy in places where the U.S. fleet was not deployed. In naval parlance, this was called patrolling, and airplanes built for this purpose were known as patrol planes. Their job was to locate and track enemy ships long before they came in contact with the fleets, thereby eliminating any surprise advantage the enemy might gain by remaining undetected in nearby waters. Because they traveled long distances over water, the Navy preferred seaplanes, which they called flying boats.[2] Too large to launch from ships, they operated instead from either fixed bases or from harbors where they could be supported by seaplane-tender ships.

Airplanes could also reinforce big ships directly by providing high-altitude lookouts to locate enemy targets for the fleet and spot the trajectory of ship's gunfire, as Trap had witnessed on *Marblehead*. Flying over a target, they could see where the salvos fell and then send back aiming corrections for the ship's guns, effectively directing ship gunfire onto targets well beyond sight of the ship, either over the horizon or hidden by smoke or weather. This scouting function was conducted by scout planes configured as small, two-seat land planes on which a large central pontoon replaced the landing wheels under the fuselage to support the weight of the aircraft, while a pair of smaller pontoons at the wing tips kept the seaplane upright on the water. Operating with the fleet, these planes were carried on board ship, launched from the ship's catapults, and retrieved from the water by cranes, allowing each big ship to have its own aerial scouting capability. By 1925, battleships and cruisers, the backbone of the battle fleet, routinely began to carry scout planes like those Trap encountered on board *Marblehead*.[3]

Scout planes enhanced the ships' visual field, extending the effective firing range of their guns, but once these planes became operational, it was evident that the enemy too could deploy scout planes, an unacceptable turn of the tables. The Navy needed a fighting airplane that could tackle and defeat enemy scout planes while defending itself and friendly scouts against enemy fighters. Such a fighter would require substantially better performance than a scout plane and could not be encumbered with heavy floats for water landings. They needed to devise a way to operate land planes within the fleet.

The idea of launching and recovering land planes from the flight deck was first tried in 1910, when Eugene Ely took off from a wooden platform jerry-built on the bow of the light cruiser USS *Birmingham*. Two months later, he landed on and took off from a platform mounted on the armored cruiser USS *Pennsylvania*. At the time, the idea of operating land planes from a ship was thought interesting but not particularly useful. By 1920, the need for seagoing fighters made shipboard operations a tactical necessity.

The fiscal 1920 budget allocated funds to convert the Navy collier USS *Jupiter* into its first aircraft carrier, renamed USS *Langley*. Commissioned in March 1922, she served as the base for the experimental development of aircraft carrier equipment and operations for the next two and a half years. The first class of Navy flight students to fly land planes on board carriers began training in July 1922. In 1924, *Langley* joined the battle fleet for line duty carrying scout planes—perhaps doubling the fleet's scouting capability—as well as fighter planes to defend against enemy scouts, inaugurating the Navy's foray into the carrier aviation age.[4]

THE GUN CLUB AND BuAer

A small cadre of young naval aviators, foreseeing the airplane's role as a naval weapon in its own right, argued that it could reliably deliver a warhead far beyond the range of ships' big guns. While ship gunnery could demolish an enemy craft at a distance measured in thousands of yards, airplanes carrying bombs and torpedoes could destroy targets a hundred miles away. By coordinating their attacks, air forces could make deadly strikes with near total surprise and effect safe retreat before the enemy knew what had hit them. In this way, these aviators reasoned, airpower would not just extend the fleet range of observation, but might replace fleet guns altogether.

These pioneers, however, were mostly junior officers, men still learning to fly while experimenting with aviation capabilities. The upper hierarchy generally regarded these mavericks as "aviation idealists," while the pioneers thought of the hierarchy as the "Gun Club." The Gun Club would be running the Navy for a long time, and although they remained uneasy about the emerging role of the "aircraft carrier," they resigned themselves to its presence in the fleet.[5]

Early ideas about how best to attack ships with aircraft envisioned the torpedo as the airplane's most effective weapon, and these ideas were borne out as early as 1918 by experiments demonstrating the ability of airplanes to launch torpedoes. Consequently, in addition to scouts and fighters, early Navy carrier airplane development focused on the torpedo plane.[6]

But the aerial torpedo had limitations. Its inherently delicate mechanisms, short range, and stringent launch requirements forced torpedo planes to deliver their weapons at low speed, close to the water, and exposed to enemy fire, a dangerous situation. Torpedoes were also heavy, with most of their weight devoted to propulsion and guidance machinery; a 1,400-pound aerial torpedo was needed to propel a 400-pound warhead. To carry the additional weight, the torpedo plane had to be larger, slower, and less agile than a bomber carrying the same or even a larger warhead. While the torpedo delivered its punch below the waterline, where a solid hit could prove lethal, a big bomb, which required no propulsion or guidance machinery, could be as deadly.[7]

The possibility of bombing planes as a serious threat to capital ships was the subject of hot debate. Could a small airplane carry a sufficiently destructive weapon? And if so, could it hit a ship traveling at high speed and taking violent evasive action? The Gun Club was doubtful.

In 1921, the Navy ran aircraft bombing tests on former German warships, trophies from the end of World War I. Although some ships were sunk and others badly damaged, the tests were hardly realistic. The target ships were sitting ducks, moored in a fixed position and unable to make evasive maneuvers, nor did they put up antiaircraft fire or defensive fighters to harass the bombers. In battle, a fast-moving and maneuvering ship made a difficult target, one unlikely to be damaged by a bomber at any significant altitude. So the results were controversial and largely inconclusive. But one fact emerged from the smoke and ash: one-thousand-pound bombs could sink or mortally wound a capital ship. An open question remained: Was there a way for an airplane to accurately deliver this bomb onto an elusive target?[8]

Mounting evidence that airplanes might prove a serious threat to big ships made the Gun Club uneasy. And like it or not, Congress and the White House recognized the growing importance of airpower in July 1921 when they created the Navy Bureau of Aeronautics, or BuAer as it was called, and appointed Rear Adm. William Moffett as its formidable chief. Moffett was one of the few senior members of the Navy bureaucracy who had stood his ground as a long-time advocate for aviation. He had BuAer up and running by September and stayed on as chief for an unprecedented twelve years, championing aviation advancement and "dragging the Navy bureaucracy into the age of airpower."[9]

THE FIRST BIG CARRIERS

In 1922, Congress gave the go-ahead to convert into aircraft carriers two partly finished battle cruisers that could not be completed as such because of limitations imposed by the Washington Naval Treaty of 1922. Aircraft carriers were under no such restriction, so these two would become USS *Lexington* and USS *Saratoga*, the largest aircraft carriers in the world and the largest ships in the U.S. battle fleet.[10]

The pending arrival of these huge new ships, each of which could carry up to eighty aircraft, gave impetus to strategic and tactical arguments for carrier-based bombers and new methods of bomb delivery. One promising idea had bombers attacking their target in a vertical dive, which enabled them to close quickly on the mark for accurate delivery, then pull out rapidly to escape anti-aircraft fire. A number of experiments were conducted in the 1920s, but the first organized vertical diving attack, later called "dive bombing," was demonstrated in a simulated attack on the big ships of the battle fleet in 1926.[11]

Planes from Fighting Squadron 2 descended almost vertically from 12,000 feet, and, although forewarned, the fleet was unable to detect the aircraft until the bombers were almost on the deck. Their nearly vertical dives came from so high and at such speed that they had pulled out and were disappearing toward the horizon before the ships' crews could get to their battle stations. The impact was stunning. Everyone on board the battleships, including the commander in chief of the U.S. fleet, agreed that the surprise and effectiveness of such an assault would overcome any possible defense.[12]

By late 1926, squadrons from *Langley* routinely used diving attacks with bombs to increase their accuracy. Within a few months, an official Navy study and related experimentation had sealed the role of dive bombing as a standard tactic in the naval arsenal. To ensure the effectiveness of this new technique against big ships, however, the bomber would have to deliver a 1,000-pound bomb. Existing airplanes could not carry such a load and still perform the necessary vertical dive and the high-stress recovery needed for accuracy and safe escape. So early dive bombing was practiced with fighter planes carrying smaller bomb loads until a new class of airplane—the dive bomber—could be created, an endeavor that became the focus of Navy aircraft development through the 1930s.[13]

When Trap began flight training in January 1926, naval aviation was firmly established as a distinct Navy function recognized by Congress. Naval aviators had won numerous air races and set world records in distance, speed, and time-to-climb performance. Aircraft carriers were accepted as an integral part of the fleet. In spite of skeptics, aviation had demonstrated its promise as an offensive weapon in its own right, and the Navy was eager to develop new types of aircraft suited to shipboard operations and able to exploit its new tactics. Still, when Trap entered a naval aviation community of proud pioneers, the Navy had a long way to go to fulfill the bold vision held by a new generation of maverick aviators.

CHAPTER 4

★ ★ ★

FIGHTER PILOT, 1926–29

Trap entered flight school at Naval Air Station (NAS) Pensacola in January 1926, receiving his wings on March 25 of the following year, when he was designated naval aviator #3358. His love of flying was evident from the start, particularly aerobatics, at which he excelled. Both physically exhilarating and technically challenging, flying provided a satisfying outlet for a range of his interests and aspirations.

His Naval Academy classmate Arleigh Burke, who later rose to the rank of four-star admiral and chief of naval operations, wrote of Trap's early affinity for flight:

> Young Trapnell was enthusiastic about flying from the moment he made his first flight with his instructor, and after he soloed he was convinced that this was the life for him. He fell in love with flying machines, and this stayed with him throughout his whole life. It was not idle to say that a good aviator flew by the seat of his britches. Mechanical instruments were good, but they were only helpful and not always reliable. They did not take the place of feel, a natural instinct that not everyone has. He intensified his sense of feel by flying at every opportunity, and the more he flew the better he got and the more he wanted to fly. He soon had a reputation of being one of the best newly fledged aviators.
>
> Fred Trapnell was a cautious man, and he learned in those very early days to check his airplane thoroughly and to know what each element of that airplane could and could not do. Above all, he learned that skill in flying was the most important characteristic that an aviator should have. He determined that he would be one

of the most skillful pilots in the Navy, and he worked at doing just that. In a very few years he had that rare combination of knowledge, caution, and skill that enabled him to be absolutely confident of what he and his plane could do.[1]

One sadness early in Trap's time in flight school was the death of his father. Trap loved and admired his father and quietly grieved the loss. Benjamin, who shared his son's respect and enthusiasm for the emerging field of naval aviation, passed away without seeing Trap earn his wings.

Following graduation from flight school, Trap remained at Pensacola, where he continued a flight schedule of thirty hours per month, mostly in an NB-1 seaplane. His flight log shows that he was sharpening his skills in radio, instrument flying, and gunnery.

In July, he transferred to the fleet Air Base in Hampton Roads, Virginia, where he joined Torpedo Squadron 1, part of the aircraft complement on board the newly commissioned USS *Lexington*, soon to join the battle fleet. He began flying Martin T3M-1s, an early Navy torpedo bomber, and his log

3. Trap, in the middle row, center, wearing a dark jacket, peers skeptically at the camera in this photo of his flight school graduating class, March 1927.

Official U.S. Navy photo, personal files of Frederick Trapnell Jr.

notes indicate emphasis on precision landings, formation flying, and bombing. His duties often gave him evenings off, which satisfied another of his growing interests.

At twenty-five, Trap cut a handsome figure, carrying himself with presence and panache that drew attention without demanding it. Though reticent to talk about himself or his profession, he readily conversed about any number of other subjects. His wry sense of humor and ready smile made him pleasing company and the object of considerable fascination to women, who were enchanted by this emerging breed of dashing aviators.

Much to his delight, Torpedo Squadron 1 transferred to San Diego to join *Lexington* in March 1928. Trap was eager to go west. The squadron's new base was NAS North Island, adjacent to the quaint island town of Coronado, California, across the bay from San Diego.

After *Lexington* had completed her acceptance tests in early June, she was ordered to sail posthaste to Hawaii to join the finale of the Navy's summer war games. Leaving her North Island–based squadrons behind, she raced westward to Honolulu, completing her record-breaking run in just over seventy-two hours.

Concurrent with *Lexington*'s return to San Diego at the end of the month, Trap transferred to one of her fighter squadrons, Bombing Squadron 1, or VB-1, familiarly known as the Red Rippers.[2] Its official designation would soon change to VF-5, or Fighting Squadron 5.[3] Commissioned the previous year at Hampton Roads, this was the first squadron designated as a "Fighter Squadron" in aviation history and would become the oldest continuously active fighter squadron in the U.S. Navy.[4] They flew the Curtiss F6C-3 fighter plane, known as the Hawk and thought by many to be "the best airplane in the fleet."[5] For Trap, this airplane was a significant upgrade in performance. The T3M he'd flown at Hampton Roads had a top speed of 109 mph, a service ceiling of 8,000 feet, and could climb to 5,000 feet in seventeen minutes. By comparison, the Hawk had a top speed of 155 mph, a service ceiling of 23,000 feet, and a climb rate of 2,000 feet per minute.[6]

Fighters offered far more interesting flying than torpedo bombers, and Trap's initiation to the fighter arena was intense. His newfound friend in VB-1, Lt. Matthias "Matt" Gardner, helped ease Trap's transition into the squadron. Not only was Matt eager to show this newcomer the ropes, but he was an outstanding pilot in his own right. The two became close and flew often together.

Trap's arrival coincided with the beginning of the fleet's July "concentration period," as designated by Rear Adm. Joseph Reeves, commander of the Aircraft Squadrons, Battle Fleet. During these exercises, the carrier squadrons met at North Island to conduct intensive drills in coordinated tactics to

4. The Curtiss F6C-3 Hawk fighter/bomber, which Trap flew upon joining the
Red Rippers at North Island, San Diego, in 1928, was said to be
the best airplane in the fleet.

Official U.S. Navy photo, National Archives and Records Administration,
Records of the Bureau of Aeronautics

unleash the largest number of airplanes ever assembled against "enemy" targets, emphasizing formation maneuvers to deliver a sudden and overwhelming deluge of bombs onto a target, or to create a dense swarm of fighters in the airspace over the enemy fleet.[7]

THE TEST

Lt. James D. Barner had recently joined the squadron after a tour of duty as a test pilot with the Navy's Flight Test Section at NAS Anacostia, D.C. One aspect of Barner's job as executive officer of VB-1 was to evaluate each pilot's fitness and to ensure that his skills were brought up to standard. New pilots treated Lieutenant Barner with the deference due this seasoned aviator, meeting his scrutiny with a mixture of dread and anticipation. He thought of his new pilots as "nuggets," because beneath their unpolished and untested exterior might reside the intrinsic skill to make a real Navy fighter pilot. But it took time in the cockpit and unrelenting discipline to burnish that rough surface. Some nuggets took longer than others. A few never made the grade.

Barner's ritual welcome included an aerial drill to test the new pilot's ability to follow him through a series of complex and violent maneuvers. More often than not, this proved a humbling experience for the nugget. He and the new man would take off together in two fighter planes and climb high up over the vast, empty mesa north of San Diego. At a hand signal, the nugget would drop behind with instructions to stay on Barner's tail through a series of coordinated maneuvers intended to make the new man lose his position. The typical young pilot pulled too hard on the controls, lost airspeed, dropped astern, and became easy prey. Then Barner rounded onto his tail, making it emphatically clear that the nugget had just been "shot down." The process was repeated, starting with the new man on Barner's tail and ending with him being shot down once again. Barner usually put the nugget through this drill three or four times, making copious notes on his knee pad.

Back on the ground, Barner reviewed the flight step-by-step with the nugget, pointing out how many times he had gotten himself shot down and reviewing his errors in painstaking detail. Tearing the sheet of notes from his pad and handing it to the new man, he would tell him to go practice with other pilots for a few weeks until he was ready for another round.

Sometimes it took two or three sessions for the nugget to meet Barner's initial criteria, at which time he introduced a whole new set of uncoordinated maneuvers: snap rolls, violent skids, high-speed stalls, and spins. It usually required several more aerial rounds over two or three months to get a new pilot up to Barner's standards.

One clear morning a few weeks after his arrival at North Island, it was Trap's turn to be tested. They took off together and climbed northward. At ten thousand feet over Kearny Mesa, Barner gave the signal, pushed to full throttle, and flicked the little F6C into a tight flat right turn. With his expertise of years in fighter planes, the roll was actually a fully coordinated maneuver, and he held the G forces of the turn precisely at the limit of smooth flight. Then, after turning ninety degrees, he rolled into a hard left turn. Here's where you start to lose them, he thought. They pull too hard and fall behind.

Glancing back over his shoulder, he expected to see Trap's Hawk struggling to follow and slipping astern. Instead, he found the airplane holding easily on a path just slightly outboard of his own. He rolled back hard into a tight right turn and again found Trap tight on his tail. And so they continued this dance in the sky—hard turns, loops, rolls, dives, and steep Immelmann turns—with Barner maneuvering hard to dislodge his pursuer. Trap trailed close at hand, pacing him move for move.

5. L to R: Jimmy James, Jimmy Barner, Trap. F4B behind, 1929.

Official U.S. Navy photo, personal files of Frederick Trapnell Jr.

Finally, down to one thousand feet over the mesa, Barner straightened out and led them climbing back to altitude. This kid is pretty damned good, he thought. Let's find out how good.

When they leveled out again at ten thousand feet, he gave the signal, slammed in full power, let his airplane run a bit and then threw it into a violent pitch-up maneuver. The airplane stalled, stopping almost dead in the air.

At the same time, he booted full right rudder, forcing the craft to cartwheel and bringing the nose down. He centered the controls momentarily to pick up speed and then hauled back into a loop, nearly stalling again at the top. He craned around to discover Trap matching his flight path and altitude, nestled close behind his right wing tip.

Barner led the duo in a long series of violent maneuvers designed to shake off an attacker, to no avail. When they reached one thousand feet of altitude, Trap was still with him, tracking smoothly astern. Finally, the two straightened out and swung gently south toward North Island.

They taxied up to the flight line, where Barner cut his engine and sat silent for a moment. It was the first time he could remember a nugget able to follow him through those maneuvers the first time out, a remarkable performance, he thought. He looked down at his knee pad, normally full of notes at this point. It was blank. He clambered down from the cockpit.

Trap stood waiting by his airplane as Barner approached with his hand extended. The older man smiled broadly as they shook hands. "I'm Jimmy Barner, and I am glad to welcome you aboard."[8]

FUN AND GAMES

Camaraderie and competition thrived among the Red Rippers, each man eager to outdo the other in mock dogfights and aerial marksmanship. At North Island, they played a game with precision landings, using a painted stripe across the east end of runway two-nine as the landing target. The object was to bring the airplane down in a perfect three-point landing, the main wheels touching the tarmac without bouncing, as close as possible to the stripe. A referee on the ground scored each pilot upon his return. The one landing farthest from the stripe bought the drinks that evening. They became so good at this that the distance of a yard or two made all the difference. Trap rarely paid for drinks.[9]

In reality, each landing was practice for shipboard operations. As the airplanes approached the runway, the pilot often leaned his head out the left side of the open cockpit so he could keep an eye on the touchdown point. Although they wore helmets, it was thought manly to let the helmet strap hang loose. Consequently, when the pilot held his head over the side of the cockpit, the helmet strap whipped in the slipstream and slapped against his left ear. Years later, Trap would say that this was how he lost his hearing on that side.

Through October, virtually all of his flying was in Hawks. Then in November, the squadron received its first F3B, the Boeing equivalent of the Hawk. While these two airplanes seem to have had similar performance, the squadron must have adopted the Boeings, since Trap's log book shows that he subsequently flew almost exclusively in F3Bs.

THE STUNNED GENERAL

Just before Christmas of 1928, Italian General Italo Balbo, head of the Italian air force, visited North Island as a guest of Rear Adm. Joseph Reeves, battle fleet commander, who had his squadrons put on a massive demonstration for the general. Flying events included an exhibition by the battle fleet aerobatic team called the Three Seahawks, flown by three crack pilots: Lt. "Tommy" Tomlinson, Lt. (jg) "Putt" Storrs, and Lt. (jg) Bill Davis. Each was a close friend of Trap's and would remain so for the rest of their careers. They practiced high-risk, low-altitude maneuvers normally forbidden in the Navy. But Reeves knew the value of an attention-grabbing show and allowed these stunts on special occasions.[10] The Italian general was moderately impressed; he had seen such maneuvers before.

But the surprise finale orchestrated by Reeves was something else altogether. As the last flight demonstration ended, Reeves walked Balbo out to the middle of the airfield. Standing alone on the tarmac, the two men in dress uniforms became the target of a simulated dive-bombing attack. High overhead, a flight of airplanes seemed innocuous in their neat V formation. Then they suddenly peeled off, plummeting straight down at the two uniformed officers and bottoming out of their screaming dives a heart-stopping few hundred feet above the runway. The astonished Balbo ducked reflexively as each airplane roared low overhead. He was speechless. That night he reported home by cable, "I have seen today a type of bombing that I did not think possible."[11] According to Trap's flight log for December 22, he flew escort for General Balbo's departure from San Diego.

TESTING THE WARRIORS

In their new fighters, VB-1 was working up to deployment in simulated wartime maneuvers on board *Lexington* in which the battle fleet was split into two opposing groups with *Lexington* and *Saratoga* in adversarial roles. The *Saratoga*'s side was to attack the Panama Canal while *Lexington*'s side defended it. Late in January 1929, *Lexington* proceeded from California to the Canal Zone with Trap and his colleagues practicing formation tactics en route.[12]

On the twenty-fifth, just as maneuvers began, the Red Rippers were launched into rain squalls and low visibility, and *Lexington* came under fire from opposing battleships fifteen miles away. After an extended search through clouds and downpour, the squadron finally located the enemy battle fleet and attacked. Meanwhile a rainstorm blanketed *Lexington*, protecting her from enemy fire but making it extremely difficult for the returning squadron to locate and land on board. The nearest airfields were three hundred miles away, well beyond the range of their airplanes. Since these airplanes were not equipped with radios, all airborne communication relied on hand signals. On board ship there was serious nail biting over whether *Lexington* would recover her aircraft.

Returning from their mission under the squadron leader's direction, the pilots looked for *Lexington* along the track she was supposed to follow, but she was nowhere to be found. By the time they located her under a low ceiling, they were nearly out of fuel. There were huge sighs of relief as the airplanes came safely on board and the pilots were duly commended for their performance.[13]

Early the next day, *Lexington*'s aircraft located and attacked *Saratoga* just after she had launched her entire contingent of airplanes on a strike at the canal. Failing to retain any fighters, she was left without air cover, so the Red Rippers and the rest of *Lexington*'s air group had a field day of simulated strafing, bombing, and torpedo attacks. Later the same day, Trap flew patrol over the enemy's main body and, on the twenty-seventh, noted in his logbook an air-to-air engagement with *Saratoga*'s fighters.[14]

These attack and defense maneuvers in the vicinity of the Panama Canal, known as Fleet Problem IX, were the most extensive Navy war games ever conducted. They were Trap's first major exercises as an aviator, but hardly his last. His flight logs show that he continued to fly fleet exercises in and around the Canal Zone during February and March before returning with *Lexington* to San Diego in April.

From May through August, he flew a heavy schedule, averaging forty-nine flight hours per month, with emphasis on bombing practice, cross-country flight, and formation tactics. That summer, the battle fleet commander required an aerial demonstration team at North Island to replace the Three Seahawks, whose pilots had been transferred to other stations. Lt. J. T. De Strazo, Lt. (jg) J. G. Crommelin, and Trap were chosen to form the new team, which flew F3B airplanes in several public stunting demonstrations.[15]

HITTING THE SILK

En route to Seattle in August, Trap made a crash landing at Marysville, California. Chagrined but unscathed, he pressed on to his final destination via ground transportation to test and take delivery of a new Boeing F4B, which promised a significant performance improvement over the F3B. While in Seattle, he checked out several different airplanes of this type before flying one of them back to North Island. Subsequently, F4B became the standard fighter for VB-1 and Trap's personal logs show that he flew nothing else from August through December.

On November 15, 1929, Trap took off on a practice bombing flight and was climbing to five thousand feet over the mesa just north of San Diego when

**6. Trap over Point Loma, San Diego, in 1929 at the controls of an F4B,
the type from which he made his first emergency parachute jump**

Official U.S. Navy photo, personal files of Frederick Trapnell Jr.

he felt a sudden burst of heat in his face. Looking down between his knees into the hull of the aircraft, he saw flame spewing like a giant blowtorch from the ruptured fuel tank. With no time to set the airplane down, he released his safety belt, clambered over the side, and pushed away from the fuselage. Floating in space, he watched the flaming airplane pull away, briefly mesmerized by the odd sensation of free falling before he pulled the ripcord to open the parachute. Moments later his airplane plunged into Kearny Mesa below, setting ablaze a broad swath of chaparral in a plume of smoke that could be seen for miles around.

Landing without injury in the brush away from the fire, he held tightly to the ripcord D-ring, knowing that this was his ticket into the Caterpillar Club, that exclusive organization of aviators saved by a silk parachute after an emergency bailout from a failed aircraft in flight. Admission to the club, whose motto is "Life depends on a silken thread," required the pilot to have the ripcord in his possession to verify his feat. Trap coiled the cord and stuffed it deep into a pocket, rolled up his chute, and walked west toward the nearest road. Years later, when the broad mesa became smothered in homes, he joked about the afternoon he'd set much of it ablaze.[16]

HOT PROSPECT

At this point in his career, Trap had demonstrated an uncanny knack for accurately diagnosing aircraft problems in the air and was often asked to test new or newly repaired airplanes. He approached these tasks with caution and precision, applying increasing rigor to his evaluations and producing ever more incisive flight reports. In addition to checking out new airplanes and repairs, he used his insight to provide the squadron with a more precise understanding of their airplanes' characteristics, their limits and expected performance under various conditions. In those days, such information was not provided by either the manufacturer or the Navy.

Trap's uncommon skill, focus, and acumen gained recognition among his peers and superiors. Certainly, his years growing up around boats and locomotives had given him a framework for grasping the complexities of airplane mechanics and aerodynamics. But his uncommon ability to infer vital information from critical airplane behaviors and to translate that insight into clear and effective remedies set him apart in a field of highly competent aviators.

This was not lost on Jimmy Barner, whose two years in the Navy's Flight Test Section enabled him to recognize a good test pilot prospect when he saw one. It was not long before Trap received orders assigning him to Flight Test at NAS Anacostia. By the time of his final log entry with VB-1 in San Diego, signed by Barner on December 4, 1929, Trap had accumulated 1,107 total flying hours.

TYING THE KNOT, 1929

Given the many hours Trap logged with VB-1, one might think he had time for little else, but that was not the case. The distance from NAS North Island to Coronado's main street, Orange Avenue, is less than a mile. The venerable Hotel Del Coronado marks the far south end of Orange Avenue, where this classic Victorian jewel has held sway since 1887, an elegant icon of gracious living and classic Southern California beachfront style. Its tropical ambience, fine cuisine, and lavishly stocked bar drew celebrities, princes, presidents . . . and the officers of VB-1.

On evenings when they were not at sea, Trap and his colleagues often congregated in the Hotel Del bar overlooking the tennis courts and the broad Pacific Ocean. They weren't simply there for the view or martinis. Between the fashionable bar and the plush Crown Room dining area, the Hotel Del drew an array of attractive and eligible young ladies eager to catch the eye of an eligible officer in blue and gold. In the bustle of bartenders and waiters in tuxedos, the atmosphere was ripe for romance; indeed, many Navy marriages began at the Hotel Del, among them Trap's to Mary Elizabeth Belcher.

It was not hard to pick Mary out in a crowd. Even among a coterie of attractive women, she was a standout beauty. Tall and dark-eyed, Mary knew how to walk into a room and be noticed. Her flare for wardrobe, her eye-catching smile, and her aura of elegance combined with a sharp wit and adroit sociability made a powerful impression. Men responded to her with open admiration, although she was particular about her associations.

Raised in San Diego, Mary was the daughter of Frank J. Belcher Jr., a prominent local banker, and Virginia Acheson Garrettson Belcher, the daughter of First National Bank president D. F. Garrettson and a second-generation Californian. Although this made Mary a westerner, which was not exactly to Trap's taste, her year as a student at Smith College in Massachusetts had given her a certain eastern cachet, as did her lineage, which traced back to ancestors along the eastern seaboard well before the Revolutionary War.

At the time of their first meeting, Mary was about to start her senior year as a drama student at the University of California at Berkeley. Her ambition was to go onto the professional stage.

It was instant attraction between these two. Their romance was passionate, though impeded by her studies and his career. Trap found her to be the most captivating and compelling woman he had ever met, and she fell hard for the dashing aviator who struck a chord of welcome drama in her life. Much to her father's chagrin, their courtship was intense. Mary was ready to quit college to marry him, but Frank Belcher had better things in mind for her than a flighty young aviator. No matter how dashing Trap was, Belcher thought he was the wrong man for his only daughter, and he made no bones about the folly of leaving Berkeley without a degree.

Headstrong Mary was not to be persuaded. So, to stem the tide of this overheated romance, her father insisted that she take time away to let things cool. In January of 1929, just before Trap was to leave with *Lexington* for Panama, Frank shuttled Mary off to Paris to study for five months at the Sorbonne. Infuriated, she reluctantly complied, brooding on the long train trip to New York, where she boarded the elegant *Isle de France* to set sail for Europe.

On her first day at sea, Mary met an older woman and her teenage daughter, also en route to Paris. In a trick of fate, the woman turned out to be Trap's mother, Ada, traveling with his younger sister Evie, who were delighted to meet the stunning beauty Trap had written home about. Mary's five months in Paris passed quickly, with much time spent in the company of the Trapnell ladies, and during this period Mary and Ada cemented a lasting friendship.

Needless to say, the European excursion only fanned the flames of the forbidden love and frustrated her father's efforts to squelch the affair.

Mary returned home at the end of July, radiant from her months in Europe and more determined than ever to marry Trap, despite her father's lingering disapproval and her unfinished degree. Her mother, Virginia, was more sympathetic. Previously quiet about the affair, she now took Mary's part in supporting the matrimony. After all, it was not hard to see what her daughter found so attractive in her Navy flier.

Lt. (jg) Frederick M. Trapnell and Mary Elizabeth Belcher were married on the evening of December 28, 1929, in a picturesque wedding held at the stately home of her maternal grandparents on Front Street in downtown San Diego. The Sunday Society section of the *San Diego Union* portrayed the candlelit service as "one of the loveliest ceremonies of the year. . . . The bride is one of the most attractive young society girls in San Diego. . . . Her brunet beauty [was] accentuated by an exquisite Spanish mantilla from Seville in place of the conventional wedding veil." The mantilla, a souvenir of her cooling-off period in Europe, was emblematic of Mary's flare for drama and style.

The article makes passing mention of the groom and his attendants, with particular reference to Trap's now close friend and colleague Lt. Jimmy Barner. It notes the couple's plans to leave for a very short honeymoon "in the north" before departing January first for Washington D.C., "where Lt. Trapnell will be stationed."

CHAPTER 5

★ ★ ★

TEST PILOT
Learning the Craft, 1930–32

The genesis of the Navy's Flight Test Section and the test divisions in today's Naval Air Systems Command lies in a letter dated August 3, 1926, from Lt. E. W. "Eddie" Rounds to Rear Adm. William Moffett, chief of the Navy Bureau of Aeronautics (BuAer). Rounds was an engineering-duty-only officer in BuAer, an aeronautical engineer and seasoned pilot. His letter to the admiral underscored the primary handicap to improving airplane design: the unreliability of data about aircraft performance. Despite the best efforts of those pilots and engineers assigned to assess new airplanes, he argued that the lack of proper equipment, consistent test procedures, a systematic approach to recording information, and common terminology undermined their ability to effectively evaluate new aircraft.[1]

Rounds recommended establishing a Flight Test Section in BuAer and a corresponding Flight Test Section at Naval Air Station Anacostia, D.C., to consolidate the Navy's expertise and provide consistency and integrity of test results. The Anacostia section would conduct the tests, maintain the equipment, and work with the BuAer section to interpret results, while BuAer would set testing ground rules, publish test results, and develop necessary special equipment. Admiral Moffett's subsequent response adhered closely to Rounds' recommendations, ordering the formation of the two new units as of January 1, 1927, and specifying the flight test mission: "to determine that the requirements in any procurement contract were met and to recommend modifications needed to make the aircraft serviceable for use in the Fleet."[2]

A YOUNGSTER AT ANACOSTIA

At the end of 1929, just three years after becoming a naval aviator, Trap's unusual abilities had gained notice, and, on Jimmy Barner's recommendation, he was transferred to the Flight Test Section at NAS Anacostia. Arleigh Burke later wrote, "This was a high honor for a youngster." A youngster indeed, although one who would change the very paradigm of flight testing in ways no one could imagine.[3]

Trap arrived in Washington in early January 1930 accompanied by his new bride. The couple moved into the Altamont Apartments on Wyoming Avenue following a hasty cross-country rail honeymoon. The following Monday, Trap reported to NAS Anacostia for duty. By Thursday he was back in the cockpit.

Anacostia, located directly across the Anacostia River from the Naval Gun Factory in Washington, D.C., was primitive by today's standards. There were no runways, just a dirt and grass field. The single large hangar opened onto a concrete runup area on one side and a ramp leading into the Anacostia River on the other, enabling the team to operate both land planes and seaplanes from the same staging ground.

Trap became one of five test pilots who made up the Flight Test Section, under Lt. Cdr. Ralph Ofstie, senior flight test officer. There was no formal training for test pilots in those days; they learned by flying and experimenting, talking to other pilots, and listening to the engineers. Nevertheless, Trap flourished in this niche. Not only was he collaborating with a highly capable team of fellow aviators, but he was also rubbing elbows with the BuAer technical staff and the contractors' top engineers.

Newly promoted Lt. Cdr. Eddie Rounds was head of the Flight Test Section in BuAer. As their relationship developed, he became a valued mentor to Trap, introducing him to a host of advanced aeronautical concepts—lift/drag ratios, turbulent flow effects, flutter, boundary-layer effects, and aeroelasticity—topics just entering the lexicon of aeronautical engineering circles. With Trap's background in sailing and experience in the cockpit, these concepts fell neatly into place, enhancing his expertise and amplifying his intuitive grasp of the flying machine.[4]

Rounds insisted that test pilots return from their flights with hard data that engineers on the ground could use to evaluate against performance criteria and to compare different aircraft. Qualitative statements about an airplane's flying characteristics—"this was good, that was bad," "response was slow," "controls were heavy"—were vain chitchat to Eddie, lending little insight into actual performance, never mind useful comparison between aircraft. His test pilots were expected to record actual instrument readings on their knee pads, using a stopwatch for timing and special instruments to derive data that was otherwise difficult to calculate. He further maintained that consistent written test reports were the only way to make meaningful comparisons between airplane types and to come up with effective design modifications.

7. The Flight Test Section at Anacostia, the entire Flight Test staff of the U.S. Navy in 1930. Trap is on the far right, his friend Lt. Bob Pirie is on the far left, and the commanding officer, Lt. Cdr. Ralph Ofstie, is in the center.

Official U.S. Navy photo, personal files of Frederick Trapnell Jr.

This made perfect sense to Trap. Concrete information was essential to making an intelligent, comprehensive evaluation of an airplane. He had long since learned that if you wanted to get something fixed quickly on an airplane, you had to be specific with the mechanics about what was wrong. So the quest for quantitative data that Eddie preached exactly suited Trap's sensibilities and fell like sweet gospel on the young man's ears.

Flight Test also afforded breadth and variety to Trap's flight experience, dramatically increasing his exposure to different airplanes. During his previous four years as a pilot, he had flown seventeen different types; within his first six months at Flight Test, that number had more than doubled, to thirty-nine. Anacostia was a virtual toy store for the inquisitive young aviator eager to gain broad experience in aircraft behavior, and he found the environment exhilarating.

Since Navy doctrine stipulated that the primary mission of aviation was to locate and track the enemy, BuAer placed primary focus on scouting and patrolling. Scout planes operated from capital ships and aircraft carriers, searching near the fleet to locate and identify enemy dispositions and to spot the trajectory of fleet gunfire. Landing gear on these airplanes could be either wheels or floats interchangeably, while amphibious designs came with both. In 1930, Flight Test evaluated the Vought O2U and O3U as scout planes, and during the months of March and April, Trap made almost forty test flights in these aircraft, which went on to become the Navy's standard in the early 1930s.

The purpose of patrol planes was to search great distances over trackless waters where the enemy might operate. Although patrol planes were not Trap's specialty, he was occasionally called upon to test them.

BuAer's other focus was dive bombing, the newly invented technique whereby an airplane could accurately hit a maneuvering ship with a bomb. They wanted a reliable airplane that could launch from a carrier with a 1,000-pound bomb and deliver the ordnance onto a target from a vertical dive. The first such aircraft to go on board ship was the Martin BM-1, which evolved out of earlier Martin torpedo planes, the T4M and T5M. Trap had made fifteen test flights in these two types before the BM-1 was delivered in early 1932. He then flew seventeen tests of the BM-1.[5]

Fighter performance, which always pushed the limits, became Trap's specialty. During his time at Anacostia, he flew 124 test flights in fighter type aircraft, including three noteworthy prototypes under test at the time. The first was Boeing's famous F4B-4. Unlike the tubular-framed fuselage of its predecessors Trap had flown at North Island, this was the first aircraft having a semi-monocoque fuselage, which got its strength from its skin made of duralumin, a hardened aluminum alloy. It was a racy airplane for its day. The second was the FF-1, informally called Fifi, Grumman's first fighter and the Navy's first airplane with retractable landing gear. The third was the Curtiss F9C Sparrowhawk, chosen to be the hook-on aircraft for the dirigibles USS *Akron* and USS *Macon*, which later became significant to Trap.

FLIGHT DEMONSTRATION TEAM

Duty at Anacostia offered another big plus. Trap was reunited with two top-notch aviators, lieutenants from his North Island days, Matt Gardner and Putt Storrs. These three enjoyed an easy camaraderie that served them well on the ground and in the air as they renewed their mutual interest in demonstration flying.

The battle fleet had created a West Coast aerial stunt team, the Three Seahawks, to perform in the 1927 National Air Races. Now David Ingalls, the Assistant Secretary of the Navy for Air, decided that the Navy should have an ongoing official aerial demonstration team to represent its flourishing aviation resources and capabilities at air shows around the country. So, at Admiral Moffett's direction, Matt Gardner, a former member of the Three Seahawks, was asked to form the new group, dubbed the Three Flying Fish. Putt Storrs, another former member of the Seahawks, and Trap completed the squad, which flew the biwinged Curtiss F6C-4s, a later model Hawk and a staple Navy fighter.[6]

The Washington, D.C., *Sunday Star* of June 22, 1930, heralded this new unit, "which promises to develop into one of the greatest acrobatic teams American aviation ever has seen." On October 17, the *Washington Daily News* ran an article describing the new flying team's debut performance. "Daring aerial acrobatic maneuvers, new to aviation science, were shown before ranking naval aviation officials at the Anacostia Naval Air Station today. . . . Flying in V formation, the three airplanes go into the section-roll maneuver out of a short dive . . . finishing upside down with the right wingman on the left and the left wingman on the right. A half loop in V formation brings the three airplanes back into normal flying position." Among the first to witness these then novel stunts were David Ingalls and Capt. John Towers of BuAer.

The Navy released a photograph of the three pilots for publication with the following caption. "Washington D.C . . . Lt. A. P. Storrs, right wing, Lt. M. B. Gardner, leader and Lt. Frederick M. Trapnell, left wing, the three best pilots of the Navy, will give demonstrations of aerial aerobatics on Navy Day, October twenty-seventh [1930]. In performing aerial thrillers, these 'three musketeers of the Navy' are said to be without peers."

According to the *Sunday Star*, "The now famous acrobatic section of the Anacostia Naval Air Station, which has covered itself with glory at Chicago (National Air Races), Cleveland and Trenton," would make its first official appearance at the national capital during the Navy Day program the following afternoon.[7]

Two days later, noted columnist Ernie Pyle reviewed the "thrilling show" for Washington readers: "the three pilots thought their show was terrible, but from the ground it looked mighty fine." He also noted the difficulty of the section roll because "it requires quite a change in speed during the maneuver. No other stunt team has ever done this before."[8]

The January 1931 issue of *Popular Mechanics* described the performance based on an interview in which Gardner gave a detailed, step-by-step walk-through of their routine. The team demonstrated "three spectacular feats of aerial aerobatics never before accomplished," including "a bewildering five minute period of upside down flying at 120 miles an hour that, for close-range

8. The Three Flying Fish: Lt. (jg) Putt Storrs, Lt. Matt Gardner, Trap, 1930

*Official U.S. Navy photo, National Archives and Records Administration,
Records of the Bureau of Aeronautics*

inverted flying, is believed to be unparalleled." In later air shows, the team flew a complete program of formation flying—upright and inverted—with their wings linked by ribbon from takeoff to landing.

LOST DOG

During his time at Anacostia, Trap struck up a friendship with David Ingalls, who took a keen interest in the young naval aviators blazing trails in the skies over the Potomac. Ingalls had been naval aviator #85, the only Navy flying ace in World War I and the first ace in Navy history. As close friend and adviser to President Herbert Hoover, Ingalls was instrumental in tripling the number of naval aircraft and proved a forceful advocate for a fully deployable carrier task force. On a more personal note, he also ensured that Trap and Mary had a place on the guest list for a number of Hoover White House functions.[9]

Besides their professional alliance, Trap was particularly intrigued by Ingalls' Irish wolfhounds, a prize breed of large dog originally trained for war and later used for hunting and guarding. In a gesture of friendship, Ingalls gifted Trap with a young pup from his private kennels in Ohio that Trap named Wally after his younger brother. The dog often accompanied him to work, where the men at the hangar were glad to keep an eye on the pup while the lieutenant was flying. Trap loved this dog.

On February 25, 1932, Wally was AWOL. The dog had been missing for four days, and Trap was deeply troubled. That morning, he shook off the worry and strapped into a rebuilt XS3C-1 for a one-and-a-half-hour extended test flight.

Meanwhile, to find the dog, Mary decided to enlist help from the *Washington Daily* newspaper office, where she spoke imploringly with the sympathetic city editor before returning to her search. Ernie Pyle's Friday column told the story. "Just before noon yesterday a beautiful young woman walked into the editorial room of *The Daily News*. She had lost her dog, and didn't know where to find him. She wondered if the city editor, thru some publicity, could help her. He said maybe he could. He asked her name. It was Mrs. Frederick M. Trapnell."[10]

As soon as Mary left the office, the editor's phone rang. "Airplane crash at Oxon Hill," the police reporter snapped. The pilot had jumped. The wreckage was burning. The downed pilot was Lt. Frederick M. Trapnell.

After completing a series of routine tests and maneuvers to evaluate recent modifications to the tail, Trap had climbed to 20,000 feet over Oxon Hill and rolled into a vertical dive. As he started recovery at 15,000 feet, the airplane lurched and the control stick went limp in his hand. Riding the "uncontrollable meteor of steel and aluminum" down to 7,000 feet, he shot a glance over his shoulder. The elevators, which the pilot controls to raise and lower the nose of the airplane, were gone. There was only one way out of this dive.[11]

He released the lap belt, shoved out of the cockpit, and spiraled free of the airplane, experiencing a flash of déjà vu at the eerie sensation of free fall before pulling the ripcord. Then, hanging in the chute, he watched his airplane crash into the Maryland countryside just east of the Potomac River. It blasted a fresh grave twelve feet across and several feet deep, splattering flaming gas and wreckage over a wide swath of woods. He landed safely and, leaving the ensuing fire to burn for several hours, the unfazed pilot hitched a ride back to Anacostia from a stunned farmer named Enoch O'Neal.

Trap held fast to the ripcord and, according to a Navy press release, became "the thirteenth second-degree member of the Caterpillar Club when he jumped with a parachute from an experimental type airplane which he was testing."[12] Two other second-degree members of the Caterpillar Club were Charles Lindbergh and Jimmy Doolittle. Upon arriving at the Air Station he was beset by reporters, eager for details of his crash and dramatic escape. Trap offered simply, "There was nothing wrong with the airplane until the elevators came off."

Among the reporters on hand was Ernie Pyle, who wrote, "Lieut. Trapnell, calm as a cucumber, sat in the flight test office at the Naval Air Station, telling this reporter, 'It was just over the side and pull the cord, and that was about all. But what I'm interested in is finding our dog. I don't care about having my picture in the paper, but if I could just get in a picture of the dog, maybe somebody would find him and bring him back.' Trap is worth any parachute's time and trouble to save him any day. He is one of the Navy's real gentlemen. It would be a more pleasant world if there were more people like him."[13]

Wally's story ran in every local paper that covered Trap's dramatic bailout from the broken airplane. "Trapnell's dog, which looks nearly as large as a horse and weighs 110 pounds . . . is 2 years old and has a shaggy light tan coat," one story ran. "A $25 reward has been offered for his safe return."

Trap subsequently received a commendation from the Assistant Secretary of the Navy, Ernest Jahncke, congratulating him on his "miraculous escape."[14] But the better news for Trap was Wally's safe recovery from Rock Creek Park the following day.

SPIN INNOVATION

A spin is a flight regime wherein the airplane is falling in a fully stalled, uncontrollable, self-sustaining yawing and rolling maneuver.[15] If the spin is left unchecked, the airplane will crash. The only safe way out of a spin is via a spin-recovery procedure. Needless to say, an uncontrolled spin is a dangerous and undesirable situation, except when teaching a student pilot how to recover from one. Many airplane designs will spin as a natural consequence of stalling unless the pilot takes special care to prevent it, and most airplanes can be made to spin. So a high-risk but essential test of a new airplane design is to determine when and how it will enter a spin and the most effective spin-recovery technique.

After witnessing a number of spin tests that resulted in losing the airplane and often the pilot, Trap determined there had to be a better way. He began to noodle through an innovation that quickly emerged as the antispin parachute, and he then proceeded to lay out a detailed design of the apparatus. This device comprises a parachute attached to the tail end of the airplane that the pilot can deploy from the cockpit. When opened, it yanks the airplane out of its uncontrolled spin and leaves it hanging nose down from the chute. With the airplane stabilized, the pilot can then shed the parachute altogether and regain control of the airplane.[16]

The original prototype was constructed in the Anacostia shops and put to the test by Trap when he made the first parachute-actuated spin recovery. The antispin parachute immediately became required equipment for Navy spin testing and was quickly adopted by the aviation industry, saving many precious first-of-its-kind prototype airplanes and keeping untold numbers of test pilots from an early grave.

A NEW KIND OF AVIATOR

With two intensive years under their belts, the cadre of crack pilots in Flight Test at Anacostia had broadened their test experience, honed their skills, developed innovative instrumentation, and gained capabilities unique in the annals of naval aviation's short history. Indeed, they had surpassed the vision posed by Eddie Rounds five years earlier when he called for formation of the test section. Largely because they accrued so much experience flying such a variety of airplane types, the Anacostia team acquired expertise and flight instincts that no airplane builder could match, and the contractors gained enormous respect for the technical wisdom and insight inherent in Flight Test Section recommendations.

By the end of June 1932, after two and a half years in Flight Test, Trap had logged 1,670 hours in 1,700 test flights of seventy types of aircraft, perhaps three times the number of flights and types flown by most aviators of his status. Not only had he strived to master the technical aspects of flight, but he drove himself hard to perfect his flying and analytical skills, his ability to quickly size up the stability and control characteristics of an airplane. For an airplane flying in equilibrium, say straight and level, stability is the tendency for it to return to that state after it has been disturbed from it, for example by turbulence. Control is the ease and predictability with which the pilot can maneuver the airplane in pitch, roll, and yaw.

Hours of intensive test flying honed his intuition about aerodynamics and aircraft behaviors in myriad flight regimes. He formulated many of the test procedures used in Flight Test to isolate a single flight characteristic from the others and to obtain quantitative data useful in evaluating and comparing airplanes.

Trap was pioneering a quantitative approach to flight testing—get the numbers and use them to guide testing—thereby advancing the safe and comprehensive evaluation of new and untried airplanes. This was laying the foundation for a new kind of test flying and a new kind of aviator—the engineering test pilot—who explored uncharted regions of flight to bring back

9. Trap, 1932

Official U.S. Navy photo, personal files of Frederick Trapnell Jr.

hard, quantitative data to describe an airplane's behavior, and then translated these data into reports and recommendations for engineers on the ground to use in designing improvements. This pilot was no longer simply determining that the airplane met its contract specification for satisfactory service; he had become integral to correcting the airplane's problems. Daredevil pilots would continue to achieve fame and set startling records, but engineering test pilots would spearhead the development of new aircraft through the twentieth century and beyond.

His test pilot colleague and later Vice Adm. Robert Pirie wrote of this period, "Trapnell was the sharpest student of aerodynamics and flight testing that we had." And, "I believe he is the best pilot and probably the best test pilot I have ever been associated with." When Trap was transferred to Naval Air Station Lakehurst, New Jersey, in the middle of 1932, his reputation in flight testing was sealed in the Navy and the American aircraft industry.[17]

ON THE HOMEFRONT

Although Mary supported Trap's ambition as an aviator, she fretted about the dangers and was not particularly good at taking a back seat. Less than two years into their marriage, his relentless devotion to his profession was beginning to rankle.

She took part-time work as a stenographer on Capitol Hill and settled tentatively into the Washington social scene, enjoying an occasional visit to the White House and attending a host of other parties and get-togethers with friends. Trap thrived on his work but spoke little of it at home, guarding the confidentiality of his profession and expecting ample rein to do as he saw fit at Flight Test.

Then, during their first summer in D.C., the gathering gloom of the Depression and increasing demands of Trap's work were compounded by a devastating heat wave that nearly sent Mary back to San Diego. She loathed the climate along the Potomac and missed her friends and family back home.

Late in the fall of 1931, Mary announced that she was pregnant with their first child. She hoped the baby would draw them together and heal the growing rift in their relationship. Although Trap warmed to the idea of being a father, he did not curtail his time at the airfield.

CHAPTER 6

★ ★ ★

AIRSHIP CARRIERS, 1932–33

At the close of World War I, rigid airships, or dirigibles, first caught the interest of the U.S. Navy for their possible effectiveness in long-range reconnaissance at sea. Both the Germans and the British had developed these colossal airships for bombing purposes, but what intrigued the U.S. Navy was their sustainable airspeed of up to seventy miles per hour, nearly three times the speed of a fast cruiser. With radar and reliable long-range airplanes still far in the future, airships seemed to offer a major advantage in patrolling ocean space.

A rigid airship is kept aloft by large bags of lighter-than-air gas contained within its rigid airframe. European dirigibles used highly flammable hydrogen gas, with sometimes calamitous results. The U.S. Navy standardized on less buoyant but nonflammable helium. Reserves of this gas, stored in high-pressure tanks, were released into the gas bags to increase lift or to replenish gas lost to leakage. Droppable ballast could also be dumped to increase buoyancy.

USS *Shenandoah*, the Navy's first airship, was delivered in 1923 and met her abrupt demise two years later when she went down in Ohio during a storm, killing fourteen of her crew. A larger airship, delivered from Germany in November 1924 as part of war reparations, was commissioned USS *Los Angeles*. Meanwhile, the Navy ordered two still bigger airships, USS *Akron* and USS *Macon*, to be built, under the guidance of imported German airship designers, by the Goodyear Company of Akron, Ohio, using a design completely different from previous airships.[1]

In 1929, the Navy began experimenting with airplanes outfitted with hooks on top to grab a trapeze bar suspended below *Los Angeles*. When these tests demonstrated that airships could indeed support routine airplane hook-on and drop-off operations, the Navy quickly ordered design revisions to *Akron* and

41

10. USS *Macon* with two tiny Sparrowhawks (see photo 11) ascending to hook onto the trapeze seen lowered from the airship's hull, 1933

Official U.S. Navy photo, National Archives and Records Administration, Records of the Bureau of Aeronautics

Macon that incorporated internal hangars and trapeze equipment to accommodate a small complement of aircraft, which would greatly enhance the airships' defensive and scouting capabilities. At the same time, BuAer launched a competition to select a fighter type airplane suitable for airship operations.

A tiny biplane fighter, the Curtiss F9C Sparrowhawk, was the prime candidate for the job. Curtiss, which had built a long line of airplanes for the Navy, designed this airplane explicitly for airship operation. In April 1931 they delivered a prototype Sparrowhawk to Anacostia, where Trap was assigned to evaluate its stability, handling qualities, and performance against two other entrants to the competition. The Sparrowhawk won the contest handily.

This airplane was small, even for its day, its compact design fitting snugly inside the limited hangar space on board the airship. It also had a particularly tight, cramped cockpit. One colleague, watching Trap finesse his lanky six-foot-two-inch frame into the awkward confines of the Sparrowhawk cockpit, commented, "He didn't climb in—he pulled it on like a pair of pants."[2]

The upper wing on most biplanes was raised above the top of the fuselage, giving the pilot an unimpeded view of the world from a position beneath the upper wing. The upper wing on the Sparrowhawk, however, was flush with the top of its fuselage, so the pilot looked out over this wing. The frame that carried the hook was mounted atop the fuselage, allowing the pilot an unobstructed view of the mechanism, so he could readily maneuver to bring it into contact with the trapeze bar. One disadvantage of the upper wing design was that it obscured the pilot's downward view of the runway or deck on conventional landings. Later models of the Sparrowhawk, armed with two .30-caliber machine guns, featured a redesigned gull-shaped upper wing raised slightly above the fuselage to improve the pilot's view.[3]

According to Rear Adm. Harold B. Miller, as long as you paid attention it was a beautiful airplane to fly, "probably the finest stunt plane I have ever flown, and I flew just about all of the early aircraft." In flight, however, it lacked inherent stability and required the pilot's constant vigilance. And because of poor downward visibility, it was always difficult to land conventionally. The Navy considered the Sparrowhawk a tricky airplane, but in the hands of those skilled aviators selected for the airships' Heavier-Than-Air (HTA) units, this airplane was accident-free for the three years it was in service.[4]

Akron and *Macon* could each carry four Sparrowhawk fighters and a modified two-seat training biplane, which they called a "running boat," to ferry people and small parts between the ground and the airship while she was airborne.

For skilled pilots, latching airplanes onto the midair trapeze was a simple procedure. With the airship flying slightly above the stalling speed of the airplane, the pilot approached the airship about twenty-five feet beneath and behind the trapeze and then, by modulating power and controlling climb rate, closed the distance between his hook and the trapeze bar. When the hook made contact, it automatically latched onto the bar, which was slightly V-shaped so that as the airplane's weight shifted from its wings onto the hook, the hook settled into the center of the V-bar. From that position, when the trapeze was hoisted into the airship, the wing tips just cleared the T-shaped hangar opening. To drop off the trapeze bar, the pilot pulled the lever to release the spring-loaded hook while keeping the throttle open, then eased back on the stick to let the wings take the load off the hook, and the airplane flew away.[5]

On October 27, 1931, *Akron* was commissioned at her new home base of Lakehurst, New Jersey, and conducted her first naval exercise in January of the following year, before her airplanes were available. While her range was impressive—she could stay aloft for several days and fly thousands of miles at a stretch—her early performance as a scouting aircraft was a disappointment. Exercises with the fleet off the West Coast a few months later underscored the problem. Without her HTA unit, the results were abysmal. Although *Akron* could locate the target ships well enough, she quickly became a sitting duck for "enemy" seaplanes, who were able to rack up a devastating round of mock

11. Sparrowhawk hooking onto the trapeze, 1933. Trap's stabilizing boom and saddle extends aft from the trapeze over the pilot's head, and the centering fork protrudes forward above the hook. Both will rotate down to stabilize the airplane without assistance from the pilot.

Official U.S. Navy photo, National Archives and Records Administration, Records of the Bureau of Aeronautics

"kills" against the vulnerable airship as she silently stalked her targets. The airship desperately needed her airplane contingent to establish her viability as a formidable scouting mechanism.[6]

Production Sparrowhawks arrived in May of 1932, and Trap transferred two months later from the Flight Test Section at Anacostia to the HTA unit on board USS *Akron* at Lakehurst. The officers and crew of *Akron* spent the next ten months working out tactics and fixing problems with the airship and her aircraft. At the root of their difficulty was a fundamental question: What was the military purpose of *Akron*? Was she a reconnaissance vehicle that carried airplanes for protection? Or was she an aircraft carrier that supported reconnaissance airplanes? The Department of the Navy, some of the higher-ups in BuAer, and many of the airship officers took the former view, which soon became her modus operandi.[7]

JUMP FOR JOY

Naval Air Station Lakehurst was not only home base for Navy airships, but was also the training ground for Navy parachute packers who then went to fleet squadrons to pack, store, and certify parachutes for pilots. Upon completing the Parachute Packers School, the final examination required students to jump from an airplane with parachutes they had packed themselves. About every twelve to fifteen weeks, there was a ceremony in which new graduates were flown up to four thousand feet over the air station, jumped from the airplane, and parachuted down to a waiting audience of celebrants.

Trap held vivid recollections of the exhilarating rush he had experienced during his free falls through the air after bailing out of his failed airplanes and before pulling the ripcord. Watching a graduating class one day gave him an idea. Paying a call on the senior instructor at the Parachute Packers School, he set about to persuade the man that as a seasoned pilot with previous experience in jumping, he should be allowed to jump with the next graduating class. Pilots like him would benefit from more practice in parachute jumping, he explained, and one more jumper would cost the Navy no more than the effort to repack his chute. Ultimately the instructor acquiesced.

Eight weeks later, Trap was the last of thirteen men to jump out the airplane door. The others pulled their ripcords immediately and started their slow descent to the ground. Trap had something else in mind. He was going to enjoy the free fall first.

On the ground, the audience watched twelve white silk chutes blossom into full flower. In the control tower, the supervising officer was counting parachutes—twelve—but there were supposed to be thirteen. Perhaps the thirteenth didn't jump after all. Then suddenly, picking out the plummeting body far below the open parachutes, he gasped. It had been ten or twelve seconds since the jumper had left the airplane, and still no parachute. He grabbed the emergency phone: "Parachute failure! Get the ambulances and crash trucks out there now!" And with that, he pushed the big red button that set the station crash siren blaring.

Trap gave it a few more seconds until he was down to roughly twelve hundred feet before pulling the ripcord. The chute popped open, suspending his body in midair. Hanging there, he became aware of the commotion below—sirens screaming, crash trucks, fire engines, an ambulance on the move—all converging around the spot where he was about to land. A welcoming committee! Still hanging in the harness above it all, he couldn't help but laugh as it dawned on him that his extended free fall was the source of the panic below. It struck him as the funniest unintended prank of his life.

Trap landed safely, but he was told to report to the station commanding officer immediately. The man was not amused; he chewed Trap out and threatened to ground him if he pulled a stunt like that again. But as he ordered Trap to leave, there was a twinkle in his eye.[8]

AN INNOVATION

Akron and her airplanes were a new and complex system, and her shakedown turned up a host of problems, among them the mechanical arrangement for stabilizing and securing an airplane while it was hooked onto the trapeze, so that it could be safely hoisted into and lowered from the airship. The original stabilizer required that the pilot, after hooking on, attach a pair of arms that dropped down from the trapeze to a corresponding pair of jaws on the wing. This provided a three-point grip on the airplane, which kept it from yawing and pitching. But connecting the arms to the clamps while the airplane was bobbing and twisting in the airstream could take several minutes, dangerously slowing the stowing and launching of airplanes. Extended hoisting time made things ticklish when airplanes returning low on fuel had to wait to come on board. Slow launches also impeded *Akron*'s ability to quickly deploy her airplanes for self-defense.

Furthermore, to Trap's eye, the stabilizing hardware was overly complex and cumbersome. He proposed a redesign that did away entirely with the concept of the arms and jaws. Instead it provided a single long arm with a padded "saddle" on the end that swung down behind the trapeze and straddled the hooked-on airplane fuselage just ahead of the vertical stabilizer, as shown in Photo 11, holding the airplane steady while a fork in front of the trapeze rotated into position to secure the airplane's hook at the center of the bar.

This proposed redesign was accepted by BuAer, and over a period of a few months Trap personally carried out the detailed design of the new rig, including all attachments to the airship. His youthful experience in boat design and his attention to design studies at the Naval Academy enabled him to tackle this kind of engineering challenge.

When the new mechanism was built in the Lakehurst shops and integrated into the airship, it not only simplified the launch and recovery process, but it reduced the weight of the airship by three hundred pounds. The pilot, no longer involved in connecting or disconnecting the apparatus, became the immediate beneficiary of this expedited hook-on procedure.

Trap received a formal commendation from the chief of BuAer for the design of this new stabilizing mechanism.[9]

PERIL

On April 3, 1933, *Akron* was preparing to lift off from Lakehurst at sundown for a several-day flight up the East Coast as far as Newport, Rhode Island. This was a significant exercise. BuAer chief, Rear Adm. William Moffett, was on board to receive a special demonstration of nighttime hook-on operations. Three Sparrowhawks planned to take off from the airfield and hook on shortly after the airship lifted off. Trap was to follow in the running boat, up to *Akron*, and stay on board to ferry the admiral back the following day if necessary.[10]

That morning, the overcast had been solid with gusting winds, which eased during the day while the ceiling lowered and visibility deteriorated. Some question arose as to whether *Akron* should go at all. Trap accompanied his good friend Lt. Cdr. Herb Wiley, *Akron*'s executive officer, to get the final weather reading from aerology. The senior aerologist expected clearing, but his junior aerologist was skeptical. The weather all around was extremely unsettled, with showers, probably thundershowers, over the Alleghenies in Pennsylvania. Still, there were always showers over the Alleghenies this time of year, and these might not move farther east. Wiley and the aerologists finally agreed that the weather posed no imminent threat to *Akron*.[11]

Though not a trained aerologist, Trap had misgivings. He had grown up with an innate sense of weather and its effects on boats, a sensitivity that carried over into his flying career, during which he had made a close study of weather, weather maps, and forecasting. As he pored over the data, he silently agreed with the junior aerology officer—very unstable indeed.

Upon Wiley's advice, *Akron*'s skipper, Cdr. Frank McCord, decided to go forward with her flight but worried that an airplane might not be able to find the airship in the dark under prevailing conditions. In view of the risks, he cancelled the Sparrowhawk hook-on demonstration. But the running boat was another matter; the admiral might need to get back. So unless weather made it impossible, Trap was to bring it on board.

Wiley spoke to him about the hazard, but Trap felt confident that he could fly through the low ceiling; all hook-on pilots were practiced in instrument flying. As long as *Akron* was in the clear above, he would find her. But Wiley was worried about visibility on top. Airborne radio direction finding remained a thing of the future. Would the airship and airplane be able to spot enough landmarks through the overcast to navigate together effectively if the airship wasn't readily visible? McCord ordered Trap to stay on the ground until they got *Akron* up above the cloud layer to assess the situation. The airship would swing out toward the west and then, if things looked reasonably clear, circle back to Lakehurst so that Trap could fly up to join them.

In the last light of day, with the admiral and several other guests on board, the airship lifted off, swung south of the airfield, and disappeared westward into the leaden mists. Trap sat on the flight line keeping the engine warm, ready to roll at a moment's notice. All he needed was the green light from McCord or Wiley. And so he waited.

The longer he waited the more troubled he became. Even in the dark, he could see that the overcast was down to three hundred feet and fog was beginning to obscure visibility further. He was anxious to get going—and soon—before the weather closed the field down altogether. He had plenty of experience flying on and off *Akron* in rough weather. In fact, he'd played a primary role in designing the airship's night approach lighting, which he'd used to hook on many times. This was their chance to demonstrate to Admiral Moffett that everything worked according to plan. Let's go, he thought.

A sailor ran out from the line shack waving a piece of paper and handed it to Trap in the cockpit. It was a message from Wiley. *Akron* was at two thousand feet altitude and west of the field, outbound. The cloud was thick around the airship and it was unlikely that Trap would be able to find them. So the skipper called off the running boat rendezvous—for now. Trap was to wait on the ground. The airship would head out west over Philadelphia and, if visibility improved, swing back to pick him up in an hour or so. If it did not, they would turn down the Delaware River and run south along the coast to try to stay in the clear. Trap would have plenty of notice if they came back, so he need not wait in the cockpit. Regardless, they wanted the running boat on board in the morning to ferry the admiral back to Washington.

Trap was disappointed. The crew had worked hard to prepare this demonstration for the admiral. Even if the airship was able to return, the weather at the field might preclude his takeoff. He clambered out of the cockpit and headed for the hangar, where he put on red-lens goggles to preserve his night vision and slipped into a chair in the ready room to wait.

The hour ticked by slowly with no word. Another hour passed. He took off the goggles and walked up to aerology, deciding they were unlikely to come back that night. The junior aerologist was still on duty, poring over the latest weather maps, shaking his head. Trap joined him as they sized up the weather picture before them.

A vicious storm front extended all the way from the Washington area, where a deep low pressure trough was centered, northwest through Allentown and all the way up to Albany. It was moving east at about thirty-five miles an hour, which would put it over Lakehurst in a couple of hours. Furthermore, a new storm system appeared to be building over Long Island Sound near Bridgeport. That too would probably move east. Finally, scattered thunderstorms were reported to the south, from just below Cape May down to Virginia Beach. This was the worst scenario the aerologist had ever seen, bar none.

As Trap studied the weather map, his frustration gave way to ominous foreboding. Big airships were fragile. *Shenandoah* had crashed eight years earlier due to weather considerably less threatening than this. He swallowed hard. His many friends and colleagues among the seventy-seven crew and passengers on board the *Akron* were in grave danger. If she went down on land, it would be bad, but they might have a chance of escape. After all, twenty-nine out of *Shenandoah*'s crew of forty-three survived the crash in fields of Ohio. On the other hand, should *Akron* go down at sea, it would be a different story. The jagged duralumin of the broken structure would tear into the gas bags, disgorging their 184,000 cubic meters of helium into the roiling waters. The metal structure, the sailcloth fuselage cover, and the huge collapsed gas bags would sprawl out across the ocean surface to form a suffocating blanket a thousand feet long and hundreds of feet wide, the crew and passengers trapped beneath a pitch-dark tangle of metal and cloth that would sink slowly into the abyss.

He phoned the control tower, but there was no word from *Akron*. Two hours later, the Army, Navy, and Coast Guard stations up and down the coast still had heard nothing from the airship. Trap lay down on a cot in the ready room, leaving word for the control tower to let him know the minute they heard anything. He didn't sleep a wink.

Akron went down that night off the New Jersey coast about thirty miles northeast of Atlantic City, killing seventy-three passengers and crewmen. Only four of the crew survived, one of them Herb Wiley, the only officer to come through the ordeal. Captured in headlines and newsreels around the world, this was at the time the most disastrous accident in aviation history.

The crash devastated the HTA pilots and everyone else at the air station. Their families suffered a collective and personal grief of unimaginable scale, and Mary was stunned to realize that Trap had come within a hair's breadth of going down with the airship. Trap was numbed by the loss of so many friends and fellow officers, and haunted by how close he had come to losing his own life. Decades later, he still could not speak of that harrowing night without deep sorrow. Furthermore, this tragedy crystallized his lingering doubts about the future of vast, ungainly, and fragile airships as weapons of war.

THE WAY WEST

Three months after *Akron*'s demise, Trap and the other *Akron* HTA pilots were transferred to her sister ship, USS *Macon*, which was commissioned in June 1933 and spent the next four months at Lakehurst shaking down her crew and HTA unit. On October 12, she left Lakehurst for the three-day trip to her new home in Sunnyvale, California. Trap flew a running boat on board and rode the airship to the West Coast while the rest of the HTA unit flew their Sparrowhawks to California.[12]

12. Pilots of the USS *Macon* Heavier-Than-Air unit in 1934. Trap stands in center; Lt. Harold B. Miller is on his right.

Official U.S. Navy photo, personal files of Frederick Trapnell Jr.

Macon arrived in Sunnyvale with much fanfare on October 16 and settled into her quarters at the newly named Moffett Field. "The new 785-foot air giant . . . seemed as silvery as if she had just taken to the air," gushed the *Palo Alto Times*. The airship soon became a familiar sight over the San Francisco peninsula, drawing crowds of admirers to watch spellbound as the luminous leviathan glided through the skies over the bay. With the country in the throes of the Great Depression and *Akron*'s tragic demise still fresh in the national memory, the stakes were high for *Macon*'s West Coast debut. The Navy had spent a considerable sum to bring these airships into the fleet, and now the pressure was on the officers and crew to perform up to expectations on her debut reconnaissance mission. During this period of heightened tensions, Trap was named head of the HTA unit.

Over the course of the next seven months, the fleet staged a series of exercises to test naval aviation in mock combat with the two sides based on islands several hundred miles apart, as might occur in the Western Pacific. Islands off the California coast were used as surrogates. Lacking long-range reconnaissance opportunities, the powers that be reverted to old habits, using the airship rather than her scout planes as the primary search vehicle.[13]

Called upon to demonstrate her usefulness to battle fleet operations in an environment crowded with ships and carrier airplanes, *Macon* did not fare well. Although she was effective in making initial contact with the enemy, she invariably found herself within antiaircraft gun range of enemy ships or put out of action by a swarm of enemy fighters before she could even launch most of her airplanes. Despite their superior performance, her covey of four Sparrowhawks was too small and unwieldy to be effective in this scenario. Consequently, *Macon*'s performance came under heavy criticism from fleet commanders.[14]

HTA pilots and other proponents of using the airship as a carrier for the Sparrowhawk scout planes were frustrated by what they saw as egregious misuse of *Macon*'s capabilities. They, as well as a few of the ship's officers and some of the enlightened heads at BuAer, thought the airship should hang back out of enemy sight and let her airplanes do the scouting.[15]

But for *Macon*, the hand of obsolescence was writing on the wall, confirming Trap's doubts about the success of the Navy experiment with airships. In late 1933, production versions of reliable long-range patrol planes, Consolidated P2Ys, were finally being delivered to the Navy. In January 1934, Trap's friend Lt. Cdr. Knefler "Sock" McGinnis led six of these flying-boat aircraft on a 2,400-mile, twenty-four-hour nonstop flight from San Francisco to Pearl Harbor, an impressive demonstration of the P2Y's range and reliability. Not only could they readily assume most of the role envisaged for *Akron* and *Macon*, but for the price of either, you could buy twenty-five P2Ys.[16]

13. Consolidated P2Y-3, the Navy's first reliable long-range patrol plane.
Trap flew these in 1936, 1938, and 1939.

Official U.S. Navy photo, National Archives and Records Administration,
Records of the Bureau of Aeronautics

In June 1934, in the throes of this disheartening situation, Trap was transferred from *Macon* to shipboard duty as the senior aviator on board USS *San Francisco*, a brand new heavy cruiser. During his years in the HTA units on *Akron* and *Macon*, Trap had become a qualified lighter-than-air pilot and watch officer, accruing 505 hours of LTA flight time, and he received a commendation for High Gunnery Merit in the 1934 annual gunnery exercises.[17]

In February 1935, after Trap's detachment, *Macon* suffered a structural failure while airborne off the California coast that brought her down at sea. Unlike the crew of her sister, all but two of her crew were saved. Still, it was the sad end to the airship era in the U.S. Navy.

ROUGH WATERS

Life at Lakehurst offered Mary little improvement over Washington. She had hoped that becoming a father would draw Trap closer. But despite his interest in their new son, she could not compete for his attentions. The intensity of Trap's work and the amount of time he spent away from home compounded their fractured relationship. The Navy was his life.

When *Macon* lifted off from Lakehurst to head for the West Coast with Trap on board, Mary and their one-year-old son Frederick Mackay Jr., nicknamed "Fritz," boarded the westbound train in New York. They were going home at last to her beloved California. The move west brightened Mary's outlook and kindled her hopes for a more normal family life.

Following a brief sojourn with family in San Diego, Mary and young Fritz made their way north to the Bay Area, where they settled into their small house in Palo Alto, a stone's throw from Trap's new station at Moffett Field. Among the bright spots in this brief time was the opportunity to renew old friendships, including that with Alice Moffitt, the spunky daughter of a renowned San Francisco doctor and a friend from her Berkeley days.

Alice was attractive and sharp-witted, and she traveled comfortably in San Francisco's most prominent social circles. Married to a mild-mannered, wealthy man and living in the tony neighborhood of Burlingame on the peninsula south of the city, Alice was delighted to reconnect with Mary and her husband, and she welcomed the couple into their circuit of friends.

It soon became evident that Trap was more than casually attracted to Alice. By the time he was preparing to go back to sea after their first Christmas in California, all was not well between him and Mary.

As she watched him walk out the door that overcast January morning with a single suitcase in his hand, Mary decided there was no point staying in Palo Alto. She packed up her things and took Fritz back to San Diego at about the same time that Alice filed for divorce.

CHAPTER 7

★ ★ ★

SCOUTING AND PATROLLING, 1934–40

Locating and tracking the enemy, knowing where to go and where to shoot was a high priority in U.S. Navy doctrine. Even their experiment with airships targeted this objective. So with the demise of *Macon*, the handful of Heavier-Than-Air unit pilots—some of the most skilled aviators in the Navy—were transferred to aircraft units on board battleships and cruisers. The Bureau of Personnel may have seen this as a way to beef up the Gun Club's scouting capability.[1]

Accordingly, Trap was directed to report for duty as senior aviator on board the new heavy cruiser USS *San Francisco* in June 1934.[2] For the next two years, he would fly some variant of the Vought O2U/O3U Corsair, a biplane scout aircraft that could be rigged by the maintenance staff for float or land operations.[3]

Trap anticipated his new post with satisfaction. *San Francisco* was a spanking new ship, free of the cranky, awkward fixtures found on the older *Marblehead* and *California*.[4] He flew Vought O3U Corsairs launched from gunpowder-driven catapults and hoisted on board from water landings using a specially designed aircraft crane. He had flown similar seaplanes at Anacostia, but the catapult launch was new for him. The job of these graceless little scout planes was to search out the enemy position, pinpoint the impact of shells fired from the ship's big guns, and radio aiming corrections back to the mother ship.

Though the airplane was not as agile as the Sparrowhawk nor was the job as demanding of pilot precision as the aerobatic team, scouting and spotting offered a novel kind of challenge. Their mission entailed expeditions many miles away from the mother ship and far from land, often in inclement and dangerous weather, making accurate navigation and instrument flying imperative. Furthermore, sighting the enemy and telling ships where to shoot was the sharp end of the Navy's spear.

Not only was Trap gaining a new kind of flight experience on board *San Francisco*, but his role as senior aviator allowed him to hone his leadership skills. More personally, his return to sea duty was like coming home, back to the passion that had drawn him to the Navy in the first place: the stiff salty breeze, the comfortable roll of the sea, the rush of water scudding along the waterline. It was gratifying to be shipboard again as part of the mainstream Navy.

Within two weeks of Trap's arrival, as *San Francisco* steamed south for operations near the Panama Canal Zone, the ship's log shows that he began serving on the ship's watch officer rotation.[5] He made his first catapult launch while she was under way during their approach to the Canal Zone. After operating in that region for a week, *San Francisco* steamed north again to San Diego, then on to Marc Island Navy Yard near San Francisco to install new guns and to convert her to a flagship. During the four-month layover for retrofitting, the floats on their airplanes were replaced with wheels for land-based operations.

Throughout that summer, Trap's flights were a mixed bag of familiarization, radio practice, and night flying, but gunnery loomed large because he and his pilots had to shoot for record at the end of September.[6] He followed this with more instrument and night flying. After becoming one of the earliest Navy pilots to earn official certification as an instrument pilot in October 1934,[7] Trap insisted that his pilots qualify as well. From mid-October through the end of November, he focused on training his rear gunners for their gunnery qualification at the end of that month. By December, Trap was flying as a target so *San Francisco*, still moored at Mare Island, could check out the tracking of her new antiaircraft guns.[8]

In February, *San Francisco* rejoined the fleet in San Diego, where Trap and his crew again operated from the ship off the coast of California before sailing north into Alaskan waters in July. Notoriously unsettled, the weather in Alaska commonly afforded only limited visibility. Trap's earlier emphasis on instrument flying and insistence on new radio direction-finding equipment paid off in spades. *San Francisco*'s airplanes flew almost daily, rain or shine. Indeed, their captain was heard to remark that his airplanes now operated in weather that scared even him.[9]

Trap remained senior aviator on board *San Francisco* for another full year. During the last three months of this tour, the squadron swapped their old Corsairs for the newer Curtiss SOC-1 Seagull,[10] which would remain in shipboard service through World War II.

ALOHA

Mary had retreated with young Fritz to San Diego while Trap took to sea. He made a point of stopping in to visit when he was in the area. But during his layovers in San Francisco, he and Alice slipped into a romantic liaison. She was smitten by his easy charm and quiet magnetism. He was intrigued by her bold elegance and gregarious sociability, and Alice's assets provided the added benefit of creature comforts generally beyond the reach of an officer's salary.

Early in 1935, while at sea in *San Francisco*, Trap wrote to Mary in San Diego asking for a divorce. It did not take her long to respond; a divorce was probably for the best. They filed in California, where it took more than a year to complete the proceedings; Alice's divorce, filed in Nevada, was finalized sooner.

Trap and Alice were married July 4, 1936, when he was detached from *San Francisco*. They honeymooned on the *Lurline*, the flagship of the Matson line, en route to his new duty station in Hawaii, where he was to become executive officer of Patrol Squadron (VP) 10.[11] They quickly settled into Married Officers Quarters L on the naval base at Pearl Harbor, where the balmy air, the perpetual clear nights and sunny days, and the easy, aloha lifestyle offered an idyllic atmosphere for a couple of newlyweds.[12]

PATROLLING THE PACIFIC

VP-10 was a squadron of long-range, twin-engine patrol planes, Consolidated P2Ys (see Photo 13), with a 2,600-mile range and cruising speed of 120 miles per hour. Patrol planes assumed the role previously envisioned for *Akron* and *Macon*, so Trap was operating on familiar turf.[13]

The Navy wanted patrol plane bases that allowed broad surveillance of the waters bounding the United States and its territories. VP-10's mission was to develop a plan that would enable the Navy to patrol the seas from the middle of the North Pacific, west to Johnson Island, and south toward the Christmas Islands. This was roughly a six-hundred-mile margin to the north, west, and south of the Hawaiian Island chain, which stretched sixteen hundred miles westward from the big island of Hawaii to the tiny dot of Kure atoll. In the days before radar, this called for multiple aircraft operating in coordinated flight patterns from carefully selected locations to cover vast tracts of ocean. Aside from Pearl Harbor and Hilo (on the Big Island), suitable locations for supporting patrol planes were Lahaina on Maui, French Frigate Shoals almost six hundred miles west of Pearl Harbor, and Midway Island, which lay another eight hundred miles beyond French Frigate Shoals and within one hundred miles of Kure.

French Frigate Shoals offered a semisheltered bay able to accommodate a seaplane tender. Midway harbored a U.S. Marine detachment to keep order and defend the 2.4-square-mile atoll already in use as a fueling stopover by trans-Pacific Pan American Clipper airplanes. Its anchorage was sheltered by a coral reef, and either of its two islands could support a shore-based patrol facility.

The Navy did not have nearly enough patrol planes in the Pacific to continuously cover the myriad approaches to the Hawaiian Islands. The best existing squadrons could hope to do was establish and maintain the necessary anchorages and bases and to work out the requisite search timing and patterns that would enable the Navy to quickly add or relocate patrol planes for maximum search efficiency in the event of an emergency. So Trap and detachments from his squadron, although based at Pearl Harbor, routinely set up temporary operations at Midway, French Frigate Shoals, Lahaina, and Hilo to devise logistics and procedures for patrolling from these disparate locations, each of which shows up on multiple occasions in Trap's log entries for the period.[14]

In addition to surveying and planning expanded search operations, Trap carried out routine searching, gunnery and bombing practice, battle maneuvers, and instrument flying. According to his log entry for September 29, 1936, he completed a seven-hour course of simulated instrument flying in what must have been one of the Navy's earliest link trainers, achieving a final mark of 3.8 out of 4.0. Occasionally Trap also borrowed an F4B fighter from a squadron at Pearl Harbor for aerial gunnery and aerobatic practice to keep his hand in with fighter planes.[15]

In December 1937, the pilots and flight crews of VP-10 went to the continental United States by ship to pick up eighteen new patrol planes from San Diego, Consolidated PBY Catalinas. These state-of-the-art flying boats

14. Consolidated PBY Catalina, the long-range patrol plane that succeeded the P2Y in Photo 13. Trap flew these in 1938 and 1940, as well as its amphibious version, the PBY-5A, in 1943.

Official U.S. Navy photo, Naval History and Heritage Command cruised faster and carried heavier loads than their P2Y predecessors. On January 18, 1938, after gaining a measure of familiarity with their new airplanes, the entire squadron flew as a unit safely back to Pearl Harbor, setting a record of 20.5 hours for the 2,553-mile crossing. It was a stunning performance for the organization and their new aircraft, and Trap, as executive officer, received accolades for his leadership in planning and executing the flight.[16]

Trap was promoted to lieutenant commander in June 1938 but remained executive officer of VP-10 until September, when he left the squadron, along with the balmy trade winds and warm sunshine of Honolulu, to take command of Patrol Squadron 21 in the less-than-aloha skies of Seattle.[17] Alice and their one-year-old son, Herbert Wallace, called Wally, joined him.

Trap's move to Seattle was a step up in responsibility but a reversion in aircraft capability. Apparently, the Navy had decided to locate its most advanced patrol planes in more threatened regions like Hawaii and the Western Pacific, so VP-21 in the Gulf of Alaska was still flying P2Ys.

VP-21 was the only patrol squadron operating along the Northern Pacific coast, and its operations extended northward from Seattle to cover the eastern Gulf of Alaska. As in Hawaii, there were not enough patrol planes to surveil this huge expanse of ocean, so the main task was to develop logistics, plans, and procedures that would allow the Navy to mobilize quickly to cover this territory in an emergency. To this end, the squadron set up a secondary base at Sitka, Alaska, where they maintained a flight of patrol planes on rotating duty. In addition, Trap personally surveyed locations in Ketchikan, Wrangell, Petersburg, Juneau, and as far north as Yakutat. Operating from Seattle and all these subsidiary locations, VP-21 patrolled the seas from the Oregon coast northwest to the Alaskan peninsula beyond Kodiak Island.[18]

The weather in the Northern Pacific proved a perennial challenge to patrol plane operations, and, not surprisingly, Trap's 1938–1939 log book shows intensive instrument flying throughout the period. Vice Admiral Pirie recalls in his oral history for 1939 that he was commanding the seaplane tender USS *Teal* when she tended VP-21 in the Gulf of Alaska. "Weather reporting in that part of the world was almost nil, and your own meteorologists had to make their own estimates based on observations that they could make from the ships or from the airplanes. . . . We were weathered in at Yakutat one time for something like five days, and Trapnell and I drew our own [weather] maps, and we predicted within one hour when the stuff would lift and we could get out of there."[19]

In July 1939, Trap changed from CO of VP-21 to CO of VP-45 in what was likely only a squadron number change. Then in October of 1939, VP-45 moved from Seattle to San Diego, where its designation was changed again to VP-14.[20] He and Alice settled into a house on J Avenue in Coronado.[21] His log books record heavy emphasis on gunnery, bombing, and tactics. But the steady drumbeat of night and instrument flying persisted; in March 1940, his log book contains a letter certifying that Lieutenant Commander Trapnell has "successfully completed the syllabus of instruction in the Link Aviation Trainer Types 'E' and 'C', as required." For this accomplishment, he received a document certifying him as Sky Jockey No. 133, an early number among many hundreds of naval aviators.[22]

In May 1940, his ongoing bombing practice won him the designation of master horizontal bombing pilot, "a title that only a very few people in the whole navy qualified for," according to Adm. John S. Thach.[23]

The longest extant document authored by Trap is one of sixty pages that he wrote in late 1939 titled "Notes for Beginners," found in the NNAM archives; it encapsulates lectures and guidance he gave to his patrol plane pilots. It begins with a section on patrol plane seamanship, how to handle these big craft when taxiing on the water in various conditions of weather and wind. He provides guidance on how to safely come alongside a mooring buoy, a ship, or a ramp on the beach without going aground. Other sections cover sea anchors (which he describes as "widely and principally used to eliminate the necessity of using good judgment"), effects of tide, crosswind landings, powered landings, and some subtle but practical aspects of night and instrument flying. A fascinating tutorial on elemental principles not taught in flight school, this treatise clearly reflects Trap's long and sensitive experience captaining sailing vessels and piloting seaplanes.

Trap's final log entry with VP-14 is for early May 1940, when he was relieved of command of VP-14 and transferred to Anacostia, D.C., for assignment as senior flight test officer in command of the Flight Test Section. His journey had taken him full circle back to Anacostia, where his flight-testing career was launched ten years earlier.

CHAPTER 8

★ ★ ★

NAVAL AVIATION 1930–40, HISTORICAL INTERLUDE

N ew technologies had transformed aviation in significant ways since Trap earned his wings. In light of the escalating air war in Europe toward the end of the decade, the impact of these developments on aircraft design and flight capability took on heightened significance.

No technical innovation was more important than the evolution of aircraft engines. Their growth in power and power-to-weight ratio, throughout aviation history, advanced aircraft performance to new levels. The continuous evolution of the air-cooled radial engine that had become the Navy standard in the 1920s was of particular importance to the work of flight test during the prewar era. The Wright Aeronautical Corporation had been the original sole producer of the Navy's radial engines until 1925, when a group of engineers split off from Wright to launch the Pratt & Whitney Aircraft Company, immediately winning a contract from the Navy to supply new engines. From this point on, these two companies battled for preeminence in bringing forward new, more powerful air-cooled radial power plants.[1]

In addition to power plant improvements, NACA (National Advisory Committee for Aeronautics, later renamed NASA) developed engine cowlings that reduced the drag and improved the cooling of radial engines. Research into propellers led to improvements in propeller efficiency by way of better propeller aerodynamics and variable pitch propellers, which allowed the pilot to optimize engine rpm and thrust across a broad range of airplane speeds.[2]

Early airplanes were constructed using frames and stringers made of wood or aluminum and covered with cloth to form the outer skin. The innovation of monocoque construction, however, allowed a rigid metal skin itself to provide much of the aircraft's structural strength. This, combined with the advent of duralumin alloys, made it possible to build all-metal airplanes with lightweight,

60

rugged structures. Furthermore, new flush-riveting techniques allowed metal skins to be attached to frames while leaving a smooth exterior surface.

Most airplanes of the 1930s were two-winged biplanes. External bracing wires and rods between wings and from the wings to the fuselage stiffened their structure. At low flying speeds, two wings were needed to generate sufficient lift to support the airplane and its load in flight. But biplane speed was limited by the inherent drag and weight of this arrangement, as well as by the low power of then-available engines. Newer metals and structural innovations enabled airplane engineers to create practical designs featuring a single wing without external bracing. This led to the now familiar monoplane, rendered feasible by increasingly powerful engines.

Wing flaps, surfaces hinged along the trailing edge of an airplane wing, can be deflected downward to increase the lift (and drag) of the wing at low speeds. The earliest wing flap seems to have been implemented by the British in 1922.[3] But, apparently to save weight, the Navy generally eschewed this facility for biplanes, the ample wing area of which provided adequate lift at their inherently slow flying speeds, including during takeoff and landing. On the other hand, the speed-seeking design of a monoplane called for a single small wing, which provided only limited lift at low speed and so made takeoffs and landings fast and dangerous on short runways and carrier decks.

Wing flaps changed all this. At low airspeeds, the flaps were lowered to increase the monoplane's lift. Although this also increased drag, more powerful engines compensated by providing more thrust to keep the monoplane flying comfortably at low speeds. At high speed, the flaps were raised to become an integral part of the wing's low-drag streamlined airfoil. This, along with its more powerful engine, enabled the monoplane to fly significantly faster than its biplane counterpart.

Retractable landing wheels first appeared on U.S. Navy airplanes with the Grumman FF-1 in 1932 as a means of reducing drag and improving performance, and they became common on production aircraft during the late 1930s.[4]

Superchargers were essential for high-altitude flight. Because engines require oxygen for combustion, they lose power at high altitude, where the engine intake air becomes thinner. The supercharger is a pump, usually driven off the engine, that compresses thin ambient air at high altitude and forces it into the engine at pressure corresponding to a lower altitude, thereby boosting available engine power at higher altitude. Important steps were made in the 1930s to improve supercharger compression effectiveness (pressure ratios) and reduce their weight.[5]

The single-stage supercharger, common even before the 1930s, comprised a single centrifugal pump that could provide output pressures limited to approximately three times the input pressure. But high-performance, high-altitude engine operation required even more pressure, which gave rise to two-stage superchargers in the late 1930s. These were essentially two single-stage superchargers, one feeding into the other, often having a cooling section between the two known as the intercooler.[6]

Thus many of the technical innovations that ultimately materialized in World War II had been introduced in airplane designs through the 1930s. Lacking the funds to replace an increasingly obsolete inventory of aircraft and to keep up with technical evolution, however, U.S. naval aviation technology began to fall dangerously behind the rest of the world.

TORPEDO AND DIVE BOMBERS

BuAer procurement and engineering during the 1930s focused primarily on torpedo and dive bombers, airplanes that could deliver a weapon lethal to a big ship. As a result, the first operational carrier airplane to integrate many of the foregoing innovations was a torpedo bomber, the Douglas TBD Devastator. This airplane, which could deliver either a torpedo at low altitude or a bomb dropped from high altitude, was ordered in 1934 and first flew in 1935. It represented a number of firsts for carrier-based aircraft: first monoplane, first all-metal airplane, first airplane with hydraulic folding wings to conserve cramped deck space on board ship, and first with a completely enclosed cockpit.[7]

The Navy was more ambivalent about dive bombers and pursued both biplane and monoplane designs. Its primary goal was to get an airplane that could deliver a 1,000-pound bomb in a vertical dive.[8] In 1934, BuAer issued a request for a new round of carrier-based dive bombers. This request specified the ability to sustain a stable, vertical dive at a speed of no more than 250 knots, which allowed the airplane to continue its dive low enough for accurate bombing and then pull out for a safe escape. Northrop answered this call with the Navy's first monoplane dive bomber, the XBT-1, which first flew in 1935. This airplane pioneered the split dive flap, which, after a long struggle to cure severe buffeting, yielded the first monoplane able to sustain a true vertical dive at moderate speed. Although the Navy procured fifty-five of these, by the time they became operational in 1940, they were already considered obsolete.[9]

The Navy's second monoplane dive bomber candidate, the Vought SB2U Vindicator, was constructed partly of cloth-covered metal framing. It first flew in 1936 and was introduced into the fleet in 1937. The final production order for this airplane was issued in 1939, and by late 1940 it was evident that it lacked the performance required for effective combat operations. A total of 169 were produced, a number of which went to the British Fleet Air Arm.[10]

Hedging their dive-bombing bets, the Navy continued to fund the evolution of the Curtiss SBC, an all-metal biplane design. The last of these, the SBC-4, was introduced as late as 1938. It was procured in greater quantities than both of its two monoplane counterparts and deliveries continued into 1941. The SBC, however, was the last combat biplane built in the United States, and in view of the capabilities of airplanes fighting in Europe, its performance was quickly deemed unsatisfactory.[11]

In September 1939, the president proclaimed the existence of a limited national emergency based on the escalating aggression of Nazi forces in Europe, and he directed measures for strengthening national defenses within the limits of peacetime authorizations. So as the shadow of the decade lengthened and the early clouds of war broke over the eastern horizon, the Navy found itself saddled with all three of its operational dive bombers on the brink of obsolescence.[12]

FIGHTERS

During this period of trial and error, high powers at BuAer held fighter planes on the back burner, believing that speed was not a priority for these planes, which lacked the range to accompany the bigger bombers to distant targets and would be superfluous to properly armed bombers capable of defending themselves.[13]

Even into early 1941, carrier squadrons continued to operate with biplane dive bombers and fighters; ominous photographs taken at the time show U.S. carrier flight decks filled with biplanes. The fighters shown in Photo 15 are biplane Grumman F3Fs, which had a top speed of just over 260 mph and packed one .50-caliber and one .30-caliber machine gun.

As early as 1936, BuAer issued a requirement for a new carrier fighter to replace the F3F. Grumman responded with a proposal for a more advanced biplane, the XF4F-1, which the Navy deemed too slow.[14] Grumman quickly presented its XF4F-2 proposal for a monoplane fighter. The Brewster Aeronautical Corporation offered a monoplane design, the XF2A-1, later dubbed the Buffalo, which first flew in late 1937. Prototypes were ordered for both of these airplanes, and flight tests in 1938 demonstrated that while the Grumman airplane was slightly faster, the Brewster's handling qualities were superior. During these tests, the F4F suffered an engine failure, and the subsequent forced landing damaged the prototype, forcing its withdrawal from consideration. Consequently, the Navy set aside plans for the Grumman airplane and pushed ahead with the Buffalo, which entered service in April 1939.[15]

The Buffalo was an all-metal monoplane featuring a flush-riveted, stressed-skin construction, a top speed of just over 320 mph, and one .50-caliber and

15. The USS *Enterprise* alongside the quay at North Island, San Diego, July 1940.
Note monoplane dive bombers and torpedo planes on her flight deck aft
and biplane F3F fighters forward.

*Official U.S. Navy photo, National Archives and Records Administration,
Records of the Bureau of Aeronautics*

one .30-caliber machine gun, which fired from the nose cowling through the propeller. Early models had snappy maneuverability and good initial climb rates, but they had neither armor protection nor self-sealing fuel tanks, and the single-row Wright "Cyclone" engine with its single-stage supercharger gave the airplane disappointing performance at altitude.[16] Even more serious was the frailty of the landing gear, which proved unable to stand up under loads routinely encountered in carrier landings. Later models added more guns, more fuel, and a more powerful version of the engine for additional speed, only to have the added weight degrade maneuverability and climb performance. The later generation still had no armor or self-sealing tanks and so remained vulnerable to enemy fire. The correction for these shortcomings would add still more weight and further degrade performance. The airplane desperately needed a more powerful engine with a better supercharger, but its airframe design precluded this improvement.

16. Brewster F2A-1 Buffalo, the Navy's first monoplane fighter, 1938

Official U.S. Navy photo, National Archives and Records Administration,
Records of the Bureau of Aeronautics

Still more damaging were continual production and management problems at Brewster, which delayed deliveries on a Buffalo design that was already
virtually obsolete. By early 1940, the shine was off this once-promising fighter,
and the Navy, increasingly disgruntled with Brewster, shelved further orders
for the airplane.[17]

Fortunately, BuAer had supported Grumman efforts to improve the
F4F under a 1938 contract, and the resulting XF4F-3 Wildcat prototype was
ready to fly on February 12, 1939. This new fighter accommodated either the
Wright "Cyclone" engine used in the Brewster airplane or the more advanced
two-row 1,200-horsepower Pratt & Whitney "Twin Wasp" engine with the
world's first two-speed, two-stage supercharger. At lower altitudes, the Wildcat offered speed and climb rates comparable to the Buffalo, though it was
less maneuverable. But the Pratt & Whitney engine, with its more advanced
supercharger, provided much better performance than the Buffalo at altitudes
above 15,000 feet.[18]

Grumman was awarded a production contract for seventy-eight F4F-3
Wildcats in August 1939, which called for essential modifications, including
armor protection and self-sealing fuel tanks. The first production Wildcats

17. Grumman F4F Wildcat fighter, mainstay of Navy and Marine Pacific fighter
units during the first year and a half of World War II in the Pacific.
For the rest of the war it remained in production and served on
board light carriers in Allied navies.

Official U.S. Navy photo, U.S. Naval Institute Photo Archive

flew in February 1940 and received formal Navy acceptance in January of the
following year.[19]

By the summer of 1940, the Luftwaffe had swept continental air forces
out of the skies, some of them flying aircraft purchased from the United States.
With the obsolescent Brewster Buffalo in limited operation, the Grumman
Wildcat not yet operational, and far superior aircraft clashing in the skies over
Europe and Britain, the U.S. Navy found itself in very deep water indeed.

In other troubling news, RAF fighters in the Battle of Britain were having
a turkey shoot every time they caught unescorted German Stuka dive bombers,
which had defensive capabilities similar to the latest U.S. Navy dive bombers.
So the notion, still held in some quarters of BuAer, that bombers could defend
themselves against fighters was demonstrably wrong. The Navy needed first-
class fighters to protect its bombers and torpedo planes.[20]

The armament of operational Navy biplane fighters and early monoplane
prototypes also stood in stark contrast to the stunning firepower of the weapons

carried by fighters on both sides of the European war. The Messerschmitt Bf 109E packed two 20-mm and two 7.9-mm (.30-caliber) machine guns. British fighters carried eight .30-caliber guns, which the RAF was rapidly upgrading by replacing them with 20-mm cannons.[21] The Navy rushed to add two .50-caliber wing guns to the existing cowling-mounted guns on the Buffalo and changed orders for the Wildcat to remove the engine-cowling-mounted guns and replace them with four .50-caliber wing guns. Even so, the German Bf 109E packed 20 percent more firepower than the Wildcat, which had yet to become operational.[22]

The Wildcat, with its top speed of 330 miles per hour and service ceiling of 35,000 feet,[23] had performance roughly comparable to the British Hawker Hurricane fighter, though the latter climbed faster and performed better at altitude.[24] The Hurricane had been in RAF service since 1937, and by September 1939 five hundred Hurricanes had been delivered to the RAF.[25] So, in the broad scheme of things, the U.S. Navy trailed far behind its allies on the other side of the Atlantic. But the really bad news was that the Hurricane had already proved no match for the Messerschmitt Bf 109E, and RAF practice called for its Hurricanes to avoid tangling with the Bf 109s whenever possible.

The RAF, though, also had a superior fighter in its inventory, the Supermarine Spitfire, which had been in service since August 1938. The Spitfire and the Bf 109E had top speeds of more than 350 mph at 20,000 feet, service ceilings above 35,000 feet, and, as noted above, packed superior firepower.[26] In 1940, these were numbers that operating squadrons of the U.S. Navy could only dream about.

U.S. ARMY AIR CORPS

The Army Air Corps, with its stable of fighters, was better off than the Navy. Eyeing the situation in Europe in 1939, it ordered 524 Curtiss P-40 Tomahawks, the largest single order ever placed for U.S. fighter planes at the time. The Tomahawk had solid low-altitude performance, with a top speed of 343 mph and service ceiling of 31,000 feet. While it compared favorably with the best European fighters at low altitude, above 20,000 feet this no longer held true.[27]

The Bell P-39 Airacobra first flew in 1939 with a top speed of 385 mph, making it even faster than the Tomahawk at low altitude. But the production airplanes lacked an adequate supercharger and failed to compete at high altitude.[28]

In January 1939 the Lockheed P-38 Lightning made its first flight. This large turbo-supercharged twin-engine fighter had truly superb high-altitude performance, and in an early cross-country flight achieved an average cruising speed of 360 mph, with a top speed approaching 400 mph. Although the prototype crashed in early 1939, its performance was strong enough for the Army to fund thirteen service test models, the first of which would not be ready to fly until September 1940. It was a long dry spell.[29] Nonetheless, the U.S. Army Air Corps had at least some vision of their path to becoming competitive in wartime operations.

NEW NAVY PROTOTYPES

In January 1938, BuAer issued a requirement for a high-performance single-engine fighter. Grumman Aircraft's submission, an upgraded Wildcat, was rejected, but two others were approved and orders were placed for their prototypes: the Bell Aircraft XFL-1 Airabonita and the Vought Sikorsky XF4U-1 Corsair.

The Airabonita, which first flew in May 1940, was derived from the Army Airacobra, which had tricycle landing gear. But the naval version was given conventional landing gear with a tail wheel and strengthened aft section to accommodate a tail hook for carrier operations. It was a pretty airplane, but its power plant, taken from the Airacobra, foreshadowed weak performance at high altitude.

The Airabonita had another strike against it: the Navy's persistent aversion to liquid-cooled engines. Since the early 1920s, BuAer had argued that for the same horsepower, liquid-cooled engines were heavier than air-cooled engines and too vulnerable to enemy gunfire; one small puncture in the cooling system and the engine was finished. This was risky for airplanes required to operate over water at great distance from their carrier.

Vought had recently built scout planes and a dive bomber for the Navy, but their entry in the 1938 competition with the XF4U-1 Corsair was their first attempt in a long time at building a fighter. Vought's chief engineer, Rex Beisel, chose for his design the 1,850-horsepower (later increased to 2,000) air-cooled R-2800 engine from Pratt & Whitney, the most powerful engine of its kind, with a two-stage supercharger for strong altitude performance. This brand new engine had not yet completed its tests and the Corsair would be the first airplane to fly with it. Beisel and his design team wrapped the engine in the slenderest streamlined fuselage and wing configuration that could handle high-speed aerodynamic forces while providing the low-speed control and lift required to make it a carrier-suitable fighter. To raise the fuselage high enough off the ground to accommodate the huge propeller while still keeping the rugged landing gear short, they gave it an inverted gull wing and mounted the main landing wheels at the low point of the wing. With its radical wing design, its highly sculpted fuselage shapes held together with novel but rugged spot-welding techniques, and its new and unproven engine, this was an altogether new airplane. The quality of the design and its expected performance were almost too good to be true. But BuAer was under no illusion. With all of its novelty, this bird would not be in service any time soon.[30]

When their submission for the 1938 single-engine competition was rejected, Grumman took another tack, and in April 1938 BuAer was delighted to receive an unsolicited Grumman submission for a twin-engine design called the XF5F-1 Skyrocket. Grumman engineers wanted to place the two engines as close together as possible on the leading edge of the wing to improve the airplane's single-engine controllability. When the fuselage was inserted between the engines, wind tunnel tests revealed aerodynamic interference with the engine nacelles (the streamlined enclosures that housed the engines), which caused the wing to stall early and raised the landing speed. To correct this, they moved the nose of the fuselage aft to the middle of the wing. Twin vertical tails were mounted at the ends of a wide horizontal stabilizer directly in the slipstream of each engine. Because the Pratt & Whitney engines with their two-stage superchargers could not be delivered in time, Grumman decided to power the airplane using the Wright "Cyclone" engine with single-stage superchargers that had powered the Buffalo. In view of the engine's known limitations in altitude performance, this was a gamble to match the schedule for the Airabonita and the Corsair. But the airplane was complex for its day and big enough to make handling it on board carriers awkward. Moreover, the choice of engine foreshadowed performance problems at altitude.

So by mid-1940, with the storm clouds gathering across the Atlantic and the Japanese stirring unrest in East Asia, the U.S. Navy found itself saddled with inadequate fighter planes and no ready prospects for real improvement.

CHAPTER 9

★ ★ ★

CHIEF OF FLIGHT TEST, 1940–41

In May 1940, the Germans had overrun Western Europe, defeated the French, and were on the verge of destroying the British army trapped at Dunkirk. With President Roosevelt's approval, the thrust of U.S. Navy war planning now shifted away from its long-standing focus on defeating Japan to prepare for battle with the Germans. And these plans called for fleet readiness to mobilize for war by September 1, 1941, sixteen months away.[1]

To fight this war, the Navy would require a whole new stable of high-performance airplanes of all types, but most especially a first-class modern fighter plane. Fighters dominated the European air war on both sides and were superior in speed and firepower to the new fighters just going into service in the Navy. If forced into war in Europe with the current roster of warplanes, U.S. Navy aviation units would be defeated.

Nor was there reason to expect any better in a contest against Japan. Although the Japanese had previously copied American airplane designs, they could now borrow better models from their German allies. So whichever way the situation turned, the Navy was in trouble, and the outlook for acquiring competitive fighters remained dire.

The tremendous advantage of European designs imposed new criteria for fighters that called for vastly increased firepower, armor protection for the pilot and aircraft vitals, self-sealing fuel tanks, and dramatically improved airplane performance, essentially a complete revision of Navy fighter design doctrine. The next generation of Navy fighters would be bigger, heavier, and more complex than any airplane in the service pipeline for the foreseeable future. In light of this daunting array of requirements, the Navy's current lineup of fighter prototypes—the Airabonita, Skyrocket, and Corsair—did not look all that promising. Worse, the standard procedures for testing and modifying to render any of these aircraft serviceable could well take three to four years.[2]

The powers in BuAer found in Trap a flight test engineer uniquely qualified to lead the Navy out of this hole and equip its forces for the impending air war. His steady rise through increasingly responsible positions to the rank of lieutenant commander had demonstrated a high level of command, creativity, and competence. His flight logs show he had flown more than 3,854 flight hours in 3,097 flights of eighty-one different types of airplanes, which was probably unmatched by any naval officer of his seniority. His skill in testing and assessing airplane problems and potential was without equal, and his experience in operating units gave him a deep understanding of Navy needs. He had displayed superb skills in engineering and rare talent for innovation. So at the height of the chaos in Europe, BuAer brought him back from patrol plane duty in the Pacific to become senior flight test officer—chief of Flight Test—at the Naval Air Station Anacostia, D.C.

BuAer was also counting on Trap to rethink and restructure the way the Navy and its contractors tested and evaluated new aircraft. They simply did not have the luxury of four years to develop the airplanes needed to win the impending war. Trap would have to figure out a way to streamline the process without compromising integrity, a radical change for the muscle-bound Navy culture. Trimming at the margins would not suffice.

TAKING CHARGE

Six flight test officers reported to Trap in Flight Test Section, all of them skilled and experienced naval aviators. His number two officer, Lt. Charles Donald Griffin, was a Naval Academy graduate from the class of 1927 with a master's degree in aeronautical engineering from the University of Michigan. He became a lifelong friend of Trap's and rose to the rank of four-star admiral. Lt. Seymour "Sammy" Johnson was also in the class of 1927 from Annapolis, and two lieutenants, Pete Carver and Carl Giese, were class of 1929. Giese appears later in this story, as does Lt. Eddie Sanders, class of 1930, who went on to become a rear admiral. Capt. William Saunders, USMC, completed the section. Trap was pleased with the seasoned aviation team he inherited. But they had some skills to sharpen.[3]

It didn't take these men long to recognize in their new commanding officer an aviator worthy of their profound respect. His cool, steady demeanor made him easy to work with, and he brought a striking combination of skill, knowledge, and intensity to his work, while demanding an equally high standard of performance from his team. Up close, you couldn't help but admire the precision and grace with which Trap executed every airplane maneuver, no matter how violent. Even more impressive was his uncanny ability to diagnose aircraft behavior—what was going on and why—and how to modify an airplane to remedy its problems.

In one case, a test pilot reported that his airplane's elevators were fluttering at high speed, an unnerving experience. Trap listened thoughtfully to his account and read the pilot's report with care. Skeptical of the findings, he took the airplane up for a forty-minute test and returned with his diagnosis. It wasn't the elevators, he determined, but the horizontal stabilizer that was oscillating. He directed the mechanics to disassemble the tail section, where they discovered metal framing that was bent and cracking from stress.[4]

In another case, a pilot reported a sharp increase in lateral control-stick forces while rolling his airplane at high speed. At low speed, the ailerons worked fine, but as he increased speed the effort to move the ailerons became nearly impossible. He concluded that aerodynamic loads were too strong for the ailerons. Trap took the airplane up and returned in short order to suggest that the problem was likely the linkage mechanism between the stick and the ailerons. On the ground, testing the movement of the ailerons against heavy resistance revealed that the linkage rods flexed under load, causing them to bind in their guide holes and rendering them virtually immoveable.[5]

NO MORE MUMBO JUMBO

For Trap, the work of flight testing was more than a matter of flying skill and mettle. It required that the pilot be alert and sensitive to what the airplane was telling him—a minor vibration here, a slight stiffening of control forces there, a wing dropping unexpectedly—the myriad facets and phenomena that make up the flight characteristics of an airplane. Test pilots needed unusual skill to sense, evaluate, interpret, and accurately record these phenomena and instrument readings while flying the airplane up to and often beyond the known limits of safe flight. Trap encouraged his crew to cultivate the same skill and sensitivity that marked his own approach to testing.

He demanded from his pilots much more detail and precision in planning, flying, and reporting than had been the norm. To conserve test time and avoid duplication, a pilot was to plan each flight carefully, laying out test cards for the exact sequence of maneuvers and settings to follow. In flight, the pilot checked off each step on these cards as it was completed.

The best test pilots combined flying skill with solid engineering knowledge, talents Trap came by naturally. He set out to instill these capabilities in his protégés, pushing them to improve their flying expertise as well as their technical grasp of aerodynamics, structures, and operational requirements.

Trap's arrival also signaled changes in the way technical discussions were conducted at Flight Test. Pilots had grown accustomed to engineers conversing in mind-boggling jargon about aerodynamic phenomena and invoking a litany of technical terms that often went over the pilots' heads. Trap insisted, however, that the engineers slow down and explain to the pilots precisely what they meant in plain English, making clear that part of the technical people's job was to school the test pilots in the more technical aspects of test flying. He later wrote:

> We got excellent pilots from the fleet, dedicated, motivated and experienced, but without any concept of testing. This came from discussions in the office on rainy days. I was very much impressed by the intense interest these guys showed in even the most primitive analysis of stability and control forces and their effect on handling qualities. . . . We had hot-shot pilots available and we had aeronautical engineers, but the two talents never seem to appear in combination. However, the enthusiasm shown by the former category [pilots] for any sort of reasoned analysis (or pseudoscientific understanding of handling and other flight test problems) clearly indicated that if properly instructed, they could approach the aeronautical engineer in managing their affairs.[6]

He wanted his pilots to become as conversant in flight characteristics as his engineers. No more mumbo jumbo.

GETTING THE NUMBERS

Trap made it clear that for flight tests to translate into effective airplane design modifications, pilots had to convince engineers of their findings by bringing back information that accurately described airplane behavior under measured flight conditions—speed, altitude, climb rate, and so forth—and precise control inputs. He pressed for hard data and instrument readings for every situation under test and each anomaly encountered. Then he and the engineers used the written reports to reconstruct the flight and form the basis for proposed design changes. He also believed that any other test pilot using that report should be able to repeat the test with the same results.

In those days before electronics, their measuring tools were primitive. Pilots eyeballed the panel of simple flight instruments and used a hand-held fish scale with a loop that dropped over the stick to measure stick forces. Trap had the shop build a self-retracting reel of cord that mounted on the stick while the other end of the cord dropped over a hook on the front or sides of the cockpit, so that deflecting the stick unreeled a measure of cord proportional to the deflection. On the ground, colored tape markers were wrapped around the cord at points that indicated deflections to be tested in the air. With the end of the cord attached to one side or the other of the cockpit, and in combination with a hand-held fish scale and a stop watch, an adroit pilot could simultaneously measure roll or pitch rate and stick load for a given stick deflection. With the cord attached to the instrument panel in front, along with a hand-held fish scale and a G-force indicator, the pilot could measure stick force per G in turns or pull-ups. Further complicating the multitasking required of the pilot, he was also expected to record these measurements with a pencil on his knee pad.[7]

Capt. Sydney S. Sherby later wrote of this period that other than the recorded temperature data from the Brown recorder, all (flight) data was obtained from notes handwritten by the pilot on a knee pad based on his visual observations.[8]

Photo panels, just coming into use, comprised a panel of cockpit-type instruments to measure airspeed, altitude, rate of climb, turn rate, and bank angle, as well as a gyro horizon, clock, and engine instruments. This was mounted in the fuselage, usually behind the pilot, and enclosed in a box with artificial lighting and a motion picture camera aimed at the panel. The pilot could activate the lights and camera to record data for selected tests. Such photo recordings were far more accurate and comprehensive than a test pilot's eyeballs. Using these crude tools, "get the numbers" became the watchword from the chief.[9]

Aeronautics is a tricky business, and in the air things often do not work as expected. Don't assume that all changes will work as planned, Trap counseled. Go up and try it out to be sure. He also insisted that notes made on the spot provided a more accurate depiction of events in the air than those reconstructed after the fact.

To minimize risk, Trap required his test pilots to explore untried regions of speed, altitude, and maneuver by incrementally probing the unknown, one small step at a time. If a pilot encountered a new phenomenon during the test, he made careful notes then and there on which to base his report. When a pilot discovered a malfunction or an unexpectedly dangerous situation in flight, he was to make notes after bringing the airplane under control, then immediately return to base. After completing the report, he and Trap reviewed the test together. Trap did not second-guess the readings, but he would often go up to replicate troublesome findings. The more risky the problem, the more likely that Trap would insist on conducting further testing himself. Either way, exploration continued one step, one risk, one reading at a time.

Bantering with his men, Trap occasionally borrowed an old test pilots' gag: "We don't so much care if you go up there and kill yourself, but you damn well better bring that airplane back in one piece—it's the only one we've got." But in fact he cared very much for the safety and welfare of his men, a detail not lost on them. When one of his pilots, Lt. Seymour Johnson, was killed in 1941 due to oxygen equipment failure at altitude, Trap was despondent for several days.[10]

He read every test report his pilots wrote. Reports had to be clear and complete, and his red penciled notes and corrections extended from the first page to the last. These edits were not merely technical; grammar, sentence structure, and spelling also mattered. He took particular exception to dangling participles. Pilots rarely received "good" ratings on their reports, though he might say so aloud on occasion. His men soon learned, the less red ink the better. And don't expect kudos from the chief for doing it right. Perfection in flying and reporting was the requisite standard.

Recognizing they were under the tutelage of a master, his pilots came to appreciate the high bar Trap set, which pushed them to ever higher levels of proficiency. It was a hard stretch when a pilot found himself stalled in the prevailing headwinds of his quest for precision, clarity, and detail. But they learned to take his criticism as a constructive boon to their careers.

Trap's respect for his men, whether officers or enlisted, was evident. While he could be demanding—no-nonsense and precise about business—he tended to be relaxed and even-keeled in his leadership style. His wit and ready smile relieved some of the inevitable stress of their work environment, giving everyone plenty of room to do their jobs without fear of tripping over a fragile ego or hair-trigger temper. The pilots often got together for problem-solving sessions mediated by the chief, round-table discussions that gave everyone an opportunity to chip in. Not only was the process instructive, but it invariably generated more insightful results.

SHORTENING THE SCHEDULE

Trap liked to fly at least once a day. Fortunately, routine test requirements made daily flight not only possible but often necessary. Nevertheless, Trap devoted significant time to scrutinizing and rethinking the flight test regimen. How could they cut testing time in half for new airplanes without sacrificing the quality of the tests and results?

Traditional Navy procurement called for BuAer to issue a request for a new airplane, inviting contractors to submit proposals. For each successful proposal, BuAer contracted for a prototype. This agreement included specific performance guarantees and tests to be conducted by the aircraft builder. Once these guarantees had been demonstrated and specified tests run, the prototype was then turned over to Navy Flight Test for further operational and service testing, for which contractors were not equipped. When the Navy found something amiss, they returned the prototype to the contractor for repair. This made reasonably good sense; once the contractor had fulfilled its contract, the Navy took over from there.[11]

Mulling this over, however, Trap came to the conviction that this approach inhibited the accelerated development of new airplanes. Instead, the Navy must get involved much earlier, not just in an advisory capacity but also in testing, evaluating, and modifying the prototype design in real time. This would allow the Navy to apply necessary changes to the prototype itself, or at least to the early production design, rather than waiting until the design was stabilized. Thus final design elements could converge sooner to deliver the airplane the Navy really needed.

Aircraft manufacturers might resist this disruption to their usual development process, but there was no other way to streamline the progression to final design. The aircraft industry would have no choice but to accept Navy Flight Test and the Bureau of Aeronautics as working partners in the evolution of new airplanes.

Trap resolved to have his pilots begin their own flight evaluations concurrent with airplane builder's tests, giving the Navy access to the prototype long before the contract was fulfilled or the aircraft fully flight checked. The builder and the Navy would work cheek by jowl to expedite the process with carefully planned, concurrent test cycles.

Aside from shortening the test schedule, this arrangement offered another clear advantage. Competent test pilots were hard to come by; each contractor usually had one or two on its roster. Navy Flight Test, on the other hand, had a designated cadre of seven seasoned test pilots supported directly by their small but capable engineering staff. Hundreds of current testing hours in a wide variety of aircraft types gave Flight Test pilots a level of expertise in analyzing flight problems that most contractors knew they could not match; as a result, they generally embraced the advice and counsel of Flight Test. Now they would have to accept their intervention much earlier than ever before.[12]

Trap was also dissatisfied with the time required to accept and integrate newly introduced airplane types into the fleet. Aside from the airplane's basic flying qualities, there were too many operational teething troubles related to aircraft carrier suitability, weapons operation, radio performance, and maintainability, the myriad characteristics that make a serviceable, rugged, seagoing weapon out of a flying machine. He determined that Flight Test protocols must probe beyond the airplane's fundamental flight characteristics to include testing all factors that might impinge upon its ultimate capability as a weapon. This represented a major shift in the Navy's concept of flight testing, and it presaged the later establishment of the Naval Air Test Center with its multiple test divisions.[13]

Trap went back to BuAer and laid out his plan to integrate Navy and contractor testing tracks for those airplanes that showed genuine promise. They approved his plan but also tasked him with getting the contractors on board. Trap enlisted his old friend, BuAer engineer Eddie Rounds, to help bring contractors around.

Navy testing—always a risky business—was about to become more so.

GETTING IN THE GAME EARLY

Trap sat at the head of the large meeting table surrounded by the officers of the Flight Test Section. All eyes were on him as he began to spell out the changes that were coming. His men listened closely, all too familiar with the problems posed by elongated time frames for turning around new airplanes; it was a matter they discussed often among themselves. The arm's-length testing procedures between Navy Flight Test and their contractors were notoriously cumbersome, and Trap had their full attention as he laid out his vision.

Those assembled in the room fully understood that the United States was headed for war. Who knew when . . . a year? Two at most. The Wildcat, which was just going into service, was a nice little fighter but no match for the aircraft that Germany, and probably Japan, already had. It would not win the war. They needed airplanes like the Corsair and the Skyrocket, but those aircraft would never be ready in time if they kept doing business as usual. A murmur of agreement rippled around the table.

On priority projects, Trap proposed that they run their tests earlier. Much earlier. In some cases, the Navy had more advanced measuring equipment and facilities than their contractors did, so they could arrange to take over those tests or overlap their tests with the contractor's. For example, they could begin to evaluate carrier suitability before all the spin tests were complete. They could prove out gunnery while the contractor was still running center-of-gravity limit tests. They could test maneuverability and control loads within the previously cleared performance envelope.[14] With contractor collaboration, Flight Test could push the envelope of explored flight characteristics wherever necessary to complete critical tests. This would require careful planning and coordination with the contractor to overlap access to the test airplane and minimize test redundancy.[15]

Trap also pointed out that Flight Test had to become much more aggressive about proposing changes early in the test cycle. They could no longer wait for the builder to complete contractual tests before accepting modifications.

Heated discussion ensued. Change would not come easy, they agreed. Contractors were jealous of their prerogatives and prototypes. However much they valued Flight Test's input and advice, they would not appreciate the Navy breathing down their necks while their baby was still in gestation. Trap knew this would be an uphill effort, but with Eddie Rounds on board he was confident they could bring key contractors around to a new way of doing business. If they were to win the coming war, they had no other choice.

Thus Trap conceived and implemented what is today called the Navy Preliminary Evaluation (NPE) test, which has become a critically important formal step in the procurement contracts for all new Navy aircraft.[16]

CHECKING OUT THE CANDIDATES

During the summer of 1940, Trap made a personal survey of two fighters on the verge of deploying into the fleet. The Brewster F2A Buffalo was a delight to handle. Below 10,000 feet, it rolled fast and turned tightly, and the speed and climb rate were acceptable. But as the airplane climbed to higher altitudes it became sluggish, and above 15,000 feet engine power faded, and the airframe was not designed to take a better engine. Moreover, the airplane lacked the fuel capacity the Navy required, and it still had no protective armor or self-sealing fuel tanks. All of these upgrades would add to the airplane's weight and degrade performance. He concluded the Buffalo was unsuitable for modern war.[17]

Trap found the Grumman F4F Wildcat less maneuverable than the Buffalo at lower altitudes, but appreciated its greater speed and longer range. More importantly, it had an engine with a two-stage, two-speed supercharger that was much more powerful at altitude. At 21,000 feet, where the Buffalo was gasping, the Wildcat demonstrated a top speed of nearly 330 miles per hour.[18] The airplane was stable and easy to manage at slow approach speeds, but the narrow spread of its landing wheels made it tricky to handle on the ground at landing speed. Fleet pilots would have to be careful. The required additional guns, bombs, and improved armor would weigh heavily on the airplane's performance. But if they went to war on the schedule set by Navy planning, the Wildcat would be the Navy's first-line fighter. They had to make it work. Grumman was one of the contractors that Trap and Eddie Rounds visited first.[19]

So Flight Test put much effort into the Wildcat between mid-1940 and early 1942, requisitioning a host of changes to make it more battle-ready:

improvements to engine cooling, more responsive controls, added guns, protective armor, folding wings for shipboard stowage, a new reflector gunsight, and more. They worked closely with Grumman to conduct ongoing operational tests, propose improvements, and evaluate modifications made by the engineers. Trap personally flew 133 hours in 170 test flights in various Wildcat models during this period, and his pilots flew it many hundreds of hours more. This airplane was too slow to be a match for a Messerschmitt, but in all other respects Trap thought it a pretty decent little fighter.[20]

THE BOMBERS

By mid-1940, the fleet was operating three types of dive bombers: the Vought SB2U Vindicator (which was dubbed Wind Indicator), the Northrop BT-1, and the Curtiss SBC Helldiver. All were considered obsolete, but BuAer had continued to fund the evolution of the Northrop BT-1, and the Northrop aeronautical engineering team, under a young Edward H. Heinemann, created a heavily modified version called the XBT-2. This variant carried forward the split dive flap and featured fully flush retractable landing gear, leading-edge wing slots to improve lift at low takeoff and landing approach airspeeds, and a newly configured canopy. Only one of these was ever built, but in 1939 Northrop merged with the Douglas Aircraft Company, and the Northrop XBT-2 changed its designation to the Douglas XSBD-1, the prototype of the SBD Dauntless airplanes that became the principal dive bombers for the Navy and Marines during the first three years of the Pacific War.[21] During its tenure, thanks to its split dive flap, the SBD was the only airplane in the world that could fly the sustained, controllable vertical dive needed for precise bombing. The Navy ordered this airplane to replace all dive bombers in the fleet.[22]

The Dauntless first flew in May 1940, and Trap's team began preliminary testing almost immediately. Trap flew the airplane at the end of June and again in August. This version went into service with the Marines in late 1940 and with the Navy in early 1941. Meanwhile, Douglas designed a new version, the SBD-3, with protective armor, self-sealing fuel tanks, and more guns.[23] This went into production in early 1941. As before, the Flight Test Section lost no time conducting preliminary tests, and Trap flew this Dauntless model six times through November and December. It was deploying into the fleet when Pearl Harbor was attacked.

BuAer contracted with Grumman in 1940 to replace the aging Douglas TBD Devastator torpedo bomber that had joined the fleet in 1937. The Grumman design, called the XTBF-1 Avenger, was a much larger and more powerful airplane than the Devastator and made its first flight at the Grumman plant at

Bethpage, New York, in August 1941.[24] On October 28, Trap visited the plant, where he conducted preliminary tests in three flights during two days for a total of just over three hours. As a result, he asked only for a minor improvement in directional stability, which Grumman fixed by adding a dorsal-fin extension on the vertical stabilizer. Two months later, he flew the airplane again at Anacostia and must have been satisfied, because Grumman put the Avenger into production immediately.

NEW FIGHTER PROTOTYPES

In Trap's estimation, none of the Navy's three new fighter prototypes offered much hope in the near term. He did not have high expectations for the Bell XFL-1 Airabonita; its mediocre performance and nasty spin characteristics made it a dubious prospect.

Grumman's new twin-engine XF5F-1 Skyrocket held more promise. Grumman reported impressive speed and climb rate. But its twin-engine configuration made it big, heavy, and complicated for a carrier fighter, and its engine installations created lots of trouble. This was not a promising basis for a new shipboard fighter plane.[25]

The Vought XF4U-1 Corsair promised stellar performance, but its myriad innovations meant a long gestation period. It made its first flight in May 1940 at Stratford, Connecticut, flown by Vought's chief test pilot, Lyman Bullard. Subsequent flights over the next two months uncovered problems. Then in July, the prototype was badly damaged in a crash landing. Despite this setback, the airplane's rugged construction allowed the prototype to be rebuilt to flying status in just three months, incorporating a number of critical changes called for by the first two months of testing.[26]

At the end of September 1940, Trap went up to Stratford, Connecticut, to visit the Vought facilities. The rebuilt Corsair prototype was ready to fly. Standing silently on the hangar floor, he studied the airplane with quiet admiration. Its lean, smooth, and racy profile gave the same impression he'd had upon seeing the old Boeing F4B-4 for the first time.[27]

Then in early October, Bullard flew a high-speed run in the Corsair from the company's facilities at Stratford, enabling Vought to report to BuAer that the airplane had achieved four hundred miles per hour. This was electrifying news. If true, it meant that the U.S. Navy was in possession of what was likely the fastest fighter airplane in the world.

Late that month, the Corsair flew to Anacostia where Trap took it up for a preliminary test on October 29. In the following two weeks, he flew it six more times. Already a number of problems with the airplane had surfaced: a deadly stall characteristic, poor visibility from the cockpit, and sluggish aileron control. Not promising.[28]

Nonetheless, on the morning of November 15, 1940, Trap was scheduled to fly a speed trial over a measured course to see whether the Corsair could officially achieve four hundred miles per hour to establish its record as the fastest fighter plane in the world.

CHAPTER 10

★ ★ ★

THE DESPERATE GAMBLE, NOVEMBER 1940

Trap shifted his gaze from the two sailboats on the water below to focus on the airfield ahead. Flaring the XF4U-1 Corsair out of its glide slope and painting it onto the runway at Anacostia, he taxied in to the apron and cut the switches.

As he clambered down from the cockpit, a colleague ran from the hangar to tell him the news: Final numbers on his speed test were in. He had done it, 402 miles per hour![1] This made the Corsair the fastest fighter in the world, a record for the Navy and for the nation. And Rear Admiral Towers sent his congratulations. Trap smiled and then headed back to his office, troubled by broader considerations.

Setting the speed record was a cakewalk compared to the challenge that lay ahead. The Navy desperately needed a markedly improved fighter plane. The war in Europe reinforced the imperative for superior performance—speed, climb rate, service ceiling—and more robust firepower than any fighter in the Navy's current inventory. Moreover, these fighters needed the range to protect dive bombers and torpedo planes from enemy fighters all the way to their targets.

None of the three new prototypes under consideration—Bell Airabonita, Grumman Skyrocket, or Vought Corsair—met these requirements. Yet they were the best the American aircraft industry could produce. The U.S. Navy was in a bind.

THE BELL AIRABONITA

The XFL-1 Airabonita prototype was a navalized derivative of the Army Airacobra fighter, powered by the same 1,150-horsepower Allison liquid-cooled engine with its integrated single-stage supercharger that limited the

Airacobra's altitude performance. The Airacobra's 37-mm nose cannon was removed and replaced with additional wing guns, which made the airplane lighter than its Army counterpart and gave it better performance at low altitude. But because of an inadequate supercharger, its high-altitude performance still lagged.

By the time the Airabonita first flew in early 1940, its proposed empty weight of 4,300 pounds had burgeoned to more than 5,100 pounds, significantly decreasing performance, even before adding the requisite protective armor and self-sealing fuel tanks. Below 15,000 feet, the Airabonita was slightly faster (330 mph max) than the Grumman F4F Wildcat just going into service, but this speed advantage evaporated at higher altitudes.[2]

Navy pilots had already determined that the Army Airacobra could easily get into a spin from which it was difficult to recover. Changes made to create the navalized Airabonita moved its center of gravity further aft, aggravating this nasty spin characteristic.[3]

These limitations, in addition to its vulnerable liquid-cooled engine, rendered this prototype almost certainly unacceptable. From the outset, Trap saw little promise in the Airabonita, and when he finally piloted this airplane months later, the flight only confirmed this earlier judgment. This was not the fighter they were looking for.[4]

THE GRUMMAN SKYROCKET

Grumman's new twin-engine XF5F-1 Skyrocket held more promise.[5] Its design was hatched in the mind of Leroy "Roy" Grumman, an old friend of Trap's and the founder and president of Grumman Aircraft Engineering Corporation, which had delivered a long line of stable, rugged carrier fighters. In the late 1930s, Roy Grumman had become convinced that a single-engine fighter could not deliver the performance sought by the Navy. This view was corroborated by a February 1937 BuAer internal document stating that "new engines of horsepower higher than the (Pratt & Whitney) R-1830 will not give any great increase in speed over the XF4F. This means . . . it will be necessary to go into a two-engine, single-seat fighter design."[6]

The Skyrocket had first flown in April 1940, and although he had not yet piloted the plane, Trap was impressed by its reported speed—nearly that of the Army's Lockheed P-38 Lightning—and spectacular sea level climb rate of four thousand feet per minute. Its flying qualities were solid, aerobatics easy, and the counterrotating propellers precluded any torque effects. Grumman pilots extolled its impressive flying qualities and cockpit visibility. Subsequent test flights, however, were plagued with engine overheating; other more serious difficulties lurked in this airplane.[7]

The twin-engine design made this machine big, heavy, and complex compared to then-current Navy airplanes. With each additional modification by Grumman engineers, its weight continued to grow, adversely affecting performance and eliciting ever more intractable criticism from BuAer. In March 1940, a Grumman memo finally admitted that the Skyrocket's weight exceeded their original commitment by more than seven hundred pounds.[8] Adding guns, protective armor, and ammunition would increase the airplane's ultimate weight, decreasing both speed and climb rate. Although the Navy had also required a self-sealing fuel tank, the Skyrocket's tank location inside the wing box beam prohibited the addition of self-sealing capability.[9]

Compounding the predicament, the Navy had also become disenchanted with the Wright Cyclone engine they had originally chosen for this airplane. With its single-stage supercharger, this was the same engine that curtailed the Brewster Buffalo performance at altitude and would likely impede the altitude performance of the Skyrocket also. The Navy wanted to switch to a newer and smaller Pratt & Whitney Twin Wasp engine with a two-stage supercharger, but this would impose substantial delays in the program.[10]

Trap met with Roy Grumman to discuss his appraisal of the Skyrocket. Troubled by its reported poor altitude capability, Trap pointed out that the Navy's requirements for further modifications would work against the airplane's performance.

But Roy was optimistic. The basic design would accept the Pratt & Whitney engines with their two-stage superchargers, which Grumman planned to install later. The engineers expected to solve the fuel problem and fix the early stall encountered in previous tests. They would also restore the long nose to the fuselage to take the new guns. Notwithstanding the myriad problems still to be solved and the additional weight these modifications would impose on the design, Grumman was unperturbed, confident that the Navy would come out of the process with a first-class fighter and "certain they had a world beater."[11]

Trap's doubts persisted. "The XF5F showed considerable promise but had certain inherent deficiencies," he wrote later. "The virtues of twin-engine fighters were perhaps not fully appreciated in those days. Its performance was excellent but did not seem to justify its size and complexity."[12]

THE VOUGHT CORSAIR

The performance of the Vought XF4U-1 Corsair pushed it to the top of the Navy's list of not-very-promising prototypes. Trap's speed runs in the airplane prompted the Navy to issue a rare press release. The resulting *Washington Daily News* article of December 20, 1940, described Trap's flight of "400 odd m-p-h" in an airplane "known technically as the F-4-U, officially the 'fastest airplane in the United States today.' Authority for the latter statement is Rear Adm. John H. Towers, chief of the Navy's Bureau of Aeronautics." The article went on to say that Trap "isn't talking about the performance or specifications of the ship . . . but he will admit 'it's a real airplane' as contrasted with stubby-winged racers [of the day]."

Indeed the XF4U-1 Corsair demonstrated many of the flight characteristics the Navy wanted most: speed, rate of climb, high altitude performance, stability throughout its speed range, and a rugged airframe. The Board of Inspection and Survey report later stated, "The model XF4U airplane was found to exhibit performance characteristics superior in most respects to any fighter previously submitted for test by this board."[13] Nevertheless, the design had serious flaws that rendered it unacceptable.

The preliminary flight test report highlighted the difficulty of rolling the airplane, poor pilot visibility from the cockpit, and a sudden power-on stall. As a Corsair slowed to stalling speed in landing configuration, the left wing stalled first, dropping abruptly without warning and throwing the airplane into a spin that would spell disaster if it occurred on landing approach. Don Griffin confirmed this risky phenomenon: "The power-on stall was vicious. The aircraft rolled violently and, even if one caught it early, was almost impossible to bring it back to normal flight before 1-2 turns." This situation was fatal on landing approach; the pilot had to remember to keep his approach speed well above stall speed.[14]

In addition, the roll control was highly nonlinear in the left-to-right direction, resulting in what Trap's flight test report describes as a "kick" when the control stick was deflected sharply. Another disturbing finding was poor visibility from the cockpit, which was "restricted by the large fuselage and wing root cord and hampered by the window arrangement." And visibility was further impaired by the low position of the pilot under the shallow canopy.[15]

These early problems were only precursors to issues that surfaced as Navy testing progressed. Perhaps the worst of these was that the airplane could not be made to roll fast enough, especially at high speed. In those days, controls were not powered; the pilot had to provide the muscle to make the airplane do what he wanted, and the stick force to roll was far too high. The pilot had to use both hands for full deflection, which was wholly unsatisfactory. A fighter plane's ability to roll quickly and easily is a vital component of maneuverability and key to combat effectiveness. Convinced that the ailerons lacked the authority to achieve the needed roll rate, Trap advocated increasing the aileron span as part of the solution. This meant decreasing the span of the wing flaps, which, given the airplane's ample flap area, seemed a reasonable price to pay.[16] Decreasing lateral stick forces was a more complicated fix that required further experimentation by Vought.

Trap later summed up the Corsair's main challenges this way. "The F4U showed very superior performance, but no aileron control, a vicious stall, and terrible vision."[17]

Another deficiency was made irrefutably evident in the Battle of Britain: to be effective, fighters had to deliver a knockout punch in a single short burst of gunfire.[18] The prototype Corsair had one .30-caliber and one .50-caliber machine gun mounted in the upper engine cowling and one .50-caliber gun in each wing, far less than European fighters. The .30-caliber popgun could be scrapped, but they had to find space to mount four—and preferably six—.50-caliber guns. The only reasonable location for these was in the wing, which was where the British put them in the Spitfire and Hurricane and where Republic was placing eight .50-caliber guns in its new P-47. But with most of the Corsair's fuel stored in the wing, it could not possibly share space with the guns.

Finally, insufficient fuel capacity had serious implications. The Pratt & Whitney R-2800 engine was demonstrating higher fuel consumption than anyone had expected, almost 65 gallons per hour at slow cruising speed and more than 250 gallons per hour at combat power, nearly three times the Wildcat burn rate![19] In addition, it was becoming clear that the Navy needed fighters with more range than previously thought. This meant that the 273-gallon fuel capacity of the Corsair was not nearly enough. The airplane simply could not range far enough from its carrier to meet the Navy's needs.

ROLLING THE DICE

None of these prototypes met the Navy's requirements, nor were any more promising prospects on the horizon. Trap wrote of this period: "I was Flight Test Officer during the era . . . and deeply concerned with the three new prototypes the Navy was evaluating—the Bell XFL Airabonita, the Grumman XF5F Skyrocket, and the Vought XF4U Corsair. . . . We desperately hoped that [one of these] would produce [a superior fighter]."[20]

In this context, "we" almost certainly refers to a BuAer team responsible for bringing forth a world-class carrier fighter, which meant a major design overhaul with questionable results and further delays in deployment of any of these prototypes. Based on the organization and its subsequent enterprise, this team likely included Trap, Eddie Rounds, and Cdr. Jack Pearson on the BuAer fighter design desk, as well as two of Trap's key pilots, Lt. Charles

"Don" Griffin and Capt. Bill Saunders of the Marines. As flight test officer with his commanding knowledge of airplanes, Trap would have functioned as their de facto leader.

"In a rather desperate gamble," he wrote, "we chose [the Corsair] in the expectation of correcting its defects."[21] Doubtless they felt this airplane was their best bet because of its intrinsic performance. Now the question before them: How to fix it?

REINVENTING THE CORSAIR

In early 1941, with the United States projected to be at war within the year, the pressure to get a new fighter into the fleet was palpable. The BuAer team evaluated further test results of the Corsair in light of the combat environment they now faced. In so many ways they liked this airplane, but it remained saddled with problems for which there was no simple fix: not enough fuel, not enough firepower, and a sluggish roll that required more muscle strength than a pilot could muster with one arm. The team agreed: no matter how long and how difficult it proved, these problems would have to be solved. Vought was not going to like their verdict.

A few days later, the BuAer team sat down with Vought engineering executives to present their critique, with Trap leading the discussion for the Navy. The airplane had plenty going for it, but its vicious power-on stall would kill people and its poor rolling ability, lack of guns, and limited fuel capacity were unacceptable.

The Vought people were unconvinced. They would look for a solution to the power-on stall problem, but pilots could be trained to avoid this condition. And yes, they could probably find a way to fit in another gun or two, and perhaps a bit more fuel, which would make the Corsair far superior to the Wildcat. After all, this was the fastest fighter plane in the world, and the Navy had already shown that it could operate from an aircraft carrier. There was, they insisted, simply not enough room in the airframe to do everything the Navy was asking for.

The meeting ground to its grim conclusion when Trap rendered the team's final verdict: either Vought would fix these problems or the Navy would be forced to scrap the Corsair and struggle along with the Wildcat. There were heavy hearts around the room as the meeting closed.

No one left that meeting more troubled than Trap. They had a promising airplane with potentially superb performance, but it was hemmed in by its own design constraints. He found it ironic that the British Spitfire had a similar flaw, a lovely airplane limited by a design that restricted its fuel capacity.[22]

Also, there was something a bit odd about storing fuel in the wings. Earlier Navy fighter planes had never carried much fuel there before; their thin wings made from fabric-covered framing precluded such an option. Besides, the wing was a nasty place to try to stow self-sealing tanks, a problem Vought had yet to confront. In current biplane fighters like the Grumman F3F, fuel was held in a big fuselage tank directly in front of the pilot and close to the airplane's center of gravity. The Corsair's cockpit position precluded Vought from putting fuel in the fuselage. But suppose . . .

The next day, Trap called together some of his pilots and a few engineers. He'd been considering a solution to their problem. He laid out a blueprint of the Corsair on the conference room table to illustrate his ideas. Determined to salvage this fighter even if it meant radical modification and major surgery to the original design, they set to work on a series of major alterations to correct the airplane's troubles.

Step one, move the fuel carried in wing tanks into the fuselage instead. To do this, the cockpit had to be moved aft, say thirty inches, to make room for a big fuel cell in the fuselage in front of the pilot, directly over the wing, where fuel state would not significantly affect the center of gravity and longitudinal trim. Since this cockpit location would impair the already questionable visibility over the nose, the pilot position should be raised six to eight inches, which would provide even better visibility than the current prototype afforded. Trap suggested a blown bubble canopy like that of the Spitfire, which would provide better headroom for the pilot and improved rearward visibility.[23] Finally, to improve the roll rate, Trap wanted longer-span ailerons and shorter-length flaps. The proposition seemed logical, but Vought was going to balk at such drastic changes. There was general agreement: these alterations were a neat solution to the problem, but the Vought people had better be sitting down when they heard this.[24] The proposal was written up as a list of line-item suggestions, likely accompanied by Trap's sketches, and presented to the BuAer team. They concurred; these recommendations should be given to Vought.

At the subsequent meeting with Vought brass, Trap explained the proposal, laying out his sketches and talking them through the changes. The Vought people listened in stunned silence. When he finished, they were visibly chagrined. This was a complete redo. They might as well start over. It would take months.

But the Navy team pressed them: Was this redesign possible? The Vought people looked skeptical, but Trap quietly reminded them that the entire project was at stake. They agreed to take a closer look; perhaps it was feasible. They would go back to Stratford and see what they could do. They left, bewildered. Since when were Navy test pilots redesigning their aircraft?

THE DODO BIRD

When Trap finally flew the Grumman XF5F-1 Skyrocket in March 1941, it unfortunately matched his expectations. At low altitude, the airplane was fast, but not as fast as the Corsair.[25] As promised, the initial climb rate was quicker, but once it reached 15,000 feet, the power waned. With all its other foibles still to be fixed, Skyrocket was not going to cut it.

Back on the ground, he once again spoke privately with Roy Grumman to spell out the airplane's shortcomings. Despite recent modifications to resolve a host of problems, Grumman's troubles were far from over. Skyrocket performance above 20,000 feet remained wholly unacceptable.

Roy explained their plan to upgrade the engines to the Pratt & Whitneys with two-stage superchargers, but this would take time. He had pushed the Skyrocket because he did not believe a single-engine airplane would meet the Navy's performance standards, and he had avoided the new Pratt & Whitney R-2800 used in the Corsair out of reluctance to launch a new airplane design with an untried engine.[26]

Trap countered. The R-2800 may have been untried when the Skyrocket project began, but this was no longer the case. The engine had been flying in the Corsair for nearly a year. The airplane was a great performer, and the engine was the least of Vought's troubles. Martin, also using the R-2800 in their new B-26 Marauder, was already starting service testing with it, and Republic was preparing to fly it in their P-47 Thunderbolt. This engine was no longer untried; it was a solid machine that delivered the power necessary for a high-performance single-engine fighter.

The two men weighed this in silence.

Then Trap looked his friend coolly in the eye and told him that if Grumman didn't stop fooling around with this twin-engine dodo bird and put their engineering talent to work on a decent single-engine fighter using one of the new big engines, the Navy would not buy any more of their fighters. Furthermore, he added, BuAer had decided to proceed with the Corsair rather than the Skyrocket.

Roy acknowledged the news with grim resolve, conceding that he'd been wrong to push twin engines at this time. He also allowed that his people had already started on a new single-engine fighter design that he thought would interest Trap. The prototype could be ready for testing as early as mid-1942.[27]

Trap appreciated Roy's accommodation but remained apprehensive. Mid-1942 might be too late.[28]

AIMING FOR PERFECTION

A few weeks later, the Vought contingent met once again with Navy Flight Test at Anacostia, their hangdog demeanor replaced by fresh excitement. They laid out calculations and drawings reflecting in detail the concepts that Trap had proposed, and they launched into specifications for the new design: six .50-caliber machine guns in the wings, the cockpit moved thirty-six inches aft, a 237-gallon fuel tank in the fuselage in front of the pilot. In addition, they'd found space for more fuel tanks to bring the total up to 363 gallons.[29] They would redesign the fuselage and a whole new wing with the larger-span ailerons. A first production airplane could be ready by mid-1942, with the new wing but not the raised cockpit. This would be cut in soon afterward.[30]

Speaking later of this unprecedented collaboration between Navy test personnel and airplane manufacturers, aviation historian Frederick Johnsen wrote, "Though impressed with its [the XF4U-1's] speed and ceiling, the service [Navy] pilots offered suggestions based on experience—suggestions that would manifest themselves as changes to the design of the F4U-1 variant to follow."[31] Trap and his pilots were pleased with Vought's response.

As contract talks progressed, the BuAer team decided that the new design was sufficiently like the prototype Corsair that a new prototype was not required. The Navy would take a chance by contracting with Vought to put the new design into limited production, initially without the raised cockpit. The early production model would go through accelerated acceptance testing to verify assumptions about the new model's flight characteristics.

This redesign removed the fundamental stumbling block for the Corsair. Many years later, Adm. Charles D. Griffin commented in his oral history on the impact that Trap and Flight Test had had on the Corsair and other designs: "We redesigned some aircraft to a large degree right there at Anacostia. Of course, Trapnell was the expert in this. . . . No [we did not merely test airplanes], we actually redesigned some of them right there. . . . This ability on the part of the test pilots was greatly sought after and much appreciated by the contractors, by the design engineers, and so forth."[32]

BuAer, however, was not about to sign a full production contract for the Corsair until Vought demonstrated improved rolling ability, a matter with which Trap was still not satisfied. He wanted the new ailerons retrofitted onto the prototype as soon as possible so they could be tested before production airplanes flew. With regard to the bulged canopy, he suggested they send someone to England to find out how Supermarine had fabricated the Spitfire canopy.

The redesign of the new wing would take time, and with plenty of test work still to be done on the prototype Corsair, Vought kept it in operation as it was. Meanwhile they would build a complete wing of the new design and then replace the original on the prototype as soon as the new one was ready.

In April 1941, Trap flew as chase pilot on the formal demonstration of the Corsair prototype's spin characteristics and recovery, another requirement for putting it into production. Vought test pilot Boone Guyton flew the Corsair and performed the demonstration. Flying a Grumman F4F Wildcat, Trap was the airborne observer and the official Navy inspector to verify that the demonstration was executed correctly and completely. Guyton's own description tells the story:

> Finally, in the early afternoon, with Trapnell always close in the sky around me, I completed the maneuvers. After each, I paused to see if he was satisfied and with his terse "okay" proceeded to the next. The Corsair [XF4U-1] performed so beautifully I childishly expected some verbal applause. Nothing. Perfection was what Trapnell expected.
>
> Starting the spins I was intrigued to see how close [Trapnell's] F4F tucked in next to the Corsair's wing. . . . It was as though we were going to perform spins together. Before proceeding, I resisted the desire to ask him to move out a bit. Trapnell wasn't going to miss anything.
>
> "I'd like to see you do that one again," he said on the radio. The F4F was so close beside the wing, I could almost read his lips. "Your elevator wasn't up for the full turn."
>
> I repeated.
>
> "Okay."
>
> He wanted several more [spins] repeated so he could precisely observe the control action on recovery. What I thought was perfect, he obviously didn't. After the last landing-condition spin, he pulled up close again, nodded, and pointed down. We returned to the field.[33]

In fact, Trap deemed the demonstration satisfactory. Back on the ground, he signed off on the Corsair's spin-trial certification and gave Guyton a casual "well done." Guyton contained his euphoria with difficulty.

GETTING THE BEAST TO ROLL

In the summer of 1941, the winds of war blew hot and heavy through Washington, raising the pressure to get the Corsair into production. But Trap held out. The airplane's sluggish roll remained a liability, and Vought had yet to correct the problem. Indeed, the flaw highlighted two closely related problems. First, improving the rate of roll required bigger, more effective ailerons. Second, heavy stick loads meant the pilot still had to use all his strength to make the airplane roll at any reasonable rate.[34]

Vought wanted to wait for the new ailerons before making further modifications, but Trap, with BuAer support, vetoed this delay. There was no time to
waste. The bigger ailerons would be even more difficult for the pilot to manage
than the current ones, and whatever they learned now by fixing the ailerons on
the prototype could be applied to the production version. No, Vought had to
start immediately.[35]

So their engineers began work on improving roll rate, which called for
alternate ways to construct the prototype ailerons and to improve the linkage
that drove them. One of their main thrusts was to stiffen the aileron control
surfaces themselves, which were made of doped fabric stretched over a metal
frame. Although they tried various arrangements to strengthen this frame,
none proved satisfactory. Finally, at the end of May, they built and installed
ailerons made entirely of plywood covered with fabric. Trap flew the plywood
ailerons and found them to be a measurable improvement. On this basis, BuAer
gave Vought the go-ahead on a limited production contract for 584 Corsairs.[36]

Vought thought it wise to hold off making further changes until the bigger
ailerons were installed, but again Trap put his foot down. Anything learned
with the prototype ailerons could be applied to the bigger ones. As it was, the
stiffened prototype ailerons had barely enough authority to achieve the desired
roll rate if you were Charles Atlas and could apply both hands to the stick,
which was not an option for the pilot in combat. The roll rate was marginal
and the stick forces to make it roll remained unacceptable. Unless they were
improved, the Navy might go no further with the Corsair than initial production. And so in the spring and summer of 1941, Vought engineers and test
pilots resignedly undertook a crash program to lighten the control forces of the
prototype ailerons, trying various control linkage arrangements, aileron pivot
points, alterations to the nose balance on the control surfaces, and tab arrangements. An exercise in trial and error, these tests of incremental modifications
were done by Vought pilots in almost daily flights.[37]

Trap also took the prototype up periodically for check flights to monitor progress and was pleased by the diligence with which Vought pursued the
goals he had set. He only wished they had more time.[38]

In *Whistling Death*, Boone Guyton writes,

> As a result of Navy evaluation, test pilots at Anacostia requested
> improved lateral control and more effective ailerons. . . . [In the
> summer of 1941] I began a round of aileron tests we expected to
> complete in two weeks. They took three months—110 nauseating
> test flights. . . . We wouldn't realize the true value of this effort
> until the first Marine Corsair squadron reached Guadalcanal 18
> months later.

I don't know whether the Navy already had advanced knowledge of the still-secretive Japanese Zero fighter and its incredible maneuverability. Perhaps they did—for their request was right on the mark, and timely. Later in the war, the Corsair's maneuvering performance would receive the highest praise from fighter pilots who had their lives on the line. Its fast rate of roll, especially at extremely high speeds, was to become legendary.

In the fall, Vought also completed a mockup of the new but still unraised cockpit and forward fuselage, known as the "birdcage cockpit" for the many metal stiffeners used to support and partition the glass. Aside from myriad details still to be corrected, the mockup confirmed that visibility from this cockpit was about as bad as expected. BuAer and the Navy pilots reluctantly agreed, however, that the visibility was not bad enough to delay production. They needed the airplane yesterday, but they would accept the raised cockpit as soon as possible.

NO STONE UNTURNED

In its search for alternative fighter planes, Flight Test also evaluated a number of foreign and non-Navy fighters. At the end of 1941, Trap flew the Army P-43 as well as the British Hawker Hurricane and Supermarine Spitfire. But for various reasons, these airplanes failed to meet Navy requirements.

The Corsair still appeared to be their only hope. And so they slogged on in the struggle to get the airplane up to par under the pressure of approaching war.

CHAPTER 11

★ ★ ★

FLIGHT TEST AT WAR, 1941–43

On Sunday, December 7, 1941, the Japanese attacked the U.S. fleet at Pearl Harbor in a smoothly coordinated and executed carrier air strike of a scope that the world had not seen. U.S. Navy war games had simulated smaller strikes by perhaps a hundred aircraft from one or two carriers on a single installation, but the Pearl Harbor strike was the real thing, involving more than 350 aircraft launched in two waves from six carriers to bomb military installations across the island of Oahu. Tactical surprise was complete, and the Americans were stunned.

The attack killed 2,400 people, wounded another 1,300, and sank or severely damaged eight battleships, three cruisers, and three destroyers, as well as a number of smaller ships. Numerous harbor and aircraft facilities were destroyed. Fortunately, none of the U.S. Navy's handful of aircraft carriers were at Pearl Harbor during the raid, and so they were spared. The alarming effectiveness of the air strike and the damage suffered by the big-gun ships of the battle fleet ended all debate about whether guns or airplanes would play the lead role in the war. This was an air war.

At the Navy Bureau of Aeronautics and the Flight Test Section at Naval Air Station (NAS) Anacostia, the immediate effect was to increase the working day from between eight and ten hours five days a week to between twelve and fourteen hours seven days a week. Urgent projects became crash programs overnight. Twenty years of training and instinct urged Lt. Cdr. Fred Trapnell to get into the fighting quickly, but his job was to stay in the trenches at Flight Test to fully equip the Navy to win this war in the air.

JAPANESE NEMESIS: THE ZERO

During the early months of 1942, Navy and Army pilots began to encounter a totally new type of Japanese fighter. Compared to American fighters in service, it was fast, had extremely long range, a surprising climb rate, and startling maneuverability. The Imperial Japanese Navy designated this deadly adversary the A6M. Its manufacturer, Mitsubishi, called it Type 00. The world dubbed it simply the Zero.

Naval Intelligence and BuAer had caught their first inkling of the Zero from a report in late 1940 out of China about the Flying Tigers' encounters with this surprising new airplane. Senior aviation officers, including Trap, had been briefed on the subject. Many in U.S. aviation circles dismissed the report of speed, climb, and maneuverability as aerodynamically impossible, but Trap, along with some of his pilots and engineers in BuAer, wasn't so sure. At low altitude, before the addition of defensive armor and self-sealing fuel tanks, the old Brewster F2A-2 Buffalo had a climb rate and maneuverability not so different from that described in the report. With the benefit of a properly super-charged engine, a lighter, more modern design than the Buffalo that sacrificed protective armor and self-sealing fuel tanks might achieve the reputed performance. So there was good reason to believe, even before the outbreak of war, that the new Japanese fighter would outperform the Wildcat. Unfortunately, no modification to the Wildcat was going to change that; the U.S. Navy was still strapped for a new fighter.[1]

Their conjectures about this new Japanese airplane went into a Fleet Air Tactical Unit bulletin that was sent to Navy fighter squadrons in late 1941, and when U.S. pilots encountered the Zero during the first months of the war, the performance anticipated by Trap and others proved true. Not everyone in the fleet paid attention to this bulletin, but one officer who took it seriously was Lt. Cdr. John S. Thach, skipper of fighter squadron VF-3 at NAS North Island. Using matchsticks on his kitchen table to simulate airplanes in combat, he devised coordinated tactics for his Wildcats to render them effective against this superior performing enemy, which he then put to the test in the air. His work prompted the Navy to adopt the two-airplane section and the "Thach Weave" as a defensive maneuver for two fighters operating together, tactics which proved crucial to many Navy and Marine war victories.[2]

Pilots learned quickly that Zeros were not only more maneuverable at normal operating speeds than their Wildcats but also faster in level flight.[3] Furthermore, the Japanese pilots who flew them were formidable. This vicious combination cost the United States dearly. Navy and Marine pilots also discovered, however, that the Zero had its limitations. As predicted, it had neither protective armor nor self-sealing fuel tanks; if hit solidly with gunfire, it usually erupted into a flying inferno. Also, above two hundred knots the Zero could not maneuver with a Wildcat. Consequently, tactics called for fighters to operate in pairs for mutual support, avoid turning dogfights with a Zero, and, if attacked by a Zero, dive at full throttle and maneuver hard. Heeding these tactical lessons, Navy and Marine pilots flew their Wildcats with grit and determination and demonstrated superior gunnery skills. So in spite of the Zero's superior performance, the Wildcat achieved a nearly six-to-one kill-to-loss ratio against all Japanese aircraft during the first two years of the Pacific War. Renowned for its stamina in the battles of the Coral Sea, Midway, and Guadalcanal, the Wildcat served valiantly as the mainstay fighter for the Navy and Marines through the first year and a half of the Pacific War until the arrival of more capable fighter planes. Furthermore, Wildcats continued in production as workhorse fighters for the rest of the war and deployed on the hundreds of light and escort carriers operated by Allied navies.[4]

THE DIVE BOMBERS

While working to resolve the fighter problem, Trap and the Flight Test Section were also invested in operational testing and perfection of the Douglas SBD Dauntless dive bomber already in service. From December 1941 through September 1942, Trap personally made thirty-three operational test flights in the Dauntless.

On June 4, 1942, the Japanese attacked Midway Island with four carriers, succeeding triumphantly in the initial skirmish. They bombed the airfield and shot down many U.S. airplanes, including thirteen of the nineteen Brewster F2A-2 Buffalos that were airborne. Following the attack, only one F2A-2 was flyable; the rest were riddled with bullet holes. Most of the airplane types lost were already recognized as obsolete.[5]

Late in the morning of June 4, two squadrons of Navy Dauntlesses from U.S. aircraft carriers found the Japanese carriers and, in a textbook dive-bombing attack, struck three of them concurrently; they sank within thirty minutes. Later that afternoon, a Dauntless squadron returned to finish off the fourth. This attack decimated the Japanese carrier fleet and ended all possibility of Japan winning the war in the Pacific. It was a stunning triumph for this airplane, for the pilots that flew it, and for the Navy's relentless struggle to develop effective dive bombing tactics and aircraft.[6]

Toward the end of 1942, Trap made a number of test flights in a new dive bomber, the Curtiss SB2C, dubbed Helldiver (like its predecessor), which had been ordered as a replacement for the Dauntless. It was considerably larger and more complex and, unlike the Dauntless, included an internal bomb bay for carrying heavy bombs. Early problems plagued the aircraft, including structural weaknesses, tricky stall characteristics, lack of stability, and poor control, as well as troubles with its Wright R-2600 engine and Curtiss Electric propeller. It first flew in 1940 but underwent a complete redesign before going to Flight Test in late 1942, when Trap and others determined it still to be unsatisfactory. After more than eight hundred changes to the airplane, it finally lumbered into combat in November 1943. Bigger, heavier, and having less range that the Dauntless it was replacing, the Helldiver was not well received in the fleet, where it continued to have problems, especially with the propeller and hydraulics, that were not resolved until delivery of a later model in mid-1944.[7]

CORSAIR OUT THE DOOR

The superior performance of the Zero over the Wildcat heightened the urgency to get the Vought F4U Corsair into service as soon as possible. On December 18, a week after the Pearl Harbor attack, Trap went to the Vought plant at Stratford, Connecticut, to conduct a test flight of the prototype Corsair with the new wing installed and the final version of the new balanced long-span ailerons that would go on the production model. Despite the rain and ominously low ceiling, and because the Corsair urgently needed to clear this hurdle, he took off and climbed through the weather for the one-and-a-half-hour flight to test the new ailerons. At long last he found them satisfactory.[8]

Finally, he wanted to resolve his one remaining reservation about the airplane, the power-on stall that a pilot might encounter upon landing. Without warning, it threw the airplane into a vicious left roll that would be fatal near the ground. Trap had tested this phenomenon at altitude before, and he did it again on this flight, just to be sure. He confirmed that while the Corsair's power-on stall would not pose a problem for the alert, seasoned aviator, it might cost an inattentive green pilot his life.

Certainly, he had flown other Navy airplanes with more dangerous idiosyncrasies. But those earlier airplanes had been piloted by the small, close-knit cadre of dedicated men that made up prewar naval aviation. In peacetime, they had been brought along slowly and carefully by their operational units until they matured into accomplished aviators. Now, however, the Navy was about to train thousands of inexperienced kids to quickly become combat pilots. And hundreds of those kids might make the very mistake that would prove fatal in this machine. Yet he could see no way around it. Corsair squadrons would have to take special care in their indoctrination and training. It was a risk that left him uneasy, but one that had to be taken.[9]

That evening, he stood in wet flight gear in a phone booth outside the Vought plant in a pouring rain, water cascading down the booth windows, engaged in a three-way conversation with Cdr. Jack Pearson on the fighter desk in BuAer and Rear Adm. John Towers, chief of BuAer. He confirmed his satisfaction with the ailerons, and they agreed to proceed with an open order for Corsairs.[10]

The first Corsair off the production line flew in June 1942. On July 20, Trap went to Stratford to determine its readiness for further Navy testing, and the following day a Vought pilot delivered the first production airplane to Anacostia. For the next several months, Flight Test put the new airplane through accelerated acceptance tests. The first prototype of the raised-cockpit version was in the fifth production model, although this feature did not become standard until later in 1943.[11]

In September, the first production Corsairs, complete with birdcage cockpits, were delivered to Marine Squadron VMF-124 at MCAS Miramar near San Diego and, in early October, to Navy Fighter Squadron VF-12 at NAS North Island. The Corsair, however, suffered two ongoing troubles that made it difficult to operate on board ship: the nasty power-on stall and wheel struts that caused the airplane to bounce in a hard landing. By early 1943, the Navy

18. Vought F4U-1D Corsair with the raised cockpit and blown-bubble canopy.
Later models had a clear canopy without the metal stiffeners shown here.
The prototype for this machine is in Photo 1.

Official U.S. Navy photo, National Archives and Records Administration,
Records of the Bureau of Aeronautics

would finally have an alternative fighter that was more stable and pilot-friendly, so the Corsair did not deploy on carriers until 1944, after its two major flaws had been corrected. Until then, it went into land-based Marine and Navy squadrons, operating in the Solomon Island campaign starting in February 1943.[12] While not easy to land on board ship, its troubles caused little difficulty in land-based operation, and the airplane proved to be exactly the fighter these island-based flyers wanted.

In mid-1944, the Corsair was integrated into both Navy and Marine shipboard squadrons, and their pilots came to love the airplane, which became one of the outstanding fighter planes of World War II, achieving an eleven-to-one kill ratio. The U-Bird, or as the Japanese called it Whistling Death, remained in production through successive model changes for eleven years and four wars, the longest production run of any U.S. fighter. And its remarkable rate of roll at any speed, the quickest of any contemporary American fighter, was one of the many characteristics praised by the pilots who flew it.

Testing airplanes remained an ever-dangerous business. In August 1942, Marine Capt. Bill Saunders, a member of Trap's team, was killed in an accident at Anacostia. Seymour Johnson had been killed the previous year, making Saunders' crash the second fatal accident under Trap's command. Ironically, Saunders had recently married Johnson's widow, accentuating the tragedy. Saunders was replaced by Lt. Charles Crommelin, an outstanding aviator and one of five Crommelin brothers to graduate from the Naval Academy. Later, he went on to fame in the Pacific, only to be killed in mock air combat over Okinawa late in World War II.

THE BIG MOVE

NAS Anacostia was located within the District of Columbia just across the narrow Anacostia River from metropolitan Washington. Even before the United States entered World War II, BuAer decided it would be a good idea to move the Navy test flying arena out of the skies over the nation's capital, so they bought the property at Cedar Point, Maryland, and started construction of the NAS Patuxent River, Maryland, at the mouth of the Patuxent River where it flows into the Chesapeake Bay.

In November 1942, Trap and the Flight Test Section were preparing to move from their cramped airfield at Anacostia, D.C., to this sprawling new air station, sixty miles southwest of Washington on a finger of placid Maryland countryside abutted on two sides by water.[13] When finished, the wide concrete runways would be three times the length of those at Anacostia and would allow landings and takeoffs in all directions over water or open country. There was no worry about an airplane crashing into dense population near the field. This was a proper test center.

The upcoming move to Patuxent added stress to the already strained Flight Test Section, but in October the grim news from the South Pacific applied more heat. The situation at Guadalcanal was said to be desperate; the Marines were in danger of getting wiped out. The truth was actually worse: Japanese air power had eroded U.S. air resistance. To protect themselves, Navy carriers providing major air support had withdrawn, and Japanese transports were unloading troops onto a beach within sight of the Marine airfield. The press made it sound like Bataan all over again.[14]

HEADING HOME

When Trap announced his transfer to the new air station at Patuxent River, Alice balked. Trap would be working around the clock, while she and Wally would be stranded in the Maryland countryside. The pull of war would take him further afield, leaving her to fend for herself out in the boondocks, more isolated than ever. The prospect was distinctly unappealing.

The onset of the war had triggered in Alice a desire to go home, to be among family and people she loved. Tensions were running high across the nation, and Alice had no affinity for life on the East Coast, especially with her husband consumed more and more by the pressures of his work.

She dug in her heels on the move to Patuxent, but was no happier about the prospect of staying alone in Washington, D.C. Looking at little Wally, she made up her mind it was time to return to more familiar turf in San Francisco, where friends and family couldn't wait to have her back. Then Trap would be free to do what he needed, and as she jokingly pointed out, they were likely to see more of him on the West Coast than they did right now in D.C.

She loved him deeply but was homesick. They agreed to sell the house on Hoban Road, and in June of 1942 she and Wally boarded a train for San Francisco, leaving Trap standing on the platform at Union Station waving farewell to his wife and son, their faces pressed against the train window. Leaving him was a gamble, and she knew it; women were drawn to her husband like bees to honey.

KOGA'S ZERO

In an attempted emergency landing, a Japanese Zero fighter flipped onto its back and skidded across the boggy tundra on Akutan Island in the Aleutians, southwest of Alaska, killing the pilot, Petty Officer Koga, instantly. A month later, on July 10, 1942, a U.S. Navy patrol plane out of Dutch Harbor discovered the wreckage. The Zero appeared to be in good condition, so the patrol plane and her crew returned to Akutan the next day by boat, and the crew hiked out to the wreck, where they determined the Zero to be in remarkably good condition. Returning to Dutch Harbor, they set in motion a salvage operation that culminated in the rebuilt Zero being delivered in flyable condition to NAS North Island in September.[15]

BuAer tracked the rebuilding progress and directed Trap, now a full commander, to make an urgent firsthand evaluation of the Japanese fighter plane. He sent one of his pilots, Lt. Cdr. Eddie Sanders, to NAS North Island to do the initial checkout, and on September 20, Sanders became the first American to fly a Japanese Zero. In a phone conversation with Trap afterward, they agreed that Sanders would continue exploring the Zero's performance to get a better handle on its strengths and weaknesses. Trap would pilot a Corsair to California, where they would fly comparative tests.

True to combat reports, the Zero proved extremely agile at low and moderate speeds, but at high speed, as in a dive, it lost this advantage and could not stay with a maneuvering Wildcat. Sanders found that above two hundred miles per hour the elevator stick forces grew heavy, making it hard to pull out of a dive, and the ailerons became stiff, making it hard to roll, especially to the right. The faster it flew, the worse these conditions became, and at 250 knots fast rolls were "physically impossible."[16] Also, its carburetor could not tolerate negative Gs; the engine would cut out, which was not the case with American engines.

On October 1, Trap left Anacostia in a brand new Corsair and flew to North Island in one day. The next day, he and Sanders flew a series of comparison tests between the Corsair and the Zero, swapping airplanes. The Corsair outperformed the Zero in every way except turning radius at low speed, and the difference was more marked in favor of the Corsair as altitude increased over 15,000 feet. Trap felt greatly relieved.

Many had expressed amazement at the Zero's superb performance, but Trap's report to BuAer makes clear that he found it no big surprise. He wrote, "The general impression of the airplane [Zero] is exactly as originally created by intelligence—including the performance." It is probable that "intelligence" refers to the original report out of China two years earlier. His report continued: Below 20,000 feet, the Zero was faster and had a faster climb rate than the Wildcat, but was more vulnerable and less maneuverable at high speed. He concluded that Wildcats' success against the Zero depended on "mutual support, internal protection [armor and self-sealing fuel tanks], and pullouts or turns at high speed."[17]

Through the following week, Trap and Sanders continued to fly comparison tests among the Zero, the Corsair, and the Wildcat. Trap flew the Zero extensively in mock combat with Sanders in a Wildcat; they focused on how best for a Wildcat or Corsair to break off contact with a Zero attacking from the rear. Some pilots had tried to evade such attacks by pulling up and turning hard, a maneuver that might have worked against a Messerschmitt Bf 109; against a Zero it usually proved fatal. Instead, Trap and Sanders determined that because the Zero's maneuvering superiority evaporated with speed, the key lay in leading the Zero into a full-throttle dive so that both airplanes accelerated rapidly. These dogfight maneuver tests enabled them to devise combat techniques that were not at first intuitive.

A Wildcat or Corsair under attack from behind should abruptly push over hard—not roll—into a vertical dive at full throttle. In order to follow, if the Zero rolled inverted before pulling into its dive, the roll would consume time and the Zero would overshoot the path of the plummeting Wildcat, which could then pull out in the opposite direction to escape. If instead the Zero pushed over, it would experience negative Gs and its engine would cut out until it stabilized in the dive, slowing the airplane and opening the distance to the plummeting Wildcat. The Wildcat should hold its dive until the Zero had followed and was about to bring its guns to bear. Then the Wildcat should roll hard to the right and pull out. The diving Zero, with stiff ailerons and heavy elevators, would be unable to follow and instead would overshoot the Wildcat, which could then escape.

Trap and Sanders repeatedly demonstrated the effectiveness of this technique with Trap mostly flying the Zero and Sanders the Wildcat. Once satisfied, they forwarded this life-saving tactical directive to deployed Navy and Marine fighter squadrons, where it was enthusiastically received and implemented.[18]

At the end of the week, Trap turned his Corsair over to VF-12 and went home on a transport flight. He was deeply grateful that all the blood, sweat, and tears invested in the Corsair had indeed produced a superior airplane. And it was reassuring to know that he and Sanders had devised a fighter tactic that might save scores of lives. A worthwhile week of work.

LIFE AND DEATH

In October 1942, reports began to filter back to Anacostia from Navy and Marine fighter squadrons engaged with the enemy in the Pacific: Wildcat guns were jamming in the midst of violent combat maneuvering. In one instance, Capt. Marion Carl, then the Marine Corp's number two ace with fifteen victories, had just destroyed a Zero using a quick burst from about one hundred yards. He immediately pushed over hard to attack another Zero coming up below him, and all six guns refused to fire.[19]

The ammunition's tendency to jam in the feed chutes under negative G forces happened only when the guns were armed with full or nearly full loads of ammunition; this was corrected in the field by adding proper restraints in the ammunition boxes. Flight Test at Anacostia had tried such maneuvers, but with only partial ammunition loads, so they had never encountered the problem.

When Trap heard about this, he was furious with himself and his organization. People might have died; there was no excuse for this problem getting past them and into the fleet. He used the occasion to hammer the point home to his team: Flight Test was required to test everything under all conditions. It was a matter of life and death.

GRUMMAN FINALLY COMES THROUGH

In early 1941, setting aside all hope of redeeming the Skyrocket, Roy Grumman drove his design team hard to develop the new single-engine fighter. Trap kept close tabs on their work. Corsair development was not going as smoothly as he'd hoped, and he was eager to have an alternative. In designing the new airplane, Grumman stuck close to proven concepts and structures, so it was no surprise that the resulting XF6F-1 Hellcat appeared to be an outgrowth of the Wildcat. On June 30, 1941, the Navy signed a contract for two prototypes.[20]

Through the following year, Trap consulted regularly with Grumman engineers, giving them the benefit of his expertise and passing on lessons learned from the Corsair and the latest aerial combat reports from the Pacific. He made several trips to the Grumman plant at Bethpage to keep tabs on the airplane's progress and provide guidance on stability, control, and cockpit layout. He was pleased with the Hellcat's straightforward design and valued the Grumman philosophy that promoted ruggedness, safety, and reliability, characteristics that had evolved over many years of building solid Navy fighters.

In Trap's estimation, the main difficulty with the Hellcat was that it was coming into play late in the game. The Japanese pounding of Pearl Harbor midway through the airplane's development cycle threw the problem into sharp relief, and in January 1942, with Trap's blessing, the Navy gave Grumman a production contract for 1,080 Hellcats, long before the prototype had flown. It was a gamble. But in view of the catastrophic forward march of Japanese forces in the Pacific and all the difficulties with the Corsair, it was a gamble worth taking.[21]

Bob Hall, Grumman's chief test pilot, first flew the prototype Hellcat on June 30, 1942. To avoid putting further demands on the production of Pratt &

19. Grumman F6F Hellcat fighter. Design work started in early 1941, and the
prototype flew first in mid-1942. In October of that year, Trap flew the first
production-level airplane, and his recommendation immediately started
the production line rolling. It entered combat in 1943.

Official U.S. Navy photo, U.S. Naval Institute Photo Archive

Whitney R-2800 engines, the prototype had been fitted with the less powerful
Wright R-2600, though its design could handle either. Engineers hoped that
the smaller engine would suffice, but that hope proved vain. The airplane had
neither the speed nor the climb rate specified; it needed the bigger engine.
Fortunately, delays in production of other aircraft using the R-2800 made the
bigger engine available. On July 30, one month after the disappointing first
flight, Hall made the second flight with the larger engine. It made all the
difference and enabled him to demonstrate unequivocally that this prototype
easily met its specifications for speed and climb performance.[22]

Further test flights by Grumman proceeded to map out the Hellcat's performance envelope, and Roy Grumman was delighted. He and his staff had already gone out on a long limb by setting up a manufacturing plant for the airplane without Navy clearance to go into production. Launching their production line for the new airplanes without Navy approval posed huge risks to the company and its shareholders. The thought of the Bethpage airfield piled high with an inventory of brand new undeliverable airplanes was sobering, to say the least. He needed assurance that the Navy would ultimately accept the new Hellcat.

Navy procedure ordinarily required a full test program before such approval could be given and a formal contract developed, which would take months they didn't have. Roy began to agitate with his friends in BuAer and likely went directly to his friend, now Vice Adm. John Towers, the bureau chief. You need this airplane now, he argued. BuAer agreed. The Corsair development was in trouble, and if the Hellcat proved as good as hoped, they needed it as fast as possible. How could they short-circuit the cumbersome Navy approval process? Grumman mulled this over before returning to BuAer with a proposition: Why not have Trap come up here and fly this machine to see what he thinks of it? If he gives it a full thumbs-up, let us go into production.

BuAer gave this plan the green light. Grumman had already built a commendable line of first-rate fighters and had established a clear track record for integrity. As Vice Adm. John McCain said, "The name *Grumman* on a plane or part is like *Sterling* on silver."[23]

On October 21, one week after flying the Zero in San Diego, Trap went to Bethpage to fly the XF6F-3 Hellcat. Roy Grumman himself helped Trap suit up for that first flight.[24] He flew it twice for a total of 2.4 hours and was impressed. With his flight test of the Zero still fresh, he readily determined that the new Grumman airplane was comfortably superior in all respects except low-speed turning radius. The Corsair was a better all-round performer, and in the hands of a competent pilot even superior. But the Hellcat was good enough to beat the Japanese, easy to fly, and forgiving of approach-speed errors that would crash a Corsair. Summarizing his opinion later, he said, "If we were going to send ten thousand young kids into an air war, then the Hellcat was the airplane to put them in."

Roy Grumman later recalled of that test flight that Trap thought the airplane lacked sufficient longitudinal stability, which was easily corrected; but otherwise he gave it an unequivocal "thumbs up." Based on Trap's evaluation, BuAer supported the Grumman decision to put the Hellcat into immediate

20. Trap, Roy Grumman, and Bob Hall at the Latin Quarter, September 1942,
probably celebrating the prototype Hellcat's debut and testing success. You
can almost hear them saying, "We think we have a winner here!"

Lat. Qtr., personal files of Herbert W. Trapnell, Trap's second son

full production without formal Navy approval. "We relied on Trapnell's opinion," Grumman said. Official approval of this airplane did not come until years later; by that time the Hellcat had destroyed more than five thousand enemy airplanes.[25]

Don Griffin, now a lieutenant commander, had recently left Trap's unit at Anacostia to take command of Air Group 9 in Norfolk, Virginia. This unit was forming up to deploy to the Pacific as soon as possible. Because of the Corsair's erratic bouncing on hard landings, the Navy was uneasy about introducing it into shipboard operation. As a result, Air Group 9 planned to deploy with either the latest version of the Wildcat, the Wildcat-4, or the Corsair, the availability of which concerned Griffin. As soon as Trap returned to Anacostia from flying the Hellcat, he phoned Griffin, urging him to go up straightaway to check out the new Grumman airplane. He relayed his assessment of the Hellcat, suggesting that Griffin would like it a whole lot better than the Wildcat-4. When Griffin flew to Bethpage, he received a warm welcome. One flight was all it took. Back on the ground, Griffin phoned BuAer requesting an immediate change order to replace his Wildcat-4s with Hellcats. All other fighter squadrons deploying on the big new carriers followed suit.[26]

And so the Navy career of the legendary Hellcat was launched. Griffin's Hellcats went on board the USS *Essex* with Air Group 9 in February 1943 and made their combat debut in a strike on Marcus Island in August, fourteen months after the first flight of the prototype and just ten months after Trap gave the thumbs up that put it into production. This airplane became the most successful fighter in Navy history during the second half of World War II, destroying 5,171 enemy airplanes, mostly in the Pacific theater.[27]

A GLIMPSE OF THE FUTURE

The sun was cresting the low rolling hills to the east, casting long shadows from a motley group of hastily constructed buildings nestled on the edge of the immense dry salt flat. This ancient lakebed stretched out to the southwest as far as the eye could see, where the San Gabriel Mountains stood tall, bathed in morning sunlight. On the other side was Los Angeles. It was April 21, 1943.[28]

Trap had arrived the evening before, landing his brand new Corsair in the marked-off area on the lakebed. Ostensibly, he was ferrying that airplane from the factory in Connecticut to NAS North Island in San Diego, where new Corsair squadrons were being assembled. But orders from the chief of the Bureau of Aeronautics directed him to make this one-day stop-off at a remote, clandestine Army air base in California—Muroc Field—one day to be known as Edwards Air Force Base. His mission was to test a new kind of airplane. The airplane, these orders, the stop-off itself, and the very existence of this special test facility were all top secret.

Trap stood for a moment outside the ramshackle operations office. Parked on the flight line to his right were four P-38 Lightning fighters that served both as chase airplanes and as air patrol for the little air base. Beyond them was parked his sky-blue Corsair. Already at this hour of the morning, Army personnel were swarming around, inspecting it closely. He guessed they had never seen one before.

On his left was the reason for his visit to Muroc. The Bell P-59A Airacomet, America's first jet airplane, was parked on the flight line outside its hangar. He understood jet propulsion and had been checked out in the cockpit inside the hangar the evening before. But this was the first time he had seen a jet airplane in profile from a distance, and the image caught him momentarily by surprise—a clean silver sculpture of smooth curves gleaming in the early morning light, a monument to some Jules Verne notion of launching into

21. Bell P-59A Airacomet, America's first jet airplane,
which Trap flew in April 1943 to become the Navy's first jet pilot

*Official U.S. Army Air Forces photo, National Archives and Records Administration,
Records of the Bureau of Aeronautics*

space, a fantasy made real on that runway laid out before him. Without a propeller, the airplane looked an absurdity. He guessed this was how clipper ship
sailors felt on first eyeing a steamship. Without sails, how could it possibly
go anywhere? He was about to find out exactly how this propellerless wonder
would fly.

Previous flights of the Airacomet had uncovered myriad issues, including
weak lateral stability and poor engine responsiveness. But the biggest drawback
was simply the lack of engine thrust; one pilot commented that the airplane
could hardly get out of its own way. Its P designation notwithstanding, this little fighter would eventually be relegated to a training and familiarization role.
In those days, the U.S. Army Air Forces called their fighters "pursuit" planes,
hence the designation P.[29]

As a matter of course for a test flight, Trap would check out these performance factors just to confirm what he had been told. But what really interested him was the jet engine performance at high altitude, where the oxygen
needed for combustion grows ever thinner. Reciprocating engines, with their
propellers, struggled to retain power with increasing altitude by using heavy,
cumbersome superchargers, which compressed the thin air and delivered it to
the engine, as discussed in chapter 8. On the other hand, the jet engine inherently tended to retain its thrust at altitude. So while checking out the known
problems on the way up, Trap was going to take the Airacomet as high as his
oxygen equipment would allow him, to assess engine behavior.

As he clambered into the cockpit, he shrugged his fur-lined flight suit up around his neck and plugged in the oxygen mask. He had forgotten how cold nights could get in the desert, but it would be much colder where he was going.

The Army major who had led him through his cockpit checkout the night before now stood on the wing and leaned into the cockpit, watching Trap run through the start-up procedure. On command, the big diesel ground generator roared as he set the controls, pouring electrical energy into the airplane's starter receptacle. Trap watched the rpm gauge as the engine's compressor and turbine rotor turned ever faster, until the rpm reached the critical number. He opened the fuel stopcock and advanced the throttle halfway. In a few seconds, the exhaust gas temperature in the jet engine tailpipe jumped to the maximum allowable; any higher and the engine might disintegrate, destroying the airplane along with anything or anyone in the vicinity. As the wailing jet engine came to life and the rpm climbed, he backed off the throttle. The tailpipe temperature dropped and the engine settled into idle rpm. He followed the same routine with the right engine.[30]

With both engines turning at idle, the major nodded and smiled broadly. Sensing the airplane was in competent hands, he clapped Trap on the shoulder and shouted over the screaming jet blast, "She's all yours, commander. Just bring her back in one piece." Trap's smile was hidden behind his oxygen mask. He nodded and gave a casual salute as the major jumped off the wing.

As Trap had been warned, it took nearly full throttle to start taxiing, and with every throttle advance he kept an eagle eye on the tailpipe temperature. Then, once the airplane started rolling, he quickly retarded the throttle almost to idle to keep from accelerating. This was nothing like a propeller airplane.

As he lined up for takeoff at the start of the runway, his chase airplane took off ahead. The Lightning was a high-altitude fighter, equipped with turbo-superchargers, the most powerful superchargers available. It would provide an interesting comparison to the jet at altitude. As the Lightning swung around the pattern to come up behind him, Trap got a green-light clearance from airfield control, which wasn't a tower but just a desk and a stack of radio equipment on the desert floor. Holding the brakes, he advanced the throttle while keeping a sharp eye on the gauges, tailpipe temperatures just below the allowable maximum, rpm climbing. Finally, the rpm reached maximum, and he released the brakes.

The response was stunning. When the brakes were released on a Corsair at takeoff, it shoved you back into the seat so you could hardly keep your head off the headrest. This thing accelerated more like a freight train, slowly, ever so slowly, picking up speed. The wheels thump-thumped over the small cracks and rough spots on the dry lakebed; the surface wasn't as smooth as it looked from a distance. After what seemed an eternity, the airspeed indicator came off its lower stop at sixty miles per hour. The thump-thump continued, seemingly forever, at a slowly escalating rate, while the airspeed crept toward liftoff speed. In a Corsair, he would already be airborne with the wheels up, but the Airacomet was still glued to the lakebed, thumping and bumping its way along. Finally, as the airspeed edged up to liftoff speed, he brought the stick back and the airplane rotated and climbed off the lakebed. He settled her into an easy climb at full throttle and retracted the wheels and flaps.[31]

My God, it was quiet inside the closed cockpit. Even with forewarning, the silence proved unnerving. He glanced quickly at the engine instruments to be sure the machinery was still working.

The chase airplane pulled up alongside and throttled back to stay even, then danced around the Airacomet to inspect it from all sides. Finally, the chase pilot saluted with a thumbs up to indicate that all looked well, and then dropped back into a loose echelon as they continued their climb.

On the way up, Trap performed some stability tests. He verified the lateral stability problem he had been warned about and also found a longitudinal stability quirk he didn't like. This was not an airplane you wanted to turn new students loose in.

At 10,000 feet he leveled off to check the throttle response. He powered back to minimum flying speed, then advanced the throttle and watched the tailpipe temperatures go nearly to their maximum limits. But nothing else happened, at least for a long time. Then, slowly, the compressor and turbine spools' rpm began to increase. Gradually he felt the slight push of acceleration at his back, and the airspeed indicator inched its way up. Good heavens, he thought, this thing will never make a carrier airplane.

They continued to climb, and at 30,000 feet and still at full throttle, the Airacomet was holding the same climb rate at a higher airspeed than at lower altitude. The chase airplane kept up easily and maneuvered all around the Airacomet for another inspection. Again, all was well.

At 38,000 feet, as they approached the limit of their oxygen equipment, the Airacomet continued to hold climb rate and speed. Trap had flown the Lightning as part of the Navy's evaluation of a broad range of fighter planes, and he knew that at this altitude, even with its turbo-superchargers, the chase airplane would labor to keep up. Looking back, he could see the Lightning flagging, but the little jet plane held its speed and kept climbing.

He leveled off at 40,000 feet, as planned. He had come this high to get a good feel for the jet's comparative performance at altitude. The Lightning lagged hopelessly behind, unable to hold either speed or climb rate.[32]

The fuel gauge said it was time to head back. Trap retarded the throttles to idle and lowered the nose until the airspeed indicator was redlined. Without a propeller the little jet was clean, and going downhill it wanted to run like a horse for the barn. Keeping below its maximum speed limit required considerable attention. As they moved into denser air, the chase airplane came alongside and again kept up easily. Down they swung toward the vast dry lakebed.

Their landing was uneventful. Back on the ground, Trap made a few notes; later he would write a full report and evaluation. He thanked his hosts and climbed into his Corsair. At the end of the runway, he got a green light from control and pushed the throttle forward. The engine roared, and he was pressed against the backrest. Amid the cacophony of usual noises, he hardly noticed the rumble of the wheels on the lakebed. The plane lifted off in a few moments and settled into an accelerating climb. As the wheels thumped home and the flaps came up, he took notice of the savage growl of the engine up front. This airplane lacked the quiet serenity of the jet; it was noisy and rough and responsive, like an airplane ought to be.

And yet, he reflected, that little jet had demonstrated potential that no propeller airplane could match. Perhaps you could even get used to the quiet. The jet needed a lot of development to become a useful combat aircraft suitable for carrier operation, but the potential was there. If they could build bigger, more responsive jet engines and put them into a decent airframe, then it would change the game. And the Navy was bound to play a vital role in that development.

The growl of his engine brought him back to the present, and he eyed his fuel gauge. It was time to get this Corsair down to San Diego. There was a war to win. Perhaps down the road a ways, the jet airplane would come into its own as player in a new age of aviation. Yes, he had seen the future, and his report would say so. He had also just become the first U.S. Navy pilot to fly a jet airplane.

OFF TO WAR

Trap had been a commander for a little less than a year when he was promoted to captain in May 1943; at the same time, he received orders transferring him out of Flight Test to a new post on the West Coast. He had guided the Flight Test Section through a highly stressful period, meeting the charge to outfit the U.S. Navy for air war. The airplanes they had tested, evaluated, redesigned, refined, and approved went on to win every key air battle in the Pacific. The challenge had been both exhilarating and treacherous; two of his pilots had been killed in the line of flight test duty.

But the bombing of Pearl Harbor and the subsequent declaration of war were a clarion call to Trap and his colleagues. They had taken a solemn oath long ago to fight for their country when called upon; for all their adult lives they had trained to protect and defend. It was now Trap's turn to go to war.

Adm. Charles D. Griffin, Trap's good friend and number two at Anacostia, spoke of this time and place in his oral history:

> The Flight Test officer was Fred Trapnell, who in my opinion was probably the greatest test pilot the world ever saw. He was absolutely terrific. He had no advanced degrees, largely through choice, but he could take an aircraft up, find out what was wrong with it, bring it back down, and not only tell the engineers what was wrong with it but the most probable way for them to proceed to cure the problem. He was absolutely brilliant in his field and was recognized as such I think by the entire aviation industry. I was his number two and felt it was really an honor and a pleasure to work with him.[33]

As chief of Flight Test for the Navy, Trap led Navy Flight Test into early testing of prototypes to shorten test-and-development cycles, thereby reducing the time from conception to deployment of new airplanes. Furthermore, he had pursued getting better fighter planes with diligence and determination, putting on a fast track the development and delivery of not one but two superb fighter types for the operational Navy: the Corsair and the Hellcat, shipboard fighters that would have been prized in the inventory of any air force in the world. These airplanes swept Japanese aviation out of the skies, saving the United States immeasurable blood and treasure while accelerating the victorious conclusion of World War II.

Trap's achievement—though not made in combat conditions for which so many of his colleagues received decorations—stands among the most important contributions made by an officer of his rank to the American war effort. For this, he received a personal commendation from Secretary of the Navy Frank Knox, which reads in part:

> The Department has been informed of your outstanding performance of duty as Head of the Flight Test Section at the Naval Air Station, Anacostia, D.C. for a period of approximately three years. Under your guidance the test section changed its nature from that of an acceptance group to determine the suitability for service to that of a semi-development group assisting in the elimination of

flight deficiencies in the early steps of flight tests, finally passing on the acceptance of the delivered airplane for service use. It further appears that you personally performed a large portion of the important flight testing, much of it being particularly hazardous in nature, since it was made in aircraft which had not been demonstrated or completely flight checked.

For the outstanding manner in which you carried out a very hazardous and difficult assignment, you are hereby commended.[34]

CHAPTER 12

★ ★ ★

HIGH NOON IN THE PACIFIC, 1943–45

Trap was not a happy man when he relieved his friend, Capt. Leslie Gehres, to take over command of Fleet Air (Patrol) Wing 4, based at Kodiak, Alaska, in early June 1943.[1] Trap's prewar experience with the patrol squadron operating in southeastern Alaska had introduced him to the region's typically primitive stations and predictably foul weather. This base, however, was farther west than his previous post; not only was everything more primitive, but the weather was considerably worse.[2] More troubling still, he was a long way from the war in the South Pacific. Why in the world had they sent him to this godforsaken wasteland? He should be down in the thick of battle with the carrier operations, where the U.S. fleet was slugging it out with the Japanese.

At the end of May, U.S. Army troops had wrested Attu, the westernmost isle in the Aleutian chain, from the Japanese, but the enemy still held Kiska, two hundred miles farther east, closer to the Alaskan mainland. Plans were also afoot to invade and repossess Kiska, and Fleet Air Wing 4 was assigned to support operations in the western Aleutians by patrolling those waters to detect attempts by the enemy to reinforce Kiska or to attack the American amphibious force. The wing had far-reaching responsibility for patrolling the waters of the Bering Sea, the Gulf of Alaska, and beyond to the westernmost Aleutian Islands.

Trap apparently wanted to assess the situation for himself. In the middle of June he caught a hop out to their base at Adak, and from there he flew a PBY-5A to Attu and back. He also made several flights to nearby islands, probably to check out harbors there for basing opportunities.[3]

But his tour with Fleet Air Wing 4 did not last long. Somebody in Washington must have gotten their wires crossed, because within two weeks of assuming command, Trap was relieved by none other than Leslie Gehres, now promoted to commodore.⁴ Trap had new orders to assume command of Fleet Air Wing 14 based at North Island, San Diego.⁵

Patrol Wing 14 was responsible for scouting waters along the entire west coast of the continental United States, from San Diego north. His wing flew Consolidated PBY Catalinas and big land-based patrol planes, Consolidated PB4Y-1 Liberators, the Navy version of the Army B-24 Liberator, from bases in San Diego, San Francisco, and Seattle. Although not measurably closer to the fighting than in Kodiak, San Diego was bustling with war preparations and training operations.

It didn't take Trap long to discover trouble. During the previous two weeks, one of his squadrons based in Seattle had lost two airplanes and both crews. The apparent cause was bad weather. Then, on the third day of his command, they lost another. This was inexcusable.

Trap immediately grounded the troubled squadron and organized his other units to temporarily cover their vacated patrol responsibilities. Then he commandeered the executive officer of one of those squadrons and together they flew to Seattle to investigate. Upon interviewing the pilots of the grounded squadron, they quickly discovered that most of them had virtually no training in instrument flying.

Their story provoked Trap's ire. How could these men be put in the position of flying through some of the foulest weather in the North American continent without appropriate instrument training? This was negligence.

Instrument flying is vital to any pilot's ability to control and navigate his aircraft reliably when fog, clouds, or darkness mask visual references outside the cockpit. It is too easy for a pilot to become disoriented. G forces generated by standard maneuvers, vibration, and turbulence induce vertigo and other sensory distortions that make it impossible to gauge aircraft orientation, much less speed, altitude, or direction. For a patrol plane pilot to survive conditions such as those in the Pacific Northwest, his instrument-flying skills had to be honed to perfection.

In their final interview, Trap asked the squadron commander why his pilots had not received appropriate training. His answer: There had not been adequate time. Urgent orders to move his newly formed unit up to their new Northern Pacific patrol left no opportunity to take time out for instruction. His first priority had been to get the job done, which meant his men would have to learn the ropes on the fly. Since no orders had been issued for instrument training, he had not asked for additional time and resources that he did not expect to receive. In his view, he'd simply done the job he'd been asked to under the constraints imposed by the situation. Trap relieved the man of his command on the spot.

After verifying that the other squadrons in his own command were fully instrument-qualified, he commandeered a handful of patrol planes and crews from his San Diego–based squadrons to move temporarily to Seattle to replace the grounded ones. He also dispatched an instrument training team to Seattle, along with qualified instrument check pilots to instruct and supervise students. The unqualified pilots were put to work around the clock on an accelerated instrument training course, and they loved it.

In a matter of weeks, the grounded squadron began to rally as more and more of its pilots completed their instrument certification. By the end of summer, they were fully operational under a new commanding officer. Rigorous and ongoing refresher instrument training became standard fare in Fleet Air Wing 14.[6]

Trap chalked up ample flying time in this job, more than thirty-six hours in September and fifty-four in October. His flight time included several trips up and down the Pacific coast, and one round trip across the country. Still, he was itching to get out to sea and into the war. A week after reporting for duty as commander of Fleet Air Wing 14, he filled out a Form 278, whereby an officer could request a change of duty, listing the following preferences in priority order: CO (commanding officer) of a light carrier in the Pacific, CO of a light carrier in the Atlantic, and CO of an escort carrier in the Pacific. A plaintive plea at the bottom of the form underscored his request: "Urgently desire C.O. of any kind of CV [aircraft carrier]," for which one can read, "Get me out of this backwater."

Meanwhile, life at North Island had its perks. Many of his old friends and acquaintances had settled in or around Coronado. Since Alice remained comfortably lodged in San Francisco, Trap lived alone in the bachelor officers quarters at North Island, practically within walking distance to town. If solitary living ever weighed on him, he never showed it. He enjoyed getting together with friends, colleagues, and their families, who welcomed his warm wit and easy charm. He was a popular addition to their plans for dinner or an evening on the town, pleasing diversions while he waited to be wheels up and into the war.

BACK TO THE SEA

Trap's escape from the tedium of West Coast patrol plane duty was not long coming. In November 1943, he was relieved as commander of Fleet Air Wing 14 and given command of USS *Breton* (CVE 23), a small escort carrier assigned to the Carrier Transport Squadron, Pacific Fleet, as part of the logistics pipeline that provided expedited transport of critical men, material, and aircraft to aviation units operating against Japanese forces in the Pacific. The ship had just returned from delivering to Efate, in the New Hebrides, a squadron of Marine Corsairs en route to Vella Lavella in the Solomons.[7] When Trap took command of *Breton*, she was tied up at a quay at Ford Island, Pearl Harbor, loading aircraft and spare parts for transport to the New Hebrides in support of the Solomons campaign.[8]

Breton was not a happy ship. The captain he relieved was reputed to be a martinet, an attitude that apparently trickled down through the ship's ranks. Some officers, Trap noted, were overly deferential toward him. Not a good sign. Officers who paid too much attention to their superiors often failed to devote appropriate attention to their subordinates. He also learned that crew resentment toward their officers was brewing. If true, this was bad news indeed. An officer's men did not have to like him, but they had to respect him. And resentment was toxic to respect.

He had seen this before in other units. The crew that did not esteem their officers tended not to respect their ship. Failing to take responsibility for keeping their equipment in top-notch working order, they aimed instead for minimum compliance and dawdled when no one was looking, all of which wreaked havoc on a ship's operating standards and efficiency. As the new skipper, Trap wondered how to turn this around. His opportunity came sooner than expected.

Late one afternoon, some of the crew were preparing for shore liberty. On the hangar deck, a young ensign was inspecting a long line of sailors to ensure that their uniforms and grooming met standards for going on liberty. Trap was passing down the hangar deck when he suddenly heard the officer berating one of the men in a raised voice. Trap quietly detoured over to the two, everyone snapping to attention as he approached.

"What's going on here, Mister?" he asked, using the proper term of address for an ensign.

"Sir, this man's hair is too long. I am denying him liberty until he gets it cut." The ensign seemed quite satisfied with his rebuke of the sailor.

As the young seaman in question stood at rigid attention, Trap quietly inspected him, passing completely around him, perusing his hair and clothing. His uniform was immaculate, he was clean-shaven, and his black shoes sparkled. He had perhaps three weeks' growth of hair—maybe a bit longer than ideal—but it was neat and carefully combed. In fact, the man looked pretty much the model sailor.

Trap turned to the officer and announced in a voice that everyone in the area could hear, "He looks okay to me, Mister."

Word flashed around the ship as if announced on the loudspeaker. The men had heard that their new skipper was a renowned aviator, said to be the best test pilot in the Navy. Now they saw that he was a reasonable man, a commanding officer who respected his crew. And they would trust and respect him in turn.[9]

The incident set the tone for Trap's leadership style and expectations on board USS *Breton*. As with the Flight Test Section, he was consistently demanding but utterly fair. And it soon became evident to everyone that he was not just a hotshot Airedale; when it came to ship handling, seamanship, and navigation, they saw that his knowledge and skill were second to none. *Breton* became notably more cheerful and efficient under her new commanding officer.

BETTER MUSIC

Another off-note met with Trap's disapproval: *Breton*'s high-pitched tinny ship's whistle. In January 1944, when the ship put into San Francisco for a general overhaul, he made a visit to the East Coast, stopping briefly in Richmond, Virginia, to visit his brother Nick, who had been recently promoted to superintendent of motive power on the Chesapeake & Ohio (C&O) Railroad. After listening to Trap's complaints about his ship's whistle, Nick suggested the two of them take a trip down to the locomotive shop. Stowed in a back corner was a fine brass whistle of the kind used by the C&O on their massive steam locomotives that hauled coal from the mines in western Appalachia over the mountains and down to the Atlantic seaport at Norfolk.

Peeling the original packaging from the whistle, Nick said that if Trap wanted it for his ship, he could have it. Trap was intrigued, but wanted to hear its sound. The two of them scrambled into the cab of one of the big locomotives that stood idling in the yard, and Nick blew the whistle, a deep melodic wail. Trap was thrilled. Yes, he wanted it, but how would the Navy pay for it? Nick refused payment; it would be part of the railroad's contribution to the war effort. The C&O would be proud to have their whistle sailing on board a U.S. Navy warship in the Pacific Fleet.

The whistle was shipped by Railway Express to San Francisco, where it replaced the original on *Breton*. Its deep-throated timbre became the envy of every ship's crew in her class, and Trap was proud to say thereafter that she had the finest ship's whistle in the Navy.[10]

SPECIAL DELIVERY

In May 1944, after the overhaul and two trips to the South Pacific, *Breton* returned to San Diego to pick up airplanes and supplies destined for the Fast

Carrier Task Groups that were slated to support the upcoming Marianas invasion. In earlier transport missions, the escort carriers had delivered aircraft and parts to shore bases, where they unloaded their cargo by crane onto a dock or quay. In a change that would enable the big carriers to remain on station in the combat area, little carriers like *Breton* were being asked to deliver replacement aircraft deck to deck at sea. The Navy Supply Corps and its ships had already learned how to manage at-sea replenishment of fuel, ammunition, food supplies, and so forth. But large-scale wartime transfer of aircraft between ships at sea in combat had not been attempted previously.

At a meeting of the Carrier Transport Squadron leadership, including the escort carrier captains, discussion centered on the feasibility of ship-to-ship transfers. With the little carriers fully loaded, as was their practice, there was not enough flight deck left for safe takeoff. So they would have go with a partial load of planes. How much deck run would they need to get the planes safely airborne? Knowing of his recent tour in Flight Test, the leadership turned to Trap for an answer. He had already done the calculation.[11]

Hellcats, with their high power-to-weight ratio, a minimum load of fuel, and no ammunition, would get off in the shortest deck run, so they would go first. With twenty knots of wind over the deck and flown by a skilled pilot, this plane should be able to launch in 190 feet. The first few airplanes to launch were the most critical since their departure would clear deck space for less seasoned pilots to follow. If the destination ships were close at hand and the planes could land quickly, their minimal loads were of no consequence. Because Trap strongly favored direct ship-to-ship transfers, *Breton* was chosen to make the first trial run, a proposal that met with quick approval from Pacific Fleet Command.

To verify his calculations, Trap took *Breton* to sea off San Diego with a handful of Hellcats and seasoned pilots. They flew the planes from a measured deck to determine the space required for takeoff, with Trap coaching the pilots in the optimum technique for achieving a minimum run. In calm air and with the ship at full speed, if their plane carried only fifty gallons of fuel and no ammunition or external stores, a good pilot could indeed get a Hellcat airborne consistently in less than 190 feet. This information became part of the training regimen for all replacement pilots.[12]

In June 1944, *Breton* sailed with a full load of airplanes from San Diego to Eniwetok, where she offloaded enough inventory to make room for the deck launch. Then she joined Task Force 58, which was supporting the landing on Saipan. This invasion precipitated the Battle of the Philippine Sea during June 19–21, also known as the Great Marianas Turkey Shoot. Hellcat fighter planes from Task Force 58 shot down more than four hundred enemy aircraft, essentially destroying what remained of Japanese naval aviation.[13] Here, under combat conditions and well within range of the enemy, *Breton* pilots used the fly-off technique developed in San Diego to quickly replace the twenty-nine American planes lost in battle.[14] Trap was awarded the Bronze Star for his handling of this resupply operation.[15]

As the battle tempo of the Fast Carrier Task Groups accelerated through the fall of 1944, *Breton* shuttled between the West Coast of the United States and the Western Pacific, resupplying the big carriers and airfields hastily established on captured islands. Carrier offloading was often done under combat conditions.

INTO THE BATTLE FLEET

At the request of Rear Adm. Arthur Radford, who would later become commander in chief of the United States Pacific Command and chairman of the Joint Chiefs of Staff, Trap left *Breton* and the Carrier Transport Squadron in October to join the battle fleet itself. The two men, who had known each other since the early 1930s, became particularly well acquainted during Radford's stint with BuAer, which began in May 1941 while Trap was at Anacostia. When Radford was promoted to rear admiral and given command of Carrier Division 6, he selected Trap as his chief of staff, and so began his role as a lifelong friend and mentor to Trap.

In November 1944, Radford and Trap came on board USS *Yorktown*, hoisted the admiral's flag, and settled down to conduct business from the flag bridge. She was anchored at Ulithi, an atoll in the western Caroline Islands that today is part of Federated States of Micronesia. Task Force 38 ships at anchor stretched across the huge lagoon to the far horizon.

This remote 212-square-mile lagoon, surrounded by some forty islets that formed the atoll, had become the unlikely staging ground for the largest air and sea operations ever undertaken by any navy. The industrial power of the United States was in evidence on all sides as fresh contingents of ships and airplanes merged into the task force. Water and sky pulsated under the massive convergence of aircraft and warships, metal and machinery, maneuvering for position and readying for war.

More than seventeen big aircraft carriers and their escorts, rigged and ready to move at a moment's notice, spread across the Ulithi lagoon as far as the eye could see.[16] Once relegated by the Gun Club to scouting and patrolling duty, the carriers and their airplanes had evolved into the Navy's primary weapon of war.

Task Force 38 was the operating name for the U.S. Navy's battle fleet and main strike force in the Western Pacific. The task force was split into three or four task groups, and the core of each group was a carrier division made up of three or four big carriers and as many light carriers. Each task group also comprised a battleship division, one or two cruiser divisions, and two or three destroyer divisions, perhaps twenty-five to thirty-five ships in all. So a task group was a formidable self-contained fighting unit that could carry out a mission independently of other task groups and provide for its own defense as needed. The carrier division commander, like Radford, was also the task group commander. A task group was identified by its task force number, followed by dot, then the task group number, where the task group number was a single digit, for example Task Group 38.4 or Task Group 58.2. The task force number was changed from 38 to 58 and back again periodically, and the task group numbers changed accordingly.[17]

Orders were already coming down from the task force commander: Task Force 38 was heading into combat again, and soon. American troops had already landed on the island of Leyte in the Philippines, and Task Force 38's mission was to prevent the Japanese from reinforcing Leyte from bases on the Philippine island of Luzon, as well as from Taiwan and the Japanese islands to the north. Carrier Division 6 comprised four large Essex-class aircraft carriers, including *Yorktown*, each carrying ninety to one hundred airplanes, and one to three light carriers, each carrying thirty to thirty-five airplanes, which together provided a strike force of three hundred plus airplanes while still retaining its own protective air cover.

In the early morning of November 5, 1944, the division departed Ulithi at twenty-seven knots for Luzon, as part of Task Group 38.1. During the next three weeks, aside from four days maneuvering to avoid a typhoon, they struck at ships and installations on Luzon, especially around Manila Bay. They sustained occasional attacks by kamikaze suicide planes, which damaged a number of ships, including *Essex*, a sister ship to *Yorktown*. The carrier air groups typically executed two or three strikes a day for two days straight and then, on the third day, retired several hundred miles to refuel at sea.[18] On November 27, they dropped anchor back in Ulithi.[19]

TYPHOON COBRA

Twelve days later, they were again under way for Luzon to support landings on Mindoro, where the Army Air Forces wanted to gain airfields from which to reinforce the invasion of Luzon itself. This was interrupted on December 17, when Task Force 38 was caught in Typhoon Cobra, perhaps the worst storm in U.S. naval experience. Sustained winds in excess of 145 miles per hour, with gusts considerably higher, tossed the fleet like tinker toys in a cauldron of waves, with heights measured in building stories, that dwarfed *Essex*-class carriers and their escorts. Waves crested above the carriers' gun decks, and at times solid green walls of water broke over their flight decks. When the storm finally receded on the morning of December 19, three destroyers, 146 airplanes, and nearly 800 men of the Third Fleet had been lost. According to Paul Frisco, an eyewitness and veteran of the Pacific War who served on board USS *Cushing*, "Every ship had sustained damage as from a major battle. Not one ship emerged unscathed."[20]

Nevertheless, Task Group 38.1 immediately went back to war, pounding targets on Luzon and Mindoro to soften up the island for the upcoming Mindoro landing before returning to Ulithi on December 24.

GUIDING THE BATTLE FORCE

While Trap had been exposed to combat in a support role on board *Breton*, these early sorties on *Yorktown* were his first experience in offensive operations against the enemy, and his role was primarily as an observer. The prior task group commander and his experienced staff planned and coordinated these operations to show Radford and Trap how it was done. The next time out, in addition to commanding Carrier Division 6, Radford would also take command of Task Group 38.1, while Trap would direct the planning and coordination of all task group operations.

This was a difficult job. Strike orders came down from the task force commander to attack and destroy installations, airfields, ships, and other enemy resources at specified locations, or perhaps to provide air cover over a designated area. Trap and his staff broke down those orders into specific targets for every strike. Each target—building, pier, tunnel, ship, gun installation, airplane dispersal area, and so on—was identified on maps or aerial photographs, then assigned the numbers and types of weapons—bombs, rockets, torpedoes and ammunition—needed to destroy that target. Targets and deliverables were allocated to each carrier air group, which in turn allotted weapons to airplanes, and airplanes to targets.[21]

Each strike force was to suppress both the enemy's interference with the strike and its retaliation against the task group. The opening mission of a strike was usually made by fighters, first to destroy aircraft on the ground, and then to put up a target combat air patrol to protect striking aircraft from enemy fighters. Enemy fighter operations from surrounding airfields also had to be suppressed. The sequence of strikes and the down-to-the-minute schedule for each element to arrive over its target were designed to accomplish the job in the shortest time with the fewest losses. This plan was mapped back into launch times for individual elements, taking into account the airspeed of each aircraft type involved.

The task group was also to provide for its own protection with continual fighter cover, so the plan had to allow for ships to launch and recover these local combat air patrols concurrent with its offensive sorties. Finally, plans had to take account of weather conditions over the task group, over the target, and in between. Thus, the planning and execution of each air strike was a complex process involving an intricate array of locations, targets, conditions, and other variables. No cookie-cutter approach would suffice.

Radford expected Trap, as his chief of staff, to ensure that all planning, communication, and negotiation with strike groups were precisely coordinated and that strike orders were ready for the admiral's signature on time. This kind of tactical planning suited Trap down to the ground. Subject to Radford's usually routine approval, he was in effect leading a major naval force in battle, a role he had aspired to since his days as a midshipman.

Following the U.S. Army's invasion of Luzon on January 3, Task Force 38's mission was to interdict Japanese attempts to reinforce their troops on that island. On December 30, 1944, Task Group 38.1 sailed northwest from Ulithi with three big carriers, one light carrier, two battleships, five cruisers, and eighteen destroyers. For the next four weeks, they conducted strikes on Taiwan, Luzon, the coasts of China and Indo-China, and Okinawa.

On January 25 they were back at Ulithi, where fleet numbers changed and Radford's command was renumbered Task Group 58.1. The influx of new carriers, along with fresh tactics that called for increasing the proportion of fighters in each air group, had created a temporary shortage of Hellcat fighter squadrons. Fortunately, the waning air war in the Solomon Islands made available Marine Corsair squadrons, two of which were initially brought on board carriers to fill out the need. They amply and decisively demonstrated what the Marines had long asserted: the Corsair had come into its own as a superb carrier fighter.[22]

"Any kid who can ride a tricycle can learn to fly a Hellcat," the Marines said. "Flying a Corsair is a bit more challenging, which was not a problem for Marines. And a Corsair could wax a Hellcat any time at any altitude."[23]

On hearing this, Trap chuckled contentedly in the quiet satisfaction of seeing the aircraft lineup he and his Anacostia team had so rigorously tested, struggled with, torn apart, and put back together—the Corsair, Hellcat, Dauntless, and Avenger—all performing so well under fire in the fleet.[24]

REVENGE

At Pearl Harbor three years earlier, the Imperial Japanese Navy had delivered a vicious blow to the United States and especially the U.S. Navy. For several months, American B-29 bombers had sporadically bombed southern Japan from China, and with the capture of Saipan, they began routine bombing of cities thought to provide the backbone of the Japanese war effort. But the U.S. Navy was now going for the jugular. The Japanese, and particularly the Imperial Japanese Navy, were about to feel the full impact of the world's most powerful naval strike force, driving its fangs deep into military and supporting installations in the Japanese homeland.

American forces were under no illusion that this would be easy. The tenacity with which the Japanese had resisted every invasion in the Pacific left little doubt about their determination to defend their home ground. They would fight to the death. The kamikaze suicide planes in evidence in the Philippines would now come in force.

On February 10, 1945, Task Group 58.4 sailed from Ulithi for Japan, and for the next two weeks, the Task Group shuttled between strikes on targets around Tokyo Bay and on Iwo Jima in support of the Marine landings there before returning to Ulithi.[25]

When they sortied again on March 18, their mission was to support the upcoming landings on Okinawa, first by interdicting Japanese reinforcements coming out of southern Japan, and then by covering the invasion directly. They initially headed for Kyushu, the most southwesterly of the Japanese islands, where the Japanese High Command deployed massive military resources and personnel in hopes of defeating the Allied forces in these waters before they ever reached the main island. The task force would be operating as close to the Japanese mainland as any U.S. Navy carrier group had ventured during the war.[26]

When Task Force 58.4 struck, the Japanese immediately retaliated with air attacks, and in the course of the day all three big carriers in Task Force 58.4 were hit. That afternoon, three planes attacked *Yorktown* to release bombs before her gunners shot them down; one succeeded in placing a bomb on her signal bridge that passed through the deck of a 20-mm gun battery before detonating outside the hull near the second deck level. Although five men were killed and twenty-six more wounded, the bomb's failure to explode on impact spared everyone on the bridge, including Trap, as well as many more crew members.[27]

The next morning, they were preparing to attack Kyushu again when USS *Franklin*, a sister ship to *Yorktown*, was struck by bombs from an attacking plane. Although in a different task group, she was clearly visible to Trap from the flag bridge on *Yorktown*, erupting into flames and enveloped in smoke from stem to stern, as reports from explosion after explosion reverberated across open sea. The conflagration raged unabated as the big ship slowed to a drift and escorts closed in to assist. Trap had friends on board *Franklin*, including the skipper, Leslie Gehres, with whom he had traded command of Patrol Wing 4 in Kodiak. Shaken, Trap later said he could not imagine how anyone had survived that attack on *Franklin*.[28] Officially more than 700 men were killed and more than 250 wounded, though revised counts make the numbers higher, and she eventually limped home to the Brooklyn Navy Yard under her own steam.

Throughout the rest of March, April, May, and into early June, Task Group 58.4 struck Kyushu and supported the invasion of Okinawa, which began April 1. They had a brief diversion on April 7 when they caught and sank the Japanese super-battleship *Yamato* under way at sea on a one-way suicide mission to Okinawa.[29]

In June, they encountered another fierce typhoon and then took two weeks of rest and recreation at the island of Leyte. In July, they headed north for sustained operations against the main islands of Honshu and Hokkaido. They made their last strike of the war on military installations around Tokyo on August 13.

The United States dropped atomic bombs on Hiroshima on August 6 and on Nagasaki on August 9. On August 15 Japan capitulated and World War II was over. Trap was awarded the Legion of Merit for his performance in this campaign. The citation highlights the immeasurable help provided by Trap's keen judgment and knowledge of the aircraft capabilities and lauds Trap's calm cool courage under enemy attack.[30]

SURVEYING THE DAMAGE

From November 1945 to April 1946, Trap was assigned as the senior naval officer to the U.S. Strategic Bombing Survey, which developed a detailed report on the effectiveness of the strategic bombing of Japan in curtailing its war-fighting ability. After his long absence of more than two years from the United States and from all flying opportunity, he did not relish this assignment. Nonetheless, he apparently carried it out with characteristic diligence, as evidenced by the awarding of a "Gold Star in Lieu of 2nd Legion of Merit" for his contribution.

The citation highlights his thorough and precise knowledge of the wartime operations in which he participated, his profound insight into the complexities of the art of war, and his diligence and analytical skill. It concludes, "Capt. Trapnell has made a significant and fundamental contribution to all future planning for the national defense."[31]

His temporary duty with the strategic bombing survey finally complete, Trap returned to the United States to undertake a challenge very much to his liking. Always emphatic about the importance of pilot qualification in instrument flying, he had worked hard to maintain his own proficiency since his formal Navy qualification as an instrument pilot in 1934. He had successfully completed a link trainer course in September 1936 and another in March 1940. His log books show routine instrument flying from 1934 through 1940, when he was engaged in scouting and patrolling, and again in 1943, when he commanded Fleet Air (Patrol) Wings 4 and 14.

Upon his return from war, he enrolled in a six-week instrument flight certification program run by the Navy on behalf of the CAA (now FAA) at Naval Air Station Atlanta. Under new postwar CAA rules, three levels of instrument flight qualification were available to pilots: the first two allowed instrument flying under certain restrictions, including the requirement that the pilot obtain CAA clearance for each flight before takeoff. Pilots qualifying at these levels were issued yellow or white cards. The third and highest level, called Special, allowed the pilot to clear himself to fly on instruments without CAA approval; a pilot qualified at this level was given a "green card." Trap's green card, dated July 19, 1946, was one of the first issued to a Navy pilot.[32]

CHAPTER 13

★ ★ ★

THE CHALLENGE, 1946

Trap's ideas about full-spectrum testing of each airplane within its operating environment had taken hold since his time at Anacostia early in the decade, when the lack of advanced testing had often led to surprises in the field: airplanes proved difficult to keep operational, weapons delivery systems failed, or—worse—young pilots got killed. Far better to have seasoned experts probing these aspects of flight by exploring problems, testing alternatives, and developing solutions in planned experiments under conditions that provided for safety and survival.

In June 1943 the Flight Test Section moved out of Anacostia to Naval Air Station Patuxent River, followed shortly thereafter by the Aircraft Armament Unit's moving from Norfolk to this new air station, where it became Armament Test. Electronic Test and Service Test were formed there soon after, and finally in August the Aircraft Experimental and Development Squadron came down from Anacostia to become Tactical Test, completing the transfer of test activities to their new central location. The Naval Air Test Center (NATC) at Patuxent was established in June 1945 as a unified command over the five test units, which became divisions of the center.[1]

Flight Test's mission was to measure the flying qualities and performance of an airplane—its speed, climb rate, ceiling, inherent stability, control forces, control effectiveness, takeoff distance, and landing run—to ensure its ultimate safety and compliance with contract specifications. Flight Test also identified and documented the envelope of safe, controllable flight. These include the limits of speed, altitude, G forces, and roll rates, as well as combinations of these with control inputs that lead to losing control of the airplane. They conducted Navy Preliminary Evaluation (NPE) tests of new prototypes, followed by a detailed evaluation to establish that the design merited production, and finally trials of production models to verify readiness for service. They also determined the airplane's suitability for carrier operations: low-speed arrested landings, short-deck takeoffs, and catapult launches.[2]

Armament Test was concerned with how well the airplane and its weapons operated together. Tests were performed to detect any flaws in the release mechanisms and to validate safe separation and accurate delivery of ordnance. They examined gun housings to ensure proper disposal of spent shells and belt links, as well as satisfactory dissipation of gun gases and heat. Armament Test established which attachment points on the wings and fuselage could carry which bombs and rockets, and it explored how each weapon behaved upon release under allowed conditions of speed, altitude, attitude, roll rate, and G force. They considered conditions under which a departing weapon might collide with and damage the releasing aircraft. Armament Test also checked out weapon-safety mechanisms for effectiveness and reliability, and determined which weapons could be safely retained on the airplane during landings on the ground or on board ship.

Electronics Test examined the effectiveness of the airplane's electronic systems and its electromagnetic signature. How did vibration, electromagnetic interference, and stratospheric conditions affect the airplane's radio, radar, and other electronic equipment? Were there weaknesses in directional radio and radar signal strength, blind spots caused by aircraft structure or antennas? They also determined the distance at which an enemy could detect the radio and radar transmission signals of a Navy airplane and calculated the level of unintended radiation from an airplane whose radio transmitters and active radars were shut down.

Tactical Test probed the operability and effectiveness of the whole package—the aircraft, its weapons, and electronic systems—within its war-fighting environment. What maneuvers, speeds, weapons sequences, and escape tactics should be used to deliver weapons with this airplane? How easy was the airplane to fly on instruments? In addition, Tactical Test evaluated myriad details impinging on aircraft effectiveness, including supercharger performance, the visibility of exhaust flames from reciprocating engines and their effect on night vision, the visual acuity through acrylic plastics, and the visibility of different paint schemes.

The Service Test Division focused on aircraft maintenance and support. Their job was to ensure that maintenance procedures, tools, and test equipment allowed field personnel to determine whether the airplane was operating properly and to diagnose problems. They tested the accessibility of equipment inside the airplane for adjustment, repair, or replacement. They evaluated manufacturer-provided manuals to ensure that documents were clear, correct, and effective. Service Test also conducted testing and training to avoid physiological problems such as carbon monoxide poisoning, anoxia in high-altitude flight, noise fatigue, stress from high speed and high-G maneuvers, and reaction to various toxic agents.

NEW INSTRUMENTATION

Prior to the middle of World War II, tools and instruments for measuring flight phenomena were mechanical. But the development of electronics, which began during the war, opened new vistas into flight-data gathering.

For example, postage-stamp-sized electromechanical strain gauges, invented just prior to the war, could be placed at selected locations on structural elements of an aircraft to sense in-flight stresses, and their tiny output signals could be electronically amplified and transmitted to recording devices. Electronics allowed simultaneous direct reading of control forces and deflections at the stick in the cockpit, along with the forces and movement of the corresponding control surfaces; test pilots no longer needed fish scales and measuring tapes. Multichannel pen recorders could track these concurrent events and effects. Magnetic tape recording provided a more rugged media for capturing data, even though multichannel magnetic recording remained a thing of the future.[3]

In this way, engineers could "see" the control inputs and results and could monitor stresses and strains throughout the airplane's structure. No test pilot could report the volume of data provided by these new electronic devices; it was a radical upgrade in getting the numbers from a test flight. Early telemetering systems even allowed one or two select measurements to be transmitted from the airplane directly to a ground station, where engineers could review what was happening in the air, pointing the way to the modern technique of near-real-time flight-data analysis.[4]

THE JET ENGINE'S PROMISE

On any given day, transport airplanes carry hundreds of thousands of passengers around the globe, powered by jet engines that deliver tens of thousands of pounds of thrust. Military airplanes occasionally fly at supersonic speeds and frequently use in-flight refueling to accomplish their missions. Navy jets take off and land on colossal nuclear-powered aircraft carriers as a matter of course. From this perspective, it is easy to forget that early jet engines had limited thrust, and even those pilots proficient in flying propeller airplanes faced daunting new challenges in jets, where high-speed flight harbored mysterious aerodynamic perils that had never been encountered before. Nothing about early jet operation was routine, particularly on board carriers. Nonetheless, by

1946 jet propulsion promised aircraft performance beyond the wildest dreams of aviation pioneers just a few years earlier.

The reciprocating engine that drives a rotating propeller was the nearly universal mode of propulsion for airplanes of World War II and earlier. The propeller-generated force that actually pushes an airplane forward through the drag of viscous air is called thrust.

For a given throttle setting, a propeller engine delivers more-or-less constant power, regardless of the speed of the airplane. And a propeller engine's thrust is proportional to its power and inversely proportional to the speed of the airplane. So at a given throttle setting, the thrust of a propeller engine is high when the airplane is moving slowly, as during takeoff, and decreases as the airplane picks up speed. For example, the Pratt & Whitney R-2800 engine was used in the Corsair and Hellcat; at full throttle, the thrust of this 2,000-hp engine was approximately 7,000 pounds at takeoff, 2,000 pounds at 300 miles per hour, and 1,500 pounds at 450 miles per hour.[5]

By contrast, for a given throttle setting, a jet engine delivers more-or-less constant thrust, regardless of airplane speed. For example, at full throttle, the General Electric J33 jet engine, which powered the Shooting Star (described later), delivered 4,000 pounds of thrust at takeoff and the same at 360 miles per hour, at 450 miles per hour, and at 650 miles per hour. So while the jet's takeoff thrust was low compared to propeller fighters of the day, its high-speed thrust was vastly superior. Not only that, but the jet engine maintained performance at higher altitude without the help of a supercharger. As a result, jet-propelled airplanes flew faster and higher than their propeller-driven counterparts.[6]

The Army Air Force's Lockheed P-80 Shooting Star was the first American airplane to effectively demonstrate this performance. In mid-1945, prior to the delivery of purpose-designed carrier jet aircraft, the Navy received a couple of Shooting Stars for test and evaluation. While not configured as shipboard airplanes, they nevertheless allowed Navy test pilots to gain familiarity with jet operations, and these evaluations quickly demonstrated that the Shooting Star outclassed the Navy's best propeller-driven fighters. Marine ace Maj. Marion Carl reported his mock dogfight experience flying a Shooting Star against another Navy ace, Cdr. Fred Bakutis, flying a Bearcat, on April 22, 1946:

> I used my speed and energy in the Shooting Star to attack and run and to avoid trying to turn with the Bearcat. I soon found that by keeping up my speed in the Shooting Star, I could pull up into a zoom climb. When he pulled up his nose to keep me in sight, pretty soon he had to push over or stall, and I would be right on him. In a dogfight, the Bearcat can beat any prop aircraft ever

built. So it was obvious that even the best reciprocating engine fighters couldn't really compare with the Jets.[7]

Although jets outperformed propeller fighters, they harbored a host of challenges, beginning in the cockpit, where the unwitting pilot could get into jeopardy in myriad ways that would be forgiven by a propeller airplane. Highly streamlined jets effortlessly approached the speed of sound until they entered the transonic speed range, in which airflow over portions of the airframe becomes supersonic, even though the airplane as a whole is not.

In this range, two potentially hazardous phenomena took effect. First, ill-understood aerodynamic forces were likely to induce buffeting, freeze control surfaces, and force the nose of the airplane down into an unrecoverable dive that could destroy the airplane. Second, the aerodynamic drag became so great that no pilot had yet surpassed the speed of sound. Aviation developed vocabulary for measuring speed relative to the speed of sound, known as Mach number, where the speed of sound is Mach 1. Because these effects were so dramatic and the ability to fly faster than Mach 1 so dubious, the press dubbed this obstacle the "sound barrier."[8]

World War II fighters, such as the Corsair, Hellcat, Lightning, Thunderbolt, Mustang, and Spitfire, all encountered these phenomena in steep, full-throttle dives.[9] Because these dives were so dangerous, they were strictly prohibited for ordinary pilots, and in propeller airplanes with their inherent high drag, they could usually be avoided by simply retarding the throttle. In contrast, the sleek new jet airplane designs practically begged the pilot to push speeds up toward Mach 1, and because care had to be taken to avoid slipping into transonic danger during routine descents, pilots had to learn to manage a new and previously unnecessary control: the speed brake.

To withstand the dynamic air pressure of high-speed flight and tolerate the stress of transonic buffeting, jet airplanes were built with stronger structures. The higher speeds of jets and the resultant dynamic air pressure also meant that cable and rod linkages between the control column in the cockpit and the control surfaces on the wings and tail alone would no longer suffice. At high speeds, pilots simply did not have the strength to move these surfaces, so jets required power-boosted controls.

Jet engines burned fuel at more than three times the rate of the current high-powered propeller engines, making it essential to build as much fuel capacity into the airplane as possible. But the weight of the added fuel reduced performance, aggravating the design tradeoff between performance and range. Even so, the maximum allowable fuel capacity for a small jet did not yield the flight duration of a comparable propeller airplane, which meant it could not afford the luxury of loitering to assemble in large formations; rather, it had to take off, execute its mission, and get back on the ground before running out of fuel.[10]

Requirements for more fuel, stronger structures, powered controls, powered dive brakes, and electronics more complex than in operational propeller fighters added substantial weight to the jet airplane, so although it flew faster, it also weighed far more than its propeller-driven counterpart.[11]

To gain the desired speed advantage, jet designs were highly streamlined and had small wings. This meant that the ratio of airplane weight to wing area, or wing loading, increased. And higher wing loading on jets meant faster landing and takeoff speeds.

As seen earlier, at low speed the jet's lower thrust compared to propeller airplanes made it hard to reach takeoff speed on a short aircraft carrier deck. Whereas propeller airplanes rarely took off by catapult, jets would routinely need catapult launching. Hence jet airframes would have to be stronger. More fuel and more robust airframes would make jets heavier and further degrade their performance.

Also, when the pilot opened the throttle in a slow-moving propeller airplane, the full thrust of the engine kicked in immediately; by contrast, a jet engine rotor took several seconds to spool up and deliver full thrust, which jeopardized a jet pilot's ability to effect a landing wave-off, an aborted landing, usually invoked by the ship's landing signal officer to alert the pilot that his airplane is not positioned for a safe landing or that the flight deck is not clear.

So jet airplanes could not fly as slowly as propeller airplanes and were more difficult to control at low speeds, both factors impinging on their suitability for carrier operations. How was the Navy to operate a heavier airplane with higher takeoff and landing speed and lower thrust from a short flight deck? And how would such an airplane with its sluggish throttle response deal with routine landing wave-offs? Was it even practical to make the jet into a shipboard airplane?

Despite these hurdles, by 1946 the world's air forces were looking to a jet-propelled future. The fact that land-based jets took off and landed faster was readily dealt with by building longer runways. And longer runways greatly diminished the problems posed by sluggish low-speed throttle response. But for shipboard operation, these characteristics raised new and daunting concerns.

Nor were these problems confined to the airplanes; jets would also radically impact carrier equipment and operation because of their weight and faster launch and landing speeds relative to propeller airplanes. Would the ships' catapults and arresting gear be able to withstand the heavier duty? And jets had tricycle landing gear, unlike their tail-dragging counterparts, so the barrier wires, which were set to halt an airplane that missed the arresting wires, were likely to damage the jet and decapitate the pilot. A new barrier design was needed. And where in the ship would they find room to store the copious quantities of fuel required for jet operations? Would the Navy have to redesign its carriers too?[12]

PULLING IT TOGETHER

During the last years of the war, the Patuxent Naval Air Test Center had focused primarily on responding to problems reported from the fleet about a specific piece of equipment or a particular aspect of an airplane's behavior. These issues were usually referred to the relevant test division without involving the other units, with each operating more or less independently from the others.

But all aspects of the new jets had to be tested in concert, requiring much greater coordination and collaboration between divisions. New leadership was needed, not only to bring naval aviation into the jet era, but also to coalesce the Test Center into a cohesive, high-performance unit able to apply new technologies to evaluate, refine, and characterize this new kind of airplane.

In June 1946, Trap's former boss and mentor, now Vice Adm. Arthur Radford, took over as deputy chief of naval operations for air. A seasoned aviator, he fully grasped the difficulty the Navy faced in adapting to the jet era. And time was critical; there were rumblings high in government that challenged the viability of naval aviation in the postwar era. For carrier aviation to maintain relevance as a key player in U.S. defense policy, the Navy would have to resolve seemingly intractable problems—and soon.

As in 1940, when the Navy faced a bleak deficit in viable fighter aircraft, they now needed someone with the vision, grit, and competence to steer the Navy through a complex metamorphosis into the jet era. Radford had no doubt who should lead the way. From their service together during the war, he knew he could rely on Trap's judgment, his broad view of the Navy's needs, and his skill with people. And when it came to technical knowledge and flying ability, Trap was unsurpassed. So in confronting the challenge to propel naval aviation into jets, the Navy again turned to Fred Trapnell to take up the gauntlet.

Adm. Arleigh Burke, Trap's classmate at the Naval Academy who rose to become chief of naval operations, corroborated this view: "[Trap] was assigned this job because he was acknowledged as being superior in the demanding work required in developing brand-new jet aircraft with their unknown characteristics. It is very unusual for any man to be universally acclaimed as being the best in his field of work, but Trapnell had the unique distinction of having the reputation of being just that—the very best flight test engineer there was."[13]

**22. Rear Adm. Arthur Radford, USN, on board the USS *Yorktown*
at Ulithi in World War II**

Official U.S. Navy photo, U.S. Naval Institute Photo Archive

Radford was eager to make Trap head of the Naval Air Test Center, but this posed a predicament. The Navy Bureau of Personnel, known as BuPers, had recently upgraded that post to a rear admiral's billet—even though it was currently occupied by a captain—and was unwilling to downgrade it again. The next commander of NATC would have to be a rear admiral. Unfortunately,

Navy protocol would not allow Trap to advance to rear admiral until he had held command of a major ship, a big carrier. But the need to move naval aviation swiftly into jets was uppermost in Radford's mind; he could not spare Trap for six to nine months of carrier duty.[14]

Radford and Trap agreed that he should step into the created post of Naval Air Test Center coordinator. As such, he would take charge of Test Center operations and report to BuAer in parallel with Test Center commander, now Capt. James Barner. Trap felt awkward about having to work around his old friend Jimmy Barner, whom he had known since his early days in San Diego, but Radford insisted and personally called Barner in to explain the situation. It must have been difficult for Barner; for the next nine months of his tenure as commander NATC, he never once mentioned Trap or Trap's activities in his chronological reports about Test Center operations.[15]

This command structure and the awkward changes that ensued cannot have been comfortable for Trap either, but he handled them stoically and pursued his assignment with vigor. Barner left Patuxent by February 1947, and, BuPers policy notwithstanding, Trap was assigned to take over as acting

23. Trap in his office at Patuxent River, 1948

Official U.S. Navy photo, personal files of Frederick Trapnell Jr.

commander NATC. Then in August of that year, Rear Adm. Apollo Soucek took command of the Test Center, and Trap stepped back into the title of coordinator of test, still in charge of Test Center operations. Given the situation, Soucek, an outstanding officer and aviator, must have wondered what exactly his own role was. Soucek left Patuxent in June of 1949 when Trap again became commander NATC, a position he held until he left Patuxent to take command of USS *Coral Sea* in April 1950. With the exception of his administrative workload, these changes had little impact on his responsibility or activities as assigned by Radford and BuAer.[16]

Radford made the case that during the next couple of years, the Navy would require Trap's undivided attention to their aviation needs. Trap would direct all aspects of testing new aircraft and acquire the jet airplanes needed to advance the Navy to the forefront of the new jet aviation age.

As Trap took stock of the situation that summer, it became clear to him that flying jets safely on and off ships presented tough challenges. These inherently high-speed aircraft would have to be unusually stable and controllable at low takeoff and landing speeds, a tricky corner of aerodynamics. Trap also concluded that operating jets on board ship was not simply a matter of bringing in new airplanes and rearranging the flight deck. Because of jet aircraft complexities, their increased weight and speed, as well as the prodigious quantities of fuel they burned, jets would impact every facet of carrier operations. The Navy would have to retool much of its shipboard equipment and procedures for handling airplanes.[17] Moreover, jet flying required naval aviation to upgrade its pilots' skills and knowledge across the board.

The pressure to get jets on board ship on a reasonable schedule reinforced the need for early testing; flight test would also have to be in on the ground floor of the design, development, and test cycle for every new prototype well before it could be proven safe in all flight regimes.

Indeed, getting the Navy into jets posed a monumental undertaking, mandating broad changes in the way the Navy operated. Trap could not hope to solve these problems by himself. His first priority was to find, develop, and motivate a deep pool of talent, men with the skill and temperament to tackle the full spectrum of hurdles they now confronted. Men able to test, evaluate, and help design these tricky machines and then carry their knowledge and wisdom out into the fleet. His hunt began for aviators with the fire to transform the very culture and fabric of naval operations. Where would he find such men?[18]

When Trap moved to Naval Air Station Patuxent River in June 1946, he came without Alice, who, liking the prospect of moving to Patuxent about as much as she had four years earlier, stayed in San Francisco. Though they were still married, she remained there throughout his tour at Patuxent.

CHAPTER 14

★ ★ ★

THE QUEST, 1946–50

Postwar force reductions to accommodate peacetime budgets took their toll at the Naval Air Test Center (NATC), where records show experienced officers and skilled enlisted personnel leaving active duty in alarming numbers. The immediate effect was to bog down testing in all divisions.[1]

When Trap returned to Patuxent in 1946, he was dismayed by this thinning of the ranks. The arrival of jet technology was about to impose an escalating burden on testing requirements and personnel. From nose to tail, jet airplanes were novel and far more complex than their propeller-driven counterparts. Their increased performance capabilities also opened a host of new problems requiring more comprehensive test regimens from NATC.

Trap immediately began to lobby BuAer and BuPers for protection from further cuts to the personnel required for the test programs. His efforts must have been effective because by early 1947, when Barner left and Trap took over as commander NATC, he was able to report a decisive buildup in electronics and jet-engine qualified personnel.[2]

Trap had long held that success in the air, particularly in testing, depended primarily on the skill and expertise of the pilot. Other things were important, even necessary, but the competence of the person at the controls ultimately determined the quality of testing results. For this reason, he despaired of losing experienced test pilots. Despite the dramatic downsizing of the postwar Navy, one factor worked in his favor: Many career naval aviators, seeing the dawn of the jet era, looked to Patuxent as the locus for aeronautical innovation. According to then Lt. Cdr. Charles Minter, "There was real excitement in going to Patuxent because the newest developments in naval aviation were certainly going to take place there, and so every aviator had as his goal in those days, getting there, if he possibly could." With all eyes on Patuxent, the Test Center was able to attract some of the most skilled pilots available to help build a jet-oriented Navy.[3]

Among these was Capt. Carl Giese, then director of Flight Test, who had served under Trap at Anacostia in 1940 and 1941. Not only did he have a proven record as an aviator with impressive flight test credentials, but he was astutely open-minded about the changes needed to gear up for a new generation of naval aviation with jets. Trap viewed Giese as an old hand with a flexible mind, a man who could be relied upon to elicit the best from the bright fleet of young aviators in his charge at Flight Test. And in Trap's view, these young officers were key to bridging the gap between a jet-focused test facility and a jet-oriented Navy.[4]

In any segment of naval aviation, there were a few duds, many solid aviators, and the occasional jewel. Trap was on the lookout for the jewels, men who would set the bar for the rest of the team, men with sensitive hands, incisive intellects, and the intuitive grasp of aeronautics that mark superior test pilots. If his two initial picks to fit this bill were any indication, the bar would be high indeed.

24. Cdr. Thomas Connolly, USN, assistant director of Flight Test 1944–46, and later director, U.S. Navy Test Pilot School

Official U.S. Navy photo, U.S. Naval Test Pilot School, Patuxent River, Md.

TOM CONNOLLY

Cdr. Thomas F. Connolly, assistant director of Flight Test, had graduated from the Naval Academy in 1931, completed the Naval Postgraduate School, and earned his master's degree in aeronautical engineering from the Massachusetts Institute of Technology. In addition to his being a thoroughly competent aeronautical engineer and gifted student of aerodynamics, Connolly's brilliant tour flying patrol planes in the Pacific theater demonstrated his exceptional abilities as a pilot.[5]

In his mid-thirties, Connolly had joined Flight Test as assistant director under Giese in 1944, and although he and Trap overlapped at Patuxent for only a matter of months, he made a marked impression on the new commander.

The admiration must have been mutual, for Connolly later wrote,

> [Trap] was really the Navy's foremost test pilot with the keenest understanding of the meaning of flight qualities, good stability and control, the right amount of stability and the right amount of control and how to know the meaning of all the intermixing forces that take place when you maneuver an airplane. He had done a certain amount of real good, individual, and original thinking and had put excellent ideas on paper. His work represented about all that anybody at that time had to go on. Trapnell was an extremely remarkable man, and I use the highest words of praise for him.[6]

MARION CARL

Another standout, thirty-one-year-old Lt. Col. Marion E. Carl, USMC, served as senior project officer in the Carrier Section of Flight Test. A 1938 Oregon State University graduate in aeronautical engineering, Carl was one of the most respected test pilots at Patuxent. His skill as a crack shot and avid hunter proved an asset in the Pacific War, where he downed a Japanese fighter in the Battle of Midway in 1942 and fifteen and a half enemy airplanes in the subsequent air battle for Guadalcanal, where he flew Grumman F4F Wildcats. He subsequently commanded a Vought F4U Corsair squadron in combat, achieving two additional victories. He was awarded two Navy Crosses, five Distinguished Flying Crosses, and a Legion of Merit for gallantry, skill, and leadership in the air.[7]

In early 1945 Carl had transferred into Flight Test at Patuxent, where he was project pilot for evaluating Germany's best World War II jet fighter, the Messerschmitt 262. He also became the first Marine to fly a helicopter and for some time was the only qualified helicopter pilot at Flight Test. In mid-1946, he conducted carrier suitability tests of a modified jet-propelled Lockheed P-80 Shooting Star, in which he made six takeoffs, two by catapult, and five landings on board USS *Franklin D. Roosevelt*.[8]

Capt. Sydney S. Sherby later wrote, "Major Marion E. Carl was a magnificent pilot and possessed the ability to express himself clearly and concisely. He was exactly the same kind of pilot that Trap was and possessed the same kind of intuitive feel for airplanes. He and Trap became fast friends, each having the highest respect for the other."[9]

Trap, who had known Carl as an officer and test pilot by reputation, developed an immediate liking for the Marine when they finally met in mid-1946.

25. Capt. Marion E. Carl, USMC. As a lieutenant colonel, he was senior project officer, Carrier Section, Flight Test 1945–46.

Official U.S. Marine Corps photo, U.S. Naval Institute Photo Archive

This was a man greatly admired and emulated by those in the aviation community. "Nobody ever touched Marion Carl as a fighter pilot—nobody," said Connolly. "[He was also] one of the great test pilots. When he came back [from a test flight] his reports to the school were very stimulating. . . . There were

[many] people [at Patuxent] trying to be like Marion." Adm. John J. Hyland Jr. called Carl "one of the finest military aviators who's ever flown." Trap welcomed him to the Patuxent River team, confident that Carl would be instrumental in the Navy and Marine transition to jets.[10]

Tom Connolly and Marion Carl represented the cream of a crop of young officers in their prime that migrated into aircraft testing after the war to become Trap's protégés; they were well-educated, combat-seasoned, expert fliers eager to move ahead in aviation, exactly the sort of men Trap wanted on his team. They were also among the most capable officers in the Navy and Marine Corps. That was the good news. The bad news was there were not enough of them to go around, and the good ones would soon be promoted and moved on to other assignments. With the test load mounting for all facets of jet airplanes, imposing tremendous pressure on already taut test center operations, it would take more than a few good men to push naval aviation over the technological hurdles Trap saw coming. NATC would require a continual influx of competent test pilots and officers of this caliber. Where were they going to find them?

SYD SHERBY

The Flight Test Division had run an informal test pilot training course on and off since late 1944, when the flight test load was expanding dramatically under wartime demands. Capable pilots with combat experience, excellent records, and many flight hours had been plentiful. Although competent in operations, tactics, strategy, and sometimes maintenance, they generally knew little or nothing about *measuring* airplane performance, stability and control characteristics, handling qualities, fuel consumption, or other factors that made an airplane an effective weapons system.[11]

To correct this deficiency, Giese called upon Cdr. Sydney S. "Syd" Sherby, chief engineer

26. Cdr. Sydney S. Sherby, USN, first director, U.S. Naval Test Pilot School, 1948

Official U.S. Navy photo, U.S. Naval Test Pilot School, Patuxent River, Md.

of Flight Test. A 1932 graduate of the Naval Academy, Sherby served in shipboard gunnery departments, completed flight training in 1938, and then joined a scouting squadron on USS *Ranger*. He transferred to Pensacola as a flight instructor in April 1941, attended the Naval Postgraduate School the following year, and then enrolled at the Massachusetts Institute of Technology (MIT) for a postgraduate course in aeronautical engineering, at some point becoming an aeronautical-engineering-duty-only (AEDO) officer. This elite cadre of highly qualified officers serves exclusively in aviation engineering positions rather than operational units. After completing the course at MIT in 1944, Sherby transferred to Patuxent as chief engineering officer in Flight Test, reporting to the deputy director Tom Connolly.[12]

At Giese's direction, Sherby convened a committee of three in early 1945 to evaluate and recommend a flight testing instruction program "to improve the overall level of test work accomplished in this unit." This improvement was expected to come from proper indoctrination of new pilots for flight test duty, increased knowledge of those pilots already on duty, and a more standardized approach and handling of flight test assignments.[13]

The committee recommended a course of instruction that would require three sessions per week over a ten-week period. "Notes on Stability and Control" by Frederick Trapnell was one of the primary texts to be used. Giese chose Syd Sherby to run the course.[14]

Sherby was not only a talented and dedicated officer but also one of the best engineers in the Navy. He followed Connolly by three years at MIT, giving the two men important background in common. On a personal level, they hit it off, working closely to develop and standardize flight test methodology and reporting. They could often be found down at Langley Field, Virginia, collaborating with NACA (now NASA) to fine-tune test and reporting techniques.[15]

Their shared dedication to enhancing pilot knowledge and more exacting flight-test procedures led to a natural collaboration in developing the course curriculum. Sherby wrote the lesson plans and taught most of the courses and, with Connolly's help, commandeered other officers and enlisted men to contribute as instructors and assistants.

CRASH COURSE

The Flight Test Pilots' Indoctrination program launched its first session in March 1945, a full year prior to Trap's arrival. The class met for two hours a day, three days per week for twelve weeks. The school's stated purpose was to "train pilots in basic flight test methods with enough background to understand the reasons for the techniques employed in flight test and to intelligently analyze and correlate the results they obtain." The course concluded with a final written examination and recognition of its fourteen graduating officers with formal certificates and pocket slide rules.[16]

This program resulted in immediate improvements in flight testing as well as more cogent and concise test reports. Thereafter, the course was repeated every eight months or so, with outreach to other test divisions at NATC to send participants to the lecture series, which boosted attendance to about twenty-five.

Upon completion of the second course in March 1946, Capt. J. D. Barner, then NATC commander, wrote to the chief of BuAer recommending that a formal test pilot school be established as a permanent division of NATC, and he received authorization to proceed accordingly. Barner soon put those plans on hold, however, due to postwar budget constraints and shortages of personnel, the situation that prevailed when Trap arrived at Patuxent in June.[17]

Not long after his arrival, Trap learned about the test pilot indoctrination class from Syd Sherby, who tells the story in his personal narrative:

> [In June 1946] The wonderful and highly respected Captain Frederick M. Trapnell reported to take over the job of Test Coordinator. I had never met Trap and went to introduce myself. I took with me a draft copy of the new Flight Test Manual, Part Two, Stability and Control, which Tom Connolly and I had prepared.
>
> About three days later he called and asked me to come to see him. He had been through the first quarter of the book and had meticulously written notes all over it. We had it drafted in double space and on one side of the page only specifically for the reviewers to write their comments, so I was horrified when I saw how much he had marked up. A bit sharply, he asked how we dared put his name as a reviewer when he hadn't even seen it and we hadn't asked him. I explained that we knew he was coming, had intended to have him review it, and had included his name in order to have it nearly correct. He finally accepted that, then he started in on his comments: "Why this? Why that? What did this equation mean? Why is this symbol used? Where did you get this terminology?" I carefully explained each little point. He then said he would go on with it and would call after he had done some more.
>
> This went on for the next two weeks. Each time there was the same great number of meticulous notes in red pencil and the detailed questions. To say that I was apprehensive and distraught was the understatement of all time. If I had to make all the changes that he had questions about, I would have to start all over.

At the end of the last session, when we had finished going over his last comments, he said to me, "Syd, I owe you a great apology. I have made you give me a complete course in stability and control aerodynamics in the most difficult manner. This has all been new to me. You have had to do it by answering my comments without any preparation. I want to thank you for the education. I think the book is great, and I would not suggest you change one thing. This kind of information has been needed for a long time."

He held out his hand. This was the beginning of a lifelong friendship and wonderful working relationship. The man had uncanny engineering instincts. He did not have graduate engineering training. You could show him any equation or a bit of technical logic, and if he said it looked OK, it invariably was OK. If he said he didn't know why but it seemed like something was wrong, it proved to be that he had sensed a problem, and he was right. This proved to be valuable more than once. He was a superb pilot, one of the very best ever. He could take an airplane out for evaluation and could qualitatively tell you everything you could determine from instrumental data analysis.[18]

Trap held Sherby in high esteem and later wrote, "He was the only officer I knew who thoroughly understood his Aero-Engineering PG [postgraduate course material]." He began to sit in regularly on Sherby's class, noting the bright, eager, and experienced pilots that filled its ranks. Trap was impressed.[19]

It dawned on him that this class might serve another vital purpose by generating a fresh pool of prime and prepared test pilots and aviation leaders. To enlarge and cultivate this pool, he wanted more than an occasional ten-week class; he conceived a permanent formal school for training test pilots who would then go on to duty for a couple of years in one of the test divisions at Patuxent before rotating back into the fleet, where their knowledge and expertise would invigorate the operational Navy as it grappled with the problems of integrating new high-performance airplanes. Envisioning a school that would transform outstanding fleet pilots into first-rate test pilots, he immediately set out to reverse the earlier decision to cancel the test pilot training program. In view of continuing budget constraints, he would have to enlist support from the top brass; but first they needed a plan.

Trap began meeting regularly with Connolly and Sherby to outline the framework for a comprehensive test pilot school. At first Connolly was uneasy about moving the school out from under Flight Test, because the atmosphere in its current configuration was relaxed and accessible, allowing the Flight

Test engineers and pilots to participate with ease; besides, the door was always open to pilots and engineers from other divisions. But Trap and Sherby saw it differently. As a separate school, students could devote their full time to the program; if the Navy was serious about training test pilots, it would have to provide more than a few hours a week for a few months to train to the level of aeronautical mastery to which the Navy aspired. The Empire Test Pilots School in England had a comparable program, which offered a full-time curriculum requiring many months to complete.[20]

THE ENGINEERING TEST PILOT

In the aviation world, there were three broad categories of test pilots. First, *demonstration* test pilots flew new airplane prototypes to demonstrate their compliance with critical contract specifications. Most demonstration test pilots worked for or contracted with airplane manufacturing companies, a risky business that received much notoriety from Hollywood. Second, *production* test pilots typically worked for airplane companies to check out each new airplane as it came off the production line prior to final delivery to the Navy or other customer.

The test divisions at Patuxent River had little use for either of these types of pilots. Their mission called for the third category: *engineering* test pilots able to explore and report on the flight characteristics of an airplane in all flight regimes, from straight and level to gentle turns to violent maneuvering, from high-speed vertical dives to low-speed landing approaches, inverted flight, spins, as well as those unpredictable effects that manifest themselves as the airplane approaches the speed of sound.

Explored flight characteristics of an airplane were said to be bound by "the envelope," beyond which lay unexplored and potentially dangerous flight conditions. Flight testing expanded and cleared this envelope with great care, probing incrementally into potentially hazardous flight situations.

Navy engineering test pilots also evaluated each airplane in the tactical situations it would encounter in the fleet: carrier launches and recoveries, instrument flying, and arctic weather operations. They tested the airplane's ability to deliver its weapons accurately and safely. They explored all uncharted regions of flight, mining for data to describe airplane behavior in terms that engineers on the ground could understand and address. Some of this data was documented via in-flight photographs of real-time instrument readings or recorded on special devices; other results were relayed by the pilot over the radio. A great deal of raw data, though, still came back in the form of handwritten notes on the pilot's knee pad.

Following each flight, the pilot huddled with assigned engineers to distill their findings into those behaviors that were acceptable and those that still needed correction. They determined where there was implied danger and what to explore next. Each step in this collaborative process had to be carefully planned and precisely executed to ensure that the airplane did not suffer an unrecoverable loss of control as subsequent flights probed untried speeds, maneuvers, and configurations. Losing an airplane was a misfortune; losing a pilot was a tragedy.[21]

Competent and conclusive flight testing relied primarily on the pilot's sensitivity and ability to interpret what the airplane's behavior was telling him, a skill developed in great test pilots by many hours of diligent observation and experience in the cockpit. It was a proficiency Trap demonstrated in every test flight and aimed to imbue in graduates of the Naval Test Pilot School.

Trap, Connolly, and Sherby wrestled with ways to address the difficulties fleet pilots, given their limited grasp of aeronautics and even less comprehension of flight testing, faced coming into test flying. Such pilots knew what they did or did not like about an airplane, but they knew nothing about how to measure flight characteristics: how to quantitatively determine and describe maneuverability or stability and control, the essence of how an airplane behaves in flight, how to quantify the myriad factors that make an airplane seem good or bad, or how to precisely describe the way an airplane handles in turbulence, its stability characteristics in carrier landing approaches, or its behavior in transitioning into flight after a catapult shot. Moreover, they were unschooled in the language needed to explain those phenomena in terms that engineers could understand, and they failed to grasp the underlying aerodynamics and mechanics well enough to hold up their end of a working conversation with engineers. The test pilots school curriculum aimed to overcome these deficiencies.[22]

This left these three with a thorny question. Was it best to start with engineers and train them to be test pilots? Trap opposed this notion. In his experience, capable engineers did not as a rule make good test pilots; since testing required superb, and largely intuitive, flying skills, Trap believed it was far better to start with top-notch pilots and give them a technical understanding of airplane behavior, as well as the vocabulary to converse with engineers. This would require rigorous training in aerodynamics, stability and control, airplane performance, engines, and structures—core tools of the aeronautical engineer—as well as how to collect data while flying.[23]

The staple textbook *Airplane Aerodynamics* was written by Sherby and Connolly (along with Daniel Dommasch, a civilian instructor at the Naval

Test Pilots School), based on their teaching notes at the school. In its foreword, written by Trap, he addresses the quandary faced in training student test pilots:

> In the flight testing of aircraft, the talents of the engineer and the pilot must be available to the maximum attainable extent in one individual. Without a sound understanding of the basic principles and a reasonable appreciation of the more advanced problems of the aeronautical engineer, the test pilot can neither gather usable data nor analyze his own experiences with sufficient clarity to convey them to others in usable form. The requirement grows more severe as the complexity of the aircraft increases. . . . Such dual personalities do not occur in nature. Very few pilots have acquired an engineering background in the normal course of events. In most cases, both time and inclination are missing during the early stages of his career. Later on, however, the inclination often appears rather strikingly. . . . When advantage is taken of this manifestation, and time and facilities are provided for study, the results are likely to be gratifying. . . . Such a procedure may not produce aeronautical engineers, but it does qualify pilots to meet the aeronautical engineer on common ground and to perform their flying duties with greatly improved insight and effectiveness.[24]

The trio's next challenge was to enroll the best fleet pilots in the full-time program they had designed as a six-month course of instruction. Classroom theory was essential, but in Trap's view there was no substitute for flying ability. So the curriculum had to be heavy on time and testing in the air, with emphasis on airplane behavior, accurate evaluation, and reporting. Students would learn to translate their cockpit experience into clear and complete reports, written in proper English with maximum specificity and minimum ambiguity.[25]

To bolster the practical training capabilities of the program, the Test Pilots School acquired an old Brewster SB2A dive bomber, an aircraft type that the Navy had quickly taken out of service early in the war because it was plagued with every known defect in flying qualities. The school stripped the plane of all military equipment and made it reasonably safe to fly, while leaving all of its bad characteristics intact. Part of the final exam required each student to take this beast out for a preliminary evaluation flight of an hour or so and accurately diagnose its myriad problems. Sherby observed, "This was very effective."[26]

To underscore the scope and rigor of the program, Trap felt strongly that the school should be established as a dedicated division of the Naval Air Test

Center, with its own permanent staff, its own facilities, and its own aircraft. Such an entity, however, would require high-level authorization from the Department of the Navy. So while Sherby and Connolly worked out details of the curriculum, Trap set out to convince the powers that be in the Department of the Navy that Patuxent should have a formal Test Pilots School. He advocated the benefits to the fleet as test pilots matriculated through the school and test environment and then returned into the mainstream of naval operations.[27]

He faced a serious obstacle, however. In those days, most senior naval aviators in decision-making posts at the Department of the Navy had not come up through the ranks as pilots. Instead, they had transferred into aviation late in their careers, been taught to fly an airplane so they could pin on the golden wings, and then stepped into aviation command positions. As a result, they lacked the depth of experience and intuition to grasp the complexity of the challenges facing the Test Center and the need for comprehensive test pilot training. This made the institutional commitment to a test pilot school a hard sell indeed, a situation further compounded by the administration's imposition of steep new military budget cuts.

Trap's disappointment with the stalemate that ensued is understandable. "The proposal was generally received with polite interest and no response. . . . I saw no further hope." Nevertheless, he continued to press Connolly and Sherby to keep working on the curriculum.[28]

Then in February 1947, Tom Connolly was detached from Patuxent and transferred to a new post as executive officer of the escort carrier USS *Rendova* (CVE 114). Trap was sorely disappointed to lose a man whose outstanding abilities as an aviator and test pilot had substantially strengthened the leadership at NATC. Moreover, Connolly had been a staunch advocate for and contributor to the proposed test pilots school. His departure confirmed one of Trap's deepest concerns: the talented officers they needed most at Patuxent would not last long.[29]

Fortunately, Giese and Barner, anticipating this loss, had brought Cdr. John J. Hyland Jr. on board as the prospective assistant director of Flight Test to replace Connolly at about the time Trap arrived at Patuxent in 1946. Although new to flight test, John was a first-rate aviator, smart, a fast study, and a natural leader. Born in 1912, he followed in his father's footsteps to graduate from Annapolis in 1934. After earning his wings in 1937, he immediately joined a fighter squadron on USS *Lexington*. In December 1941, he flew patrol planes over the waters of the Philippines, the Dutch East Indies, and Australia, returning to the United States in late 1942. A year later, Admiral King, chief of naval operations, selected Hyland as his personal pilot, a position he

27. Adm. John Hyland, USN.
As a commander, he was assistant director, Flight Test, 1947–50.

Official U.S. Navy photo, P. Hyland

held for a year before returning to the Pacific as a carrier air group commander for the final six months of the war. Not only was he highly decorated for his wartime service, but he was also a skilled aviator with experience flying many different types of aircraft. This, along with his cool head and analytical ability, made him another of those rare men Trap singled out as a top-notch test pilot and leader.[30]

BILL DAVIS

February 1947 was a tough month. On the heels of Connolly's departure, Carl Giese received orders transferring him from Patuxent, and Trap was faced with finding a new director of Flight Test. It was a captain's billet, so the younger men who had come into aviation during the war were not senior enough for the post. He wanted someone who could successfully lead and inspire these younger men, an accomplished aviator they would look up to. There were not many, and fewer still that Trap thought qualified; most of those were busy commanding ships or important stations around the world. But, determined to find the right man, he refused to settle for second best.

During a trip to D.C. that spring, he was discussing the problem when a friend in BuPers suggested, "What about Bill Davis?" It was an epiphany: Trap had all but forgotten about Bill Davis, with whom he had served in San Diego during the early days. But the man was as good a fit for the job as he could imagine.[31]

William V. Davis Jr. had graduated from the Naval Academy in 1924, one year behind Trap. After ritual sea duty, he enrolled in flight school and flew in the air group on board USS *Langley* and USS *Lexington*. In 1927, three months after Lindbergh crossed the Atlantic, Davis navigated the airplane that won the Dole Air Race from Oakland to Honolulu. Lindbergh's navigation challenge was child's play compared to finding the Hawaiian Islands in the middle of the vast Pacific. And Davis hit the finish mark right on the money: across the Molokai Channel, directly over Honolulu, and on to Wheeler Field to finish the race two hours ahead of the next airplane, receiving the Navy's Distinguished Flying Cross for his accomplishment. Later, while serving in a fighter squadron at North Island, he flew with the Three Seahawks, the battle fleet aerobatic team on the West Coast that preceded the Three Flying Fish at Anacostia. He flew carrier airplanes off *Saratoga*, scout planes from *Idaho*, and commanded a torpedo squadron on *Yorktown*. He served a brief stint as a test pilot at Anacostia during the time between Trap's two tours there. During the war, he started and commanded the Aircraft Armament Unit at Norfolk that moved to Patuxent, where it was renamed the Armament Test Division. Later he commanded a composite group of long-range bombing airplanes in the South Pacific that attacked Japanese ships and bases. Near the end of the war, he took command of USS *Tulagi*, an escort carrier (CVE 72). Bill Davis was an ideal candidate for Trap's director of Flight Test.[32]

28. Capt. William V. Davis Jr., USN, in the cockpit of the
Douglas D-558 II after a supersonic flight in 1949

Official U.S. Navy photo, M. D. Martin

Was he available? Trap wanted to know. His colleague thought Davis could be sprung from his staff position in Norfolk for the post at Patuxent. Nonetheless, Trap wondered how Davis would feel reporting to him; after all, Davis was nearly as senior as he. Two days later, he flew down to Norfolk to find out, making a personal appeal for Davis to take the job at Patuxent that would put him squarely alongside Trap in their campaign to guide the Navy into jets.

Davis was delighted. Not only was he eager to return to Patuxent and get back into a flying job, but he was enthusiastic about working alongside Trap. By April, Davis was back on board at Patuxent, where his added leadership skills came as a godsend to the Test Center coordinator. [33]

John Hyland spoke of this period later: "There were two wonderful aviators down at Patuxent when I was first there; Admiral Trapnell was one, and Admiral Bill Davis was another. They were sort of our old mentors . . . super aviators [and] highly respected people."[34]

The summer of 1947 was also the end of Marion Carl's tour at Patuxent; the Marine Corps wanted him back. In September, he received orders sending him to Marine Corps Air Station Cherry Point, North Carolina, to take command of VMF-122, the Marines' first jet squadron of McDonnell FH-1 Phantoms. Carl had proved a superb asset to the test program, and Trap was sorry to lose him. Carl wrote with similar affection for his former commander. "Fred Trapnell was the premier test pilot of all time. . . . I admired him as much as anyone I ever knew." Carl's departure confirmed once again that the good ones would not last long at Patuxent.[35]

MATTAPANY

Separation provided a degree of freedom between Trap and Alice that seemed to suit them both. During much of Trap's postwar stay at Patuxent, he lived in the Test Center commander's quarters, called Mattapany (pronounced "mat-a-pan-EYE"), a gracious two-story antebellum plantation mansion surrounded by magnificent poplars, oaks, and magnolias that long predated Naval Air Station Patuxent River. Poised on a broad lawn, overlooking the mouth of the river where it flows into Chesapeake Bay, Mattapany's broad verandas, beautifully appointed lounge areas, and gardens were the ideal place to host parties and social gatherings. Weekend entertainment frequently included a sailing party on the bay on board the Naval Academy yawl Trap had brought down from Annapolis or water skiing behind the Chris Craft kept at the air station boathouse. Occasionally, Trap was seen in the company of an attractive woman, down from D.C. for the weekend festivities. Life was good, and Trap seemed to strike a balance between work and leisure during this period, notwithstanding his long-distance relationship with Alice.

OFF THE GROUND

Trap continued to ply the halls of the Department of the Navy for authorization to launch the test pilot school, but still those efforts proved fruitless. The postwar depression was taking a steep toll on the Navy, where drastic budget cuts left little enthusiasm or resources for a new division at Patuxent. Trap waited patiently for a window of opportunity, certain that the proposed school would prove crucial to the Navy's ability to keep its edge in the years ahead.

Then in early 1947, that opening came. Following a brief tour commanding the Second Fleet, Arthur Radford was named vice chief of naval operations, and Trap once again had a friend and ally in high places. He promptly paid a visit to Radford to lay out his plan for the new school, and it didn't take long for Radford to gauge the proposal's significance. As Trap later wrote: "He

[Radford] listened and immediately understood. Then one day, in the depths of the [downsizing], and to my great surprise, he called and asked what was the absolute minimum of authorization we would require to start such a school."[36]

On May 1, 1947, Trap responded to Radford in a letter with the subject line: Flight Test Pilots' School, establishment of. In it, he spelled out the rationale for the school:[37]

> It is impossible now to obtain pilots who are properly qualified to take over Flight Test duties. Pilots with previous experience in flight testing are not available; competent service pilots have, in general, no knowledge of the procedures and principles involved and have inadequate grounding in the theory to permit rapid indoctrination. Consequently the normal turnover in pilots of this group causes severe interference with progress and efficiency. Instruction heretofore carried out collaterally within the Flight Test Division, has been in direct conflict with operations and has not been adequate. Intensive full-time instruction of a group of service pilots will not only provide ideal selection to fill the requirements of Flight Test, but will make available a most valuable type of qualification for other specialized assignments.

He further explained the immediate need for the funds and personnel to run the test-pilot training program:

- A director and a chief flight instructor—both experienced in flight testing—and two civilian engineers as instructors in aerodynamics and engineering. He specifically mentioned Syd Sherby, who was on site, presumably available and fully qualified to serve as director. He observed, "It will be difficult to find individuals properly qualified to fill the other three billets and these positions must be established on a relatively high level." With the foregoing staff, he believed the school could handle a student body of thirty to thirty-five individuals. The bulk of these "should be naval aviators, carefully selected for their proficiency, enthusiasm, and experience." Others "may be officers of other services or civilians."

- $25,000 per year for equipment, building modifications, and civilian staff salaries.

- "8 to 10 airplanes permanently assigned and fitted with standard flight test instrumentation. These may consist largely of inactive prototype models, having no other particular usefulness."

The letter further specified, "selection of students under the proposed plan would be in direct conflict with existing personnel demands and limitations, and that it would cut across all other lines of classification or qualification presently governing assignments of naval aviators." In other words, since no provision had been made previously to divert outstanding aviators to test pilot school, student selection was going to mess up normal personnel progression plans. In conclusion, Trap made the case for unrestricted student selection as a condition for the venture: "The recommended plan for nomination and selection of students is reserved for later discussion, contingent on approval of the school project. However it is felt that the mission of the school would be seriously prejudiced by restrictions on selection and that the extent of such restriction must determine the advisability of undertaking the project."

Tom Connolly later recalled, "Trapnell was forceful; he was highly respected in Washington. Admiral Radford was Deputy Chief of Naval Operations for Air, and he supported Trapnell's desires. When Radford moved up to be Vice Chief, he continued to support Trapnell, who wanted to form a test pilots school that was not a part of Flight Test but a part of the Naval Air Test Center."[38]

As in many branches of government, the wheels of Navy bureaucracy grind slowly. In August 1947, two months after Trap's memo to Radford, Rear Adm. A. M. Pride, chief of BuAer, forwarded a recommendation to deputy chief of naval operations for air to move ahead with the establishment of the Test Pilot School at Patuxent River.[39] This included an organization statement reiterating Trap's earlier missive and defining the school's mission: "To train naval aviators to perform duties as flight test pilots for the conduct of flight tests and trials of naval aircraft." In January 1948, a further memo to Admiral Pride laid out in more detail the proposed curriculum, requisite student background, source of student billets, and anticipated costs.[40]

Finally on March 4, 1948, Rear Admiral Soucek, then commander NATC, issued the order establishing the Test Pilot Training Division (TPTD) of NATC. The first class convened in July 1948.[41]

"In due course," Trap later wrote, "this [the Test Pilots School] was authorized—all due to Radford's interest." Crediting Admiral Radford was both fair and characteristic of him; but the energy, influence, and drive that saw the school to fruition came directly from the man who foresaw its potential to generate the kind of leadership required to muscle the Navy into the jet age.[42]

Trap was determined to have Syd Sherby as the first director of the Test Pilot Training Division. But in the midst of the one-year run-up to launching the school, things almost went awry. Trap faced one more battle to get the program up and running, about which he wrote:

He [Sherby] was finishing a tour as Chief Engineer of Flight Test; the AEDO [aeronautical-engineering-duty-only] office immediately ordered him to the Naval Aircraft Factory. I hit the ceiling, because I never dreamed they would interfere with this assignment [as director, Test Pilot Training Division]. I went to all the senior AEDO types in the Navy Department and got turned down cold—career planning and all that stuff. Sherby wanted the TPTD job very much. So I went over their heads to Radford—and he fixed that.[43]

Once again, Trap stood his ground to get the right person for the job, and Syd Sherby became the first director of the U.S. Naval Test Pilot School.[44]

Starting the school raised another problem: How to select student candidates. Trap described the process best:

It was obvious that a request for volunteers would result in a flood of applications which could never be evaluated properly, but . . . BuPers allowed us to get away with a most unusual procedure: I wrote a letter to all fleet squadron commanders explaining what was required and suggesting that they listen to no volunteers or requests—but put the finger on some one subordinate whose skill, qualifications, and performance of duty merited a reward. And we furnished a long form to set forth the info. The response to this was very satisfactory, and Sherby and I made the final selections. The support BuPers gave was also very gratifying; we got most of those we asked for and they were certainly a wonderful group.[45]

Thus Trap was instrumental in founding the U.S. Naval Test Pilot School as a permanent Navy facility and in setting the emphasis of its curriculum on test flying and gathering flight data. This established a sound technical foundation for future Navy flight testing while providing the depth of leadership necessary to keep naval aviation in the vanguard of aeronautics.

Since 1948, the Test Pilot School has graduated more than four thousand students from all U.S. services and many allied countries. Marion Carl called it "perhaps the finest flight test school in the world."[46]

THE BIG BIRD

When Tom Connolly left Patuxent, John Hyland moved up to take over as deputy in Flight Test. He and Trap had numerous opportunities to work together, but none more poignant than the events of May 28, 1948. On this beautiful clear day, a private air show was planned at Patuxent for representatives from the Bureau of Ships and other senior officers and civilians in the Department of the Navy. The goal was to convince this group that the existing antiaircraft guns and fire-control systems on board Navy ships were inadequate to deal with the emerging threat of attacking jet aircraft. These new airplanes were just too fast.

The audience stood in front of the control tower as a Grumman F9F-2 Panther flown by Trap and a McDonnell XF2H-1 Banshee flown by Hyland lifted off and joined up in loose formation, heading north up Chesapeake Bay, climbing gently to several thousand feet. Then Trap brought the Panther around in a left turn until it was headed south toward Patuxent, slanting downhill at full throttle. Hyland followed a mile behind in the Banshee. The Panther streaked down over the middle of runway two-zero to cross in front of the audience with a terrific roar, then pulled up and rolled away, arcing into the blue overhead. Those on the ground were just catching their breath when the Banshee rocketed in from the left. As it blazed past, there was a sound like a 5-inch gun going off, and the Banshee's vertical stabilizer disappeared in a cloud of metal fragments.

In the Banshee cockpit, Hyland just caught a glimpse of the big bird, an osprey, as it flashed in front of his windscreen. He ducked. It barely cleared the canopy, and he heard and felt a heavy thud aft. Unclear about what had happened, he eased the stick back to put the airplane into a gentle climb. Then on the radio, he heard the control tower: "All hands stand clear of the field. The Banshee's lost its tail." Hyland quickly adjusted the rearview mirror to discover that his vertical stabilizer was sliced off cleanly. Holding the wings level, the airplane remained stable as Hyland climbed steadily ahead to 10,000 feet, where he started a gentle turn using only the ailerons and circled out over Chesapeake Bay with the airplane under control.

At 12,000 feet, Trap joined up on him, and they conferred over the radio. Trap noted that the Banshee still had a shred of rudder and suggested that Hyland try it. The rudder pedals wouldn't budge. They wanted to save the airplane if possible and decided that at this altitude, Hyland should try the airplane in the landing configuration. The Banshee's pitot head (for sensing airspeed) had been located on the vanished vertical stabilizer, so Hyland could no longer gauge how fast he was going. Trap began calling airspeed indications and as they slowed he continued checking to see that Hyland still had control. He replied, "Yes, as long as I keep straight and level, I'm alright."

Over Chesapeake Bay they continued to slow, with Trap calling the airspeed numbers. Finally, Trap gave Hyland a sober warning: "Johnnie, something to remember, when that gear goes down, it probably won't come down symmetrically, and the airplane could yaw and then go into a spin from which you are unlikely to recover without the stabilizer."

Hyland hesitated a moment to let the warning sink in, then hit the landing gear switch. The wheels started down, and the Banshee swung violently to the right. He used the ailerons, but got nowhere. The airplane went into a sort of snap roll followed by a turn and a half-spin partly inverted. He pulled the wheels up again, but it was no use. The airplane came out of the spin, yawed violently, then rolled over and spun again. These gyrations repeated three or four times.

By then, Trap was calling the tower for a crash boat and giving directions for where it should go. Hyland was still in the cockpit fighting the airplane and coming to realize that he might have to bail out, when Trap shouted over the radio, "Johnny, get out of that thing! Now or never!"

Trusting Trap's judgment, Hyland scrambled over the side in the nick of time. The chute opened, and he was still swinging wildly beneath it when he hit the water and the parachute canopy settled over him. Fortunately, he was a superb swimmer and able to get clear of the chute before drowning. The crash boat picked him up, and an hour later he was standing in front of the air show audience in a fresh uniform, telling the story of his near demise.[47]

Many years later, over a drink in the back garden of his house in Kahala, Honolulu, retired four-star admiral John Hyland told the author, "I was astonished at Trap's ability to predict exactly what would happen when my gear went down, and I believe I owe him my life for getting me out of that airplane in time."

He also wrote about that period: "In those days, [Fred Trapnell] was more or less our idol. He was still a very active pilot and a very skilled one. He flew as much as any of us. . . . He was perhaps the most distinguished test pilot in the Navy—very much a perfectionist . . . [who] set the standards for all of us at a very high level."[48]

CALLING IN SOME OLD HANDS

When Radford granted the reprieve on Syd Sherby's transfer from Patuxent, Trap knew they were running on borrowed time; sure enough, the AEDO community was breathing down his neck to spring Sherby loose as soon as possible. Trap needed a replacement quickly, and in his assessment, there was only one choice. Tom Connolly had been executive officer on board USS *Rendova* for just a year, and was due to stay for another. Connolly tells the story:

At the end of my first year [May 1948], I get this letter from Capt. Trapnell, who was the boss at the Naval Air Test Center:

> *Dear Tom,*
>
> *How would you like to come back and be the Director of the Test Pilots School. We've got it all set up now. Syd Sherby is going to go to Washington and he's got it all set. The first class is going to convene on the 1st of September. I've checked and you could be back here in time to take over the school.*

> . . . I wrote to Trap . . . sent him a reply, but before anything really came of the reply, I had dispatch orders . . . to be the Director of the Test Pilots School.[49]

There can be little doubt that Trap went up to Radford to swing Connolly's detachment ahead of time from *Rendova*. In September 1948, Connolly was back at Patuxent as the prospective director of the Test Pilot School, and in December he relieved Sherby, who moved up to take over the Fighter Desk at BuAer. Trap had lost one good man but had reclaimed another.[50]

Since Marion Carl's departure from Patuxent two years earlier, Trap had wondered how to get him back. Carl was senior enough to return as deputy director of Flight Test, but that job would not open up for a while. Then, in late 1949, the chief of the Carrier Section of Flight Test was scheduled to be transferred to a new assignment. Offering Carl the top post in Carrier Section was one notch down from director, but it would still afford plenty of opportunity to fly, and flying jobs were few and far between for lieutenant colonels.

Trap had a hunch this would appeal to Carl, and he got on the phone to his friends in Marine Corps headquarters to see if he could arrange to get Carl back. When they told him that they were thinking of moving Carl to a nonflying job, Trap nearly went through the roof.

It is easy to imagine his side of the conversation. Carl was a truly outstanding naval aviator, indeed one of the best test pilots Trap had ever known. NATC was on the verge of testing the next generation of jet fighters having swept wings—almost as big an upgrade for the Navy and Marine Corps as getting into jets in the first place—and Carl was desperately needed at Patuxent to help navigate this transition. It verged on criminal to move him to a nonflying assignment at this point in his career, particularly with pressure mounting to deliver the right new airplanes for the Navy and Marines.[51]

The Marine Corps eventually relented, allowing that if Carl wanted the Patuxent job, they would let him come. Trap phoned Carl immediately to make a determined pitch to get him back.

"He asked if I would like to return to my old Flight Test job at Pax River," Carl remembered. "The prospect had tremendous personal appeal to me, but I was concerned that returning to the same job wouldn't look good on my record.

However, once I made my decision I didn't have to do anything—Trapnell made all the arrangements."[52]

Carl reported to Patuxent in December 1949. Trap had another of his best men back on board. Additionally, the Test Pilot School had by that time graduated two classes and deployed nearly fifty new test pilots into the Patuxent test divisions.

LACOUTURE'S SUMMATION

Capt. John Lacouture, USN, whose brilliant career as a naval aviator and test pilot included a tour as assistant director of Tactical Test at Patuxent, wrote in an article for the NNAM Foundation magazine:

> Trapnell instilled in all his pilots his motto of "get the numbers." Once the airplanes' flight characteristics were determined, he then had all his pilots work on converting the test results into design-change recommendations for the contractors, who would [use them to] improve the capabilities of the aircraft being tested. He also insisted that an airplane worthy of Navy procurement had to be able to operate well and safely over a broad range of flying conditions.
>
> He was admired by all pilots as being both very knowledgeable and competent in all aspects of test flying as well as being very fair and having great integrity in his work. He personally flew all planes assigned in many of the test projects assigned them. He himself read and signed out all test reports. If he ever disagreed with results obtained by a pilot, he would call the pilot in to discuss their differences and then go out and fly the test in question himself. If he substantiated the pilot's results, he would be the first to acknowledge it; but if he came up with different results, the pilot would be asked to re-fly his flight and in most cases would end up agreeing with the figures determined by Captain Trapnell.
>
> The Navy was indeed fortunate to have Trapnell in charge at Patuxent, where he was universally acclaimed as being the best in his field. His tenure there of almost four years is by far the longest tour anyone served at that station. For sure, the Navy had their best test pilot in the top test pilot job at a very critical time in the fast-changing shift from propeller aircraft to jet aircraft, from mainly fair-weather capabilities to all-weather capabilities. As for Capt. Trapnell he could not have chosen a job for himself anywhere that he would have enjoyed more.[53]

CHAPTER 15

★ ★ ★

HARNESSING THE JETS, 1946–49

When Trap arrived at Patuxent in 1946, he found the Naval Air Test Center poised at the threshold of the jet age yet still immersed in trials of propeller airplanes. Several of these had been introduced late in the war and never got into combat, such as the Grumman F7F Tigercat, the Grumman F8F Bearcat, and late models of the Chance Vought F4U Corsair. Strides in electronics had made way for improved night-fighter versions of the Hellcat, Tigercat, and Corsair, and testing for this full spectrum of machines was in full swing.

In addition to fighters, a new and remarkable propeller-driven attack airplane was under test: the Douglas XBT2D-1, a single-seat carrier-based aircraft with a twenty-five-hundred-horsepower engine. Trap flew the first preliminary evaluation stability-and-control test of this airplane in November 1946 and a second in January 1947; he considered it a fine airplane. This was the prototype for the legendary AD-1 Skyraider, which could take off from a carrier packing four 20-mm guns and a bomb load greater than the Boeing B-17 Flying Fortress, fly four hundred miles to a target, where it could loiter, deliver its weapon load, and then return to ship. Later designated A-1, it served as a front-line aircraft in the Navy and Air Force from 1947 through the Korean and Vietnam Wars.[1]

NATC was also evaluating the early jets. A captured Messerschmitt Me-262, Germany's best World War II jet fighter, was delivered to Patuxent in August 1945. Marion Carl was the project pilot who evaluated this vaunted aircraft. The airplane, which had gone into Luftwaffe service in April 1944, was still years ahead of current American designs; it featured twin engines, leading edge slats, ejection seat, dive brakes and other innovations that would not appear together in Navy airplanes until the production McDonnell F2H

Banshees and Grumman F9F Panthers arrived in 1949. Impressed with the Messerschmitt, Carl wrote, "Its main failing was the material, not the design."[2]

Trap flew the Lockheed P-80 Shooting Star twice in August 1946, finding it stable and easy to fly with light control forces. Its landing speed was high for a carrier airplane, but its outstanding performance was consistent with the Navy's aspirations for their first round of jets.[3]

NAVIGATING THE THICKET

Following World War II, new military equipment orders dropped off sharply, forcing contractors to lay off personnel and shut down factories. It quickly became clear to Trap that in order to ensure continued development of new Navy jets, contractors would need incentives, encouragement, and guidance.

Douglas, Grumman, and Chance Vought had significant experience in the design and manufacture of naval aircraft, were in reasonably sound financial shape, and had secured positions as promising suppliers of new Navy jets. But North American Aviation was also keen, and another newcomer had emerged: McDonnell Aircraft.

So began Trap's routine travels to meet and consult with the Navy's leading manufacturers. North American and Douglas were in Los Angeles. Chance Vought's newest airplane, though built in Dallas, was to be tested at Muroc, California. McDonnell operated from St. Louis, and Grumman from Bethpage, Long Island. Consequently, Trap's flight log book entries show frequent trips from Patuxent to each of these destinations, with occasional stops in Dallas.

Neither the Navy nor the aircraft industry was entirely sure what a jet carrier fighter should look like. Jet propulsion offered higher potential speed, but shipboard operations posed stringent and conflicting low-speed requirements. The stress of mandatory catapult launches and the aerodynamic loads of high-speed flight required that jets have a more robust and heavier airframe. Their enormous fuel consumption meant they would have to carry much more fuel, adding to their weight. And airplane weight was the arch-enemy of performance.

These speed and weight considerations exemplified the myriad conflicting trade-offs in jet airplane design for which there were no clear-cut answers. In his new position, Trap was responsible for guiding the contractors through this thicket of compromises, but his message on hard requirements was the same for all. The Navy wanted the best speed and climb performance they could deliver, but their products had to be whole airplanes: stable and controllable in all normal flight regimes, rugged enough to withstand the rigors

29. Trap in flight gear modeling a new experimental crash helmet developed by the University of Southern California, 1948.

Official U.S. Navy photo, personal files of Frederick Trapnell Jr.

of sustained shipboard operation, and never departing from controllable flight without warning.

In addition to providing consultation, direction, and encouragement to airplane builders, Trap decided to personally fly the preliminary evaluation tests of all new jet airplanes before bringing them to Patuxent.[4] A primary purpose of these tests was to ferret out any tendency for the airplane to suddenly and without warning depart from controllable flight, thereby endangering machine and pilot. This could happen in a low-speed stall when a wing suddenly dropped, as with the Corsair, or in a rapid roll, when the airplane might yaw violently despite drastic corrective rudder application. But of special concern were dangers that lurked for airplanes flying at transonic speeds.

In this speed range, the aircraft itself was subsonic, but the air flowing over parts of its surface, especially the wings, accelerated to supersonic speed, causing shock waves to form and leaving turbulent airflow in their wake. Previously smooth airflow from the wing onto the tail suddenly became turbulent and might render those control surfaces ineffective. In another dangerous scenario, shock waves rapidly shifting fore and aft across the wing could cause the airplane to pitch up and down in a buffet violent enough to destroy the aircraft. At the time such conditions were ill-understood, and as aviation scholar and noted author Richard Hallion points out, in the throes of these transonic forces "all the engineers' calculations go out the window."[5]

Too many accidents of this kind had proven fatal since 1941, when a Lockheed YP-38 in a test dive broke up at Mach 0.675, killing the pilot. Still fresh in everyone's mind was Geoffrey de Havilland's early death in September 1946 during a high-speed test in a de Havilland DH.108 Swallow; the airplane had suddenly gone into violent pitching oscillations before breaking up over the Thames Estuary. As pilots began to push into the transonic speed range, it was essential that their airplanes provide early warning signals—a gradual increase in buffeting or control forces—so the pilot could safely reduce speed and bring the airplane back under control.[6]

Trap did not want to risk having his test pilots be the first ones to encounter such nasty surprises. Not only was he quicker and more sensitive than most at detecting anomalous behavior and avoiding serious problems, but his long experience with myriad airplanes enabled him to quickly identify those aircraft that would ultimately prove acceptable. Wesley Price wrote in the *Saturday Evening Post* of this "professional skeptic's" knack for expedited evaluation: "He can detect quirks in experimental airplanes as deftly as a Treasury agent can pick out engraver's mistakes in a counterfeit bill. His skill is uncanny to younger pilots."[7]

For these reasons, Trap chose to make all preliminary evaluations himself, although he occasionally took along another seasoned test pilot to help with the assessment, on the grounds that two heads are better than one.[8]

CHANCE VOUGHT'S STRUGGLES

When Chance Vought Aircraft's first-round jet fighter design, the single-engine, straight-wing XF6U-1 Pirate, first flew in October 1946, it displayed a number of aerodynamic problems that delayed its delivery for Navy testing. In August and September of the following year, after Trap made seven short flights in the reconfigured prototype, his report does nothing to mask his disappointment: "Throttle limitations imposed to protect the engine only accentuated the airplane's lack of adequate power. In landing condition, the airplane showed unsatisfactory stall characteristics, including a sharp roll without warning, and very little control-fixed stability [that is, stability when the controls are held a fixed position]. Finally, vibration of the elevators at Mach 0.75 limited its top speed."[9]

In conclusion, he rated the airplane unsatisfactory, expressing reservations as to whether it could ever be made right. Indeed, the design required two more years of tinkering before the first production Pirate was ready to fly. Even then, it offered performance too poor to be effective in combat; only thirty were ever built.

Undaunted by the failure of the Pirate, Chance Vought responded to a 1945 Navy request for a new carrier fighter by proposing what became the XF7U-1 Cutlass, a radical tailless, semi–flying wing design with twin vertical stabilizers mounted on the wing trailing edges. For additional thrust, its two jet engines featured afterburners, the first in an operational Navy airplane. The design strove for supersonic flight before supersonic aerodynamics were fully understood, which led to an exotic, elegant-looking airplane that was underpowered, unreliable, and dangerous.

In November 1948, two months after its first flight, Trap made four preliminary evaluation flights in the Cutlass. BuAer must have been concerned about its basic flying qualities because in the middle of his series of test flights, he posted a brief report. Short, almost cursory, his comments focus exclusively on stability and control in normal landing, takeoff, and level flight. Based on his preliminary findings, he gives the airplane a pass, while making clear that neither he nor the contractor had yet pushed the envelope very far.[10]

Marion Carl later wrote, "[The Cutlass was] a fighter that Vought hoped would be the jet equivalent of its F4U [Corsair]." In 1950, he and another Navy test pilot flew the airplane several times. The more they flew it, the less they liked it. The consensus among the Navy and Marine Corps test pilots was that the F7U-1 was unsatisfactory for service use, and they recommended against the Navy's procuring it.[11]

Even after a significant redesign, Navy test pilots argued against bringing this airplane into the fleet. Nevertheless, BuAer ultimately overruled their objections, issuing Chance Vought a contract for the F7U-3 Cutlass. So in 1951, after extensive testing uncovered myriad problems, the Cutlass went into operation in both fighter and attack squadrons but continued to be plagued with reliability issues, especially with the engines and the hydraulically boosted flight controls. Of the 320 Cutlasses built, 78 were destroyed in accidents, killing four test pilots and twenty-one other Navy pilots before it was removed from service in 1959.[12]

Despite disappointing results with both the Pirate and the Cutlass, Chance Vought continued to seek Navy business, winning the 1953 competition for a true supersonic fighter, the XF8U-1 Crusader, a single-engine airplane having a conventional swept-wing layout that incorporated all the supersonic design expertise gleaned from research and accident case studies since 1948. The Crusader achieved supersonic speed on its maiden flight in March 1955, went into service in 1957, and earned accolades as the best air combat maneuvering fighter of the Vietnam conflict. More than twelve hundred were built for the Navy and Marine Corps before the airplane was retired in 1999.[13]

FURY GOES TO THE FLEET

North American Aviation's first-round jet fighter candidate for the Navy, the XFJ-1 Fury, was a single-engine, straight-wing design, ordered late in 1944. Trap inspected it at Muroc as it was being readied for its first flight in September 1946 and returned for his first test flight on February 3 and 4, 1947. His report on two preliminary evaluation flights reflects a lackluster first impression of the Fury. Though nearly as fast as the Shooting Star, it had a number of troubling deficiencies. Unlike the Shooting Star, control forces were heavy, longitudinal stability was just barely positive, and the airplane's static stability during landing and takeoff could be improved by moving the center of gravity forward.[14] It took little elevator movement to control the airplane in normal flight, but on takeoff it required full strength and elevator deflection to get the nose wheel to lift off and the airplane to rotate slowly to takeoff attitude. Trap attributed this to the main wheels being too far aft of the center of gravity; he wanted these flaws fixed but acknowledged this would mean a major rework. He also complained about cockpit noise, weak directional stability, and a persistent secondary stall or prolonged buffeting after recovery from a normal stall. But he reported no tendencies to deviate from controllable flight without warning.[15]

30. North American FJ-1 Fury. On Trap's recommendation, it became the
U.S. Navy's first operational jet fighter.

Official U.S. Navy photo, U.S. Naval Institute Photo Archive

Trap thought the prospect of correcting the Fury's most significant defects looked reasonably good and appreciated the airplane's many desirable features: ailerons were extraordinarily effective at high speeds and roll rate was striking. Stall-approach warning was very slight, but the stall itself was mild and aileron control remained good throughout the stall. "Performance appeared to be excellent in respect to climb after takeoff, normal climb, speed, and wave-offs."

This previous sentence is the only comment in Trap's five-page report concerning factors normally considered key to fighter plane prowess. But for him, these were only part of the picture. In addition to doing its intended job well, the airplane had to be fundamentally safe and serviceable.

The report reveals another aspect of Trap's thinking. Getting the right jet fighter for the Navy was just the beginning; preparing the Navy to operate jet airplanes posed an equal challenge. This meant training and reorienting personnel to working in this new jet operating environment: faster-paced operations, shorter turnaround times, heavier deck loads, rapid-fire catapult launches, and prodigious quantities of fuel to be managed and dispensed. Upgrades to shipboard equipment and flight deck handling practices were also critical to managing the higher energy of faster and heavier airplanes. They would have to develop new tactics for airplanes that carried insufficient fuel to loiter; as it was, they had to fly immediately to their targets upon launching and hustle back before running out of fuel. These complications weighed heavily on Trap as he worked through the prerequisites for the Navy's effective transition to jets. Jets would have a monumental impact on the workings of carriers, and it was imperative to get them on board ship as soon as possible so the Navy could learn to operate them safely and effectively.

Mindful of this urgency, Trap decided that the Fury was a good candidate for the Navy's first well-rounded jet fighter. The airplane impressed him as serviceable and, in the hands of well-indoctrinated pilots, capable of sustained jet operations on carriers and suitable for the development of jet tactics. He wanted this airplane pushed ahead into limited production with few changes.

North American modified the Fury per Trap's requirements. He flew it twice again in August 1947 and was apparently satisfied. A total of thirty production Furys were built, with the first delivered in October to VF-51 at North Island, San Diego, the Navy's first operational jet fighter squadron.

Through 1948 and the first half of 1949, Trap made a number of trips from Patuxent to the West Coast. He visited contractors and flight tested several airplanes, often at Muroc, but in addition, he followed closely the progress and problems in VF-51 as they took their Furys on board USS *Boxer* in 1948, making them the first operational jets on board a United States aircraft carrier. Trap followed their debut closely, gleaning practical information about jet operation on board carriers.[16]

The man in VF-51 who most impressed Trap was the squadron executive officer, Lt. Cdr. Robert M. Elder. Born in 1918, Elder graduated from the University of Washington in 1939 and went on to receive his commission and wings in 1941. He engaged the Japanese in the battle of the Coral Sea, flew one of the dive bombers that destroyed the Japanese carrier fleet at Midway, and severely damaged a Japanese seaplane carrier in the Battle of the Eastern Solomon Islands. Elder was a natural flier of exceptional talent who received two Navy Crosses for skill and gallantry in combat. In 1944, he had spent nearly two years as a test pilot at the Ship's Experimental Unit at Mustin Field, Philadelphia, Pennsylvania, precursor to the later Carrier Suitability Section of Flight Test at Patuxent. There he tested a modified version of the long-range P-51 Mustang for shipboard operation, which the Navy was considering as a possible escort for B-29s bombing Japan. He also performed carrier suitability tests of the Grumman F7F Tigercat and F8F Bearcat.[17]

31. Lt. Cdr. Robert Elder, USN, executive officer of VF-51,
the Navy's first operational jet squadron

Official U.S. Navy photo, Society of Experimental Test Pilots, Lancaster, Calif.

Having met Elder previously on his occasional visits to Patuxent, Trap considered him a superb aviator and test pilot. His experience in VF-51 gave the thirty-year-old as much jet flying time as anyone in the Navy, and Trap found him to be the most lucid, logical, and astute of the squadron officers on the subject of jets. Trap very much wanted Elder to join the NATC team at Patuxent; although Elder was eager to come, he was sorely needed in the hot seat, working VF-51 through its jet teething problems.

Elder considered the Fury a good start for the jet Navy. "It was easy to handle," he recalled, but "way underpowered—basically a good airframe looking for an engine." In 1949, the squadron replaced its Furys with Grumman F9F-3 Panthers, and VF-51 leadership had its hands full with the newer airplanes. So it was not until early 1950 that Elder was sprung loose to attend the Test Pilots School, where he became the honor student in his class before heading over to the Fighter Section of the Tactical Test Division.[18]

The Fury's wings were straight, rather than swept backward from root to tip. While German research on swept-wing designs during the war showed great promise in reducing aerodynamic drag at high Mach numbers, the Germans had not yet actually flown a full-scale swept-wing airplane. Nonetheless, North American proposed to build a swept-wing version of the Fury for the Navy. There were, however, serious questions about the low-speed stability and control of swept-wing aircraft, and little research had been done on the subject. These uncertainties posed unacceptable risks for Trap and others in BuAer. The rest of the world might operate their jets from six-to-eight-thousand-foot-long runways, but Navy jets had to operate safely from cramped flight decks measured in hundreds of feet. Therefore, despite the performance potential of swept-wing airplanes, he insisted that early Navy jets adhere to a conventional straight-wing configuration, even if it cost them a speed penalty. He was willing to gamble that the Navy and the American aviation industry would quickly correct this deficiency.[19]

In 1945, North American Aviation proposed a design variant of the Fury in response to a U.S. Army Air Force request for a new fighter. Wind tunnel tests, however, showed the airplane with the Fury's configuration would not meet the required top speed. So, based on the German research, North American substituted a swept-wing version, and without the constraints of carrier operation, the Army Air Forces were definitely interested.

This derivative of the Fury evolved into the legendary F-86 Saber, whose prototype rolled out in August 1947 and first flew in October, concurrent with the flight of the first production Fury. Introduced into service in 1949, the Saber became the U.S. Air Force's standard fighter and acquitted itself well in the Korean War. Fully occupied at that time in supporting and improving the Saber, North American was unable to devote effort to naval variants of this type. As a result, swept-wing versions of the Fury did not come into naval service until 1954. A further design evolution from the Fury and Saber, the F-100 Super Saber went into service in 1954 as the U.S. Air Force's first truly supersonic fighter.[20]

TRAP AND THE TIGERCAT

By early 1947, Trap had adopted a propeller-driven Grumman F7F Tigercat as his personal official mode of transport. This elegant looking, single-seat twin-engine propeller fighter, developed during the latter stages of World War II, though too late for combat, had its roots in Roy Grumman's unsuccessful prewar twin engine F5F Skyrocket. Trap used it mostly for longer trips to visit manufacturers and to attend meetings across the country.

The Tigercat had a spacious cockpit and was a comfortable airplane to fly, though the propeller location just outside the canopy made it noisier than most. With its twin R-2800 engines and clean design, this airplane could move, cruising at more than three hundred miles per hour if you weren't trying to save fuel.[21] Marion Carl agreed, "The Tigercat was a terrific cross-country airplane."[22]

A Tigercat was kept at the ready for Trap by the Flight Test Division. Rear Adm. Edward "Whitey" Feightner recalls, "One of my jobs [in Flight Test] was to ensure that one of my F7F Tigercats was equipped with a six-hundred-gallon drop tank and available for [Trap] on short notice [for] non-stop flights to the West Coast and back." Trap's flight logs do not show that he actually made any nonstop flights to the West Coast; though he often made the trip in one day, he always made two or three stops. Perhaps the machine was more capable than the man.[23]

In the period between January 1947 and March 1950, Trap logged 595 hours in 563 flights in a Tigercat. Notwithstanding the temperamental behavior of its landing gear, propellers that refused to feather properly, and occasional engine outages, he apparently developed affection for the type and seemed eager to introduce it to fellow aviators still unfamiliar with the airplane. Feightner recalled, "At one point Trap called me to his office, introduced me to his friend Charles Lindbergh, and directed me to check Lindbergh out in the Tigercat and to keep the airplane available for as long as Lindbergh wanted it."[24]

Admiral Minter remembered other encounters with Trap and the Tigercat: "[Trap was] a superb aviator, but he also was a top-flight engineer. He knew more about what made an airplane tick than anybody I have ever known. He was a bachelor at the time . . . and his idea of a good time was to call the Flight Test Division at ten o'clock at night and say, 'Crank up a Tigercat for me. I'm going out to fly for an hour or two. Don't know when I'll be back.' And he'd go out in the middle of the night and fly it." Toying with airplanes in the middle of the night was probably not Trap's idea of amusement; in all likelihood, he took the Tigercat out to hone his nighttime and instrument flying skills, which he would have found rewarding.[25]

One crystal-clear afternoon, Trap returned to Patuxent from a trip in a Tigercat. After turning into the landing pattern, he attempted to lower the landing gear only to find the indicator showing the nose wheel not to be in its proper "down and locked" position. He cycled the landing gear, but to no avail. He tried some sharp pull-ups to increase G forces in an attempt to push the nose wheel down. That did not work either; the indicator still showed the wheel not down and locked. This was not an uncommon problem with this airplane,

32. Grumman F7F Tigercat, which Trap adopted as his personal air taxi

Official U.S. Navy photo, U.S. Naval Institute Photo Archive

and he was annoyed. Believing the gear to be down despite indications to the contrary, he made a slow fly-by of the control tower, which confirmed that the nose wheel appeared to be in a normal down position. There was still a very real danger, however, that the locking mechanism had malfunctioned and the nose wheel would collapse as soon as the aircraft weight settled onto it. Trap asked the tower for a deferred emergency landing clearance, to alert the crash trucks, and to have a mechanic standing by.

When word got around that the captain was about to make an emergency landing with a flaky nose wheel, spectators began to gather out on the front steps of the control tower where they could get a good view of the action. Among them, a group of young pilots who had flown the Tigercat were discussing how impossible it was to keep the nose wheel off the ground once the weight of the airplane had settled onto the main wheels and the speed bled off a little; the elevators simply could not hold that attitude as the airplane slowed. If the wheel collapsed when the nose came down, the nose itself would settle to the ground at sixty or seventy miles an hour, which would likely tear the nose wheel off altogether, bend the propellers back, and possibly twist one or both engines out of their mounts, creating a high risk of fire.

The audience was tense and the nervous conversation turned quiet as Trap brought the Tigercat around in a wide, flat turn and onto a shallow final approach. The landing was slightly fast, but he painted the main wheels onto the concrete about two hundred yards from the base of the ten-thousand-foot-long runway 13. The nose was high and the tail down as the airplane rolled past the tower. The audience held its breath. Behind the airplane, two crash trucks picked up speed racing down the runway; a jeep followed carrying two mechanics.

On and on the Tigercat rolled along the concrete, nose high and tail down, as it gradually slowed. Surely that nose is coming down any time now, they thought. But on it rolled, decelerating little by little, nose high. Farther and farther it rolled, slower and slower, nose high, until it had rolled for nearly a mile. From the control tower, it seemed that the airplane had practically come to a stop with the nose still up.

"How in the world can he do that?" someone asked aloud. There was no answer as the others gazed on the phenomenon in silence. Finally the nose came down, ever so gently, the nose wheel held, and the airplane rolled another three hundred yards to a full stop. The mechanics pulled up alongside the airplane. One jumped from the jeep and, with a quick check in the nose-wheel well, verified that the wheel was fully down and properly locked.

Trap taxied the Tigercat back to the control tower, shut it down, and clambered out of the cockpit. As he walked up the tower steps, the audience clapped, and the young pilots crowded around him. One young man asked the question they'd all been pondering, "Captain, how did you keep the nose of that airplane up for so long."

"Simple," he replied with a grin. "Leave the flaps up . . . stay off the brakes."

For a moment, there was dead silence, before they erupted into ebullient chatter as the light dawned: No landing flaps! They had just got a lesson from the master.[26]

McDONNELL DOUBLES DOWN

McDonnell Aircraft Corporation had been an airplane parts manufacturer since 1939, when it responded to an Army request to build an interceptor fighter in 1941. Their proposal had been a radical twin-engine design called the XP-67, which struggled to achieve desired performance and never went into production. But in 1943, when other manufacturers were fully occupied building warplanes, the Navy was sufficiently impressed with the design and construction to ask McDonnell to work on a shipboard jet fighter model. The result was the FH-1 Phantom, which made its first flight in January 1945.[27]

By mid-1946, the Phantom was the only pure jet airplane designed for shipboard operation that had been delivered for Navy testing. In July it made several landings and takeoffs on USS *Franklin D. Roosevelt*, becoming the first jet to operate from an American aircraft carrier. In August 1947, the Phantom deployed with the first Navy squadron for land-based and carrier training, and in November Marine squadron VMF-122 received its first Phantoms at Marine Corps Air Station Cherry Point, North Carolina. As mentioned earlier, this unit was commanded by none other than Marion Carl, recently transferred from Flight Test at Patuxent.[28]

Trap first flew the Phantom in early 1947 and made several more flights during that year. He thought it to be a nice, stable airplane, a step up from the Bell P-59A Airacomet but a long way behind the Army's Shooting Star in speed, climb rate, and armament, which rendered it unsatisfactory for a modern fighter. The Phantom, however, made a fine airplane on which Navy and Marine pilots could cut their jet teeth.

In 1944, while the Phantom was still in development, McDonnell engineers recognized that newer, more powerful jet engines were just around the corner. So they proposed a variant of this airplane that would harness the power of these bigger engines. A mockup of the straight-wing, twin-engine subsonic design was available in April 1945, but it soon became evident that this variant needed even bigger engines and more fuel. So a whole new airplane emerged with twin jets mounted in the wing roots alongside the fuselage, as with the Phantom. This was the prototype XF2H-1 Banshee, which first flew in January 1947.[29]

The Banshee and the North American XFJ-1 Fury prototypes were available for preliminary evaluation flights in early 1947, and BuAer asked NATC to examine both to help decide which to pursue. Trap asked Marion Carl to accompany him in making this evaluation, and in February they each made flights in both airplanes.

After flying the Banshee four times for a total of 4.3 hours, Trap thought it demonstrated satisfactory stability and control in all flight regimes and spectacular climb rate but barely acceptable top speed. This airplane, he decided, had the makings of a serious naval weapon. Carl concurred. "Trapnell and I agreed that the twin-engine Banshee had more potential than the Fury, and McDonnell received a major contract [for a redesign] based on our recommendation."[30] While the Banshee was held up for this major redesign, the more straightforward, less promising Fury was ready for immediate operational use, as discussed earlier.

33. McDonnell F2H-1 Banshee. Trap said its "performance in takeoff,
wave off, and rate of climb remain[s] superior in all respects."

Official U.S. Navy photo, Naval History and Heritage Command

That contract enabled McDonnell to make a number of changes, the biggest of which was the design of a whole new thinner wing to improve the Banshee's critical Mach number, or top speed, which took nearly a year. In addition, the airplane would get more powerful engines, more fuel capacity, and would incorporate advanced features (many of which were found in the Messerschmitt Me-262) such as electrically operated landing gear, flaps, and speed brakes, as well as a pressurized and air-conditioned cockpit. The design also accommodated an ejection seat, which was not installed in early models.

One year later, in April 1948, Trap returned to St. Louis to fly the new, thin-wing version of the Banshee, this time accompanied by John Hyland. The two men flew the requisite preliminary evaluation, during which Trap made four flights in two days, as Hyland likely did also.

Trap's written preliminary evaluation of the airplane makes the following key points.[31]

- At 18,700 ft altitude, the Banshee achieved a level flight speed of 551 mph at Mach 0.785. At this speed, transonic buffeting in the tail begins and becomes sharper as speed increases. This limits the airplane at present to Mach 0.8 for satisfactory operation.

- At Mach 0.82, transonic airflow essentially freezes the elevator—control forces are too high to move it, and only the elevator tab is effective for longitudinal control and trim. This must be corrected to provide the control needed at higher speeds where strong tucking may be encountered. [Tucking means the tendency for the plane to pitch nose downward at high speeds because of the loss in normal downward flow of air coming off the wing onto the horizontal stabilizer when shockwaves form on the wing.]

- At lower speeds, the elevator forces are still heavy, but this may be corrected by a spring tab. The roll rate is less than the Fury or the Pirate. Directional stability is satisfactory but with no margin to spare.

- When the flaps are lowered, there is a marked trim change in the wrong direction—the tail gets heavy. And there is not enough down-elevator deflection available to easily control the airplane in landing configuration. The contractor expects to fix this by adjusting the pitch of the horizontal stabilizer, which may also help the elevator forces at critical Mach number.

With this preamble, one might expect Trap to condemn the airplane outright—too slow, too heavy control forces, and erratic trim changes—but one line later in his report gives the game away. "The performance in take-off, wave-off, and rate of climb . . . remains superior in all respects."

The report concludes:

> This airplane is urgently desired for service even with its presently known deficiencies, and it is felt that production should not be slowed. Its performance and the impression it makes on pilots are most favorable, but the critical Mach number is still a very serious limitation to its effectiveness. . . . It appears necessary to continue intensive efforts to clean up the tail and eliminate or postpone the freezing of the elevator—and the buffet; thereafter it will be easier to analyze critical Mach number effect on the wing. . . . The remaining deficiencies are mostly mechanical problems which would seem possible of solution with reasonable effort.

Even with its laundry list of problems, the Banshee appealed to Trap, and presumably to Hyland as well. They found no tendencies for sudden departure from controllable flight, the thrust and responsiveness of its twin engines were commendable, and the airplane appeared capable of delivering on promised performance. It was immediately ordered into production for the Navy and went into service four months later.

With its clean design, high-lift wing, and relatively powerful engines, the Banshee had excellent high-altitude performance and was able to operate effectively at altitudes above 50,000 feet. To demonstrate this capability, a Banshee was dispatched in February 1950 to take photographs from that altitude of New York City, which Trap would later use in testimony before Congress.[32]

Nearly nine hundred Banshees of various models were ultimately built, and the issues cited in Trap's evaluation were resolved along the way. The airplane fought in the Korean War and served as a first-line fighter in the Navy and Marine Corps until 1961. The Banshee, and the Phantom before it, pioneered McDonnell's twin-jet design philosophy for fighters. They were followed by four successful twin-engine supersonic fighter designs that served in the Navy and Air Force well into the twenty-first century: the F-101 Voodoo, the F-4 Phantom II, the F-15 Eagle, and the F-18 Hornet.[33]

GRUMMAN GETS IN THE GAME

Grumman Aircraft Corporation came into the jet fighter business too late to participate in round one with the Fury and the Pirate. Grumman test pilot Corwin H. Meyer, known to everyone as Corky, addressed the matter of their tardiness as follows: "The long-term Grumman policy of cautious prudence in approaching all new challenges was the only answer." But at the time, the company was also busy supplying and supporting propeller-driven Tigercats and Bearcats, the first-line Navy fighters of that period.[34]

Grumman began their homework early on jet airplane designs. In October 1945, two Grumman engineers, Charles Tilgner and Joseph Lippert, went to Europe to see what they could learn from captured German research on high-speed aircraft. Some key findings:[35]

- The [German] background material on high speed flight was further advanced than in the U.S., but the actual airplanes were not appreciably better.

- Innovations suggested by German [wind] tunnel investigations [such as swept wings] had not yet been proven in flight.

- The big problem remained control in the transonic range, and little of value was obtained [from German research]. They were as far from a solution as was the U.S.

- No record was found of man-carrying flight beyond Mach 0.86.

Nevertheless, the German research was intriguing, and the Navy contract for Grumman's first jet, the XF9F-2 Panther straight-wing fighter, also provided for the development of a swept-wing version.[36]

Four months after the Panther's first flight in November 1947, Trap went to Bethpage, where he made three preliminary evaluation flights in the airplane over a two-day period and produced an extensive report. At the time, Grumman's project pilot on the Panther, Corky Meyer, was the only pilot who had flown the airplane.

Trap's report is notable for its scope of commentary. Weak longitudinal stability was a problem, especially in the carrier approach condition. Aileron authority was commendable and provided a good rate of roll, but aileron forces were high and there was much friction in these controls, which made them feel "sticky" when trying to make small lateral trim changes. The airplane's directional stiffness was good and there was no noticeable Dutch roll, a common phenomenon in other small jets. Dutch roll is a sustained (unstable) side-to-side

34. Grumman F9F Panther. Trap reported, "The takeoff run was surprisingly short and the subsequent climb out was excellent."

Official U.S. Navy photo, U.S. Naval Institute Photo Archive

yawing and rolling motion in level flight. Even when it is not divergent, it is annoying to the pilot and can induce motion sickness.[37]

In level flight, there was, however, a definite and inconsistent "snaking" tendency in the ride. Corky Meyer had noticed it, and Grumman engineers were mystified. Trap concluded that the problem was due to fuel sloshing in the main tank, explaining, "The faster you flew the Panther, the faster it snaked. All these jets carry huge gas tanks. When the fuel sloshes back and forth, it can make the airplane sway in imitation of a natural oscillation." His report suggested that the problem could probably be corrected by baffling the fuel cells. Grumman engineers were skeptical, but after trying several other fixes without success, they followed Trap's recommendation, which solved the problem.[38]

His report also indicates that the Panther's stall was mild, with increasing buffeting and a slow drop of the right wing and nose; also there was no sharp roll and the ailerons remained effective throughout. Although satisfied with this, Trap recommended they add a stall warning device. Regarding high-speed operation, he noted an apparent sharp drag rise at Mach 0.80 and a marked airframe vibration at 0.84.

The takeoff run was surprisingly short and the subsequent climb out was excellent, though not as good as the Banshee. Carrier landing characteristics were entirely satisfactory, except that low longitudinal stability combined with highly effective elevator control meant that when flaring out, the pilot could easily put the airplane into a full stall resulting in a rough and dangerous landing. Wave-off power and climb were good, but the Banshee's were better. He was also critical of the cockpit layout.

His report concluded that the contractor was proceeding immediately to increase longitudinal stability, reduce aileron forces and friction, and add a stall warning device. Reading this report, one gets the impression that Trap regarded this airplane's performance as quite acceptable, but not as impressive as the McDonnell Banshee.

Nearly twenty years Trap's junior, Corky Meyer had been in flight testing for just over five years. He well remembered his first encounter with Trap: "[Trap's] full report on the Panther had only one minor hydraulic system deficiency that I had failed to note. The elevator and ailerons were assisted by a highly boosted (33-to-1) hydraulic power system. When this failed, the manual pitch control forces required to fly carrier landings were high, but I had thought they were acceptable. He did not. We then designed a mechanism in the system so that when the boost failed, the stick was then provided a double mechanical advantage. He approved it with a grinning comment, 'I am a little older than you are, Corky.'"[39]

"THE BEST DAMN FIGHTER I'VE EVER FLOWN"

At the end of the second day of testing the Panther, Trap was getting ready to fly his Tigercat back to Patuxent. Meyer takes up the story:

> Captain Trapnell was the only test pilot in the Navy whose word was law both in the Navy and industry flight-test circles. . . . We were walking out to his F7F-4N Tigercat for his return trip to the Naval Test Center. I proudly told him that I was the project pilot of the Tigercat from 1943 to 1947. He immediately burst into a diatribe of the many deficiencies of the Tigercat, naming over-cooling of the engines, under-cooling of the oil system, lack of roll stability, excessively high dihedral rolling effect with rudder input, the high minimum single-engine control speed, etc., etc. He ended his oration with my exile sentence: "If I had been chief of the test center at the time, I would have had you fired!" Every one of his comments was absolutely true. I was devastated and fervently wished I hadn't got out of bed that day.
>
> Just as we reached his Tigercat I finally blurted out, "If you dislike the Tigercat so much, why do you always fly it everywhere you go?" He continued: "The power in the two engines is great for any aerobatics, the forward visibility in the carrier approach is the best in any fighter ever built, the tricycle landing gear will make much faster pilot checkouts, the roll with the power-boosted rudder is faster than the ailerons, it has the greatest range of any fighter in the inventory, etc., etc." He was absolutely right again. As he climbed up the ladder to the cockpit he turned around, grinning from ear to ear, and stated, "It's the best damn fighter I've ever flown." He closed the canopy and disappeared over the horizon. I realized he had thrown the entire test pilot school book at me with his few words and that he and I were pretty close regarding characteristics that make up a really good fighter. I went home happy that night.[40]

In November 1948 a huge international air show officially opened the new Idlewild (now Kennedy) Airport in New York. The audience included the president of the United States and a reported crowd of a half-million eager spectators. As part of the Navy's contribution, Meyer made a 625-mph flyby in the Panther. As Meyer tells the story, "With the help of high humidity . . . a massive white visible shockwave occurred on the back half of the Panther during my very low pass over President Truman's grandstand and continued

35. Corky Meyer, Grumman's test pilot for the Panther

Society of Experimental Test Pilots, Lancaster, Calif.

until I disappeared in a steep climb out." The next day's *New York Times* reported the Panther stole the show. Meyer says, "I ate it up, humbly of course."[41]

Then somebody in BuAer got the bright idea that a Navy pilot, rather than a civilian, should fly the Panther in future air shows, so the next day Grumman received a message from Washington stating that they would like to have Captain Trapnell fly those events in the future. When Trap heard this, he flatly disagreed, and Washington relented. Meyer wrote, "Trapnell asserted that he didn't have the experience that I did in the Panther and that I should continue the remainder of the shows, which I did with great pleasure. What an ego trip for me."

Corky Meyer became one of Trap's favorites. He was not on the Navy team at Patuxent, but as a key man at Grumman, Trap considered him an important asset to their collaborative efforts. The Navy would continue to depend on Grumman to supply outstanding airplanes for many years to come.

Trap returned to Bethpage to fly the Panther again in April, May, and June 1948, presumably to check modifications made by Grumman. In addition to those mentioned previously, these included the fuel tank baffles and several changes to the fixed wingtip tanks that came to characterize the Panther. On May 18, they held a comparison fly-off at Bethpage between the Panther and the Fury; subsequent history suggests that the Grumman airplane came out on top.[42]

Starting in May 1949, almost fourteen hundred Panthers were delivered to the Navy and Marine Corps. In 1952, Grumman delivered a faster, swept-wing subsonic variant, the Cougar. More than twelve hundred of these were built as fighters and more than three hundred as two-seat advanced training airplanes. Grumman continued its string of feline-dubbed Navy fighters with the single-engine supersonic F11F-1 Tiger delivered in 1956 and the outstanding twin-engine F-14 Tomcat in 1974.

A TRUE ALL-WEATHER JET FIGHTER

By 1948, it was clear that air warfare in conditions of limited visibility (night and foul weather) would be standard operating procedure and that in the Navy's environment, an all-weather fighter must be able to locate and track its targets unassisted by ground or sea-based facilities. The sophistication, and hence complexity, of satisfactory airborne radar facilities meant that a warmed-over version of a day fighter toting radar would no longer suffice, as it had in World War II. So the Navy issued a requirement for a true, purpose-designed, all-weather fighter.

Douglas Aircraft submitted the winning proposal, and the contract for its XF3D-1 Skyknight was issued in April 1946. The design team fitted the airplane around the heavy and bulky vacuum-tube radar electronics available at the time and furnished a side-by-side seating arrangement for the pilot and radar operator. The result was a robust, clean, straight-wing twin-jet fighter with the prominent vertical stabilizer that characterized the designs of Ed Heinemann, chief engineer for Douglas Aircraft Corporation.[43]

It first flew in March 1948, and Trap flew to California to do the initial evaluation in July. His flight log shows he made four flights for a total of just over four hours, and his remarks for the second flight say "smoke and fire." It would be interesting to know more, but apparently the airplane was not destroyed since he flew it again two days later. We do not have his report for these flights, but he almost certainly found this airplane satisfactory, as he consistently did with Heinemann's designs.[44] The first production Skyknight flew in February 1950 and went into naval service in December, ultimately serving in both the Korean and Vietnam wars.[45]

A PERSONAL SPEED RECORD

In 1945, the Navy issued a contract with Douglas Aircraft for several airplanes designed specifically to probe the puzzling dangers of transonic flight. The research, a joint Navy/NACA program to study the nature of these problems and explore solutions, resulted in a two-phased program with two different aircraft designs called the D-558-1 Skystreak and the D-558-2 Skyrocket.[46]

The Skystreak was a straight-wing, single-engine jet airplane with a nose air intake. The fuselage made extensive use of magnesium alloys, and its aluminum wings were extremely thin. The structure was designed to withstand eighteen-G acceleration to accommodate the violent loads anticipated in the comprehensive exploration of transonic speeds. The Skyrocket was a swept-wing airplane of similar construction, but having both jet and rocket power plants.[47]

In July 1947, when Douglas delivered the first Skystreak, there was a move afoot for the Navy to capture the official world speed record of 623 mph set by Col. Al Boyd of the U.S. Army Air Force in a Shooting Star a month earlier, a record that barely matched the unofficial one established in 1941 by the German rocket-powered prototype of the Messerschmitt Me-163 fighter.[48]

Marion Carl and Cdr. Turner Caldwell, USN, were selected to make the speed runs over a low-altitude measured course at Muroc, the remote lakebed where four years earlier Trap had first flown the Airacomet and later the Fury. In August, the airplanes and pilots were ready. By a coin toss, Caldwell flew the first run on July 20, setting a new world's record of 641 mph. Five days later Carl broke that record by clocking 650.6 mph at Mach 0.82.[49]

Three days after Carl set the new record, Trap arrived at Muroc to fly the Skystreak. He made two flights that day "for the purpose of evaluating general flying characteristics" of the airplane. The first run with the bubble canopy installed gave more headroom but restricted the airplane to three hundred miles per hour. For the second flight, they installed the high-speed canopy, which Trap noted wryly "was unsuitable for a tall pilot wearing a crash helmet";

36. Douglas D558–1 Skystreak transonic research airplane that
Trap flew to Mach 0.86

Official U.S. Navy photo, U.S. Naval Institute Photo Archive

it constrained head movement and visibility of the instruments, a condition that would be uncomfortably evident to the six-foot-two-inch test pilot. Nevertheless, he achieved Mach 0.86 at seven thousand feet altitude, a performance comparable to Carl's record-setting speed. At the time, this was probably as fast as any man, including German jet pilots, had flown in controlled flight.[50]

Seven weeks later, Capt. Charles "Chuck" Yeager went faster when he broke the sound barrier piloting the Bell X-1 to a speed of Mach 1.06.[51]

CHAPTER 16

★ ★ ★

TURMOIL, 1949–52

The Revolt of the Admirals was a high-ranking conflict over war-fighting doctrine between the U.S. Navy and U.S. Air Force, staged on Capitol Hill in 1949. The Air Force, stalwart in its commitment to strategic bombing as the way to achieve victory over an enemy at low cost in men and money, postulated that naval aviation would prove neither cost-effective nor decisive in future wars. To economize and consolidate resources, they wanted naval aviation brought under the banner of the Air Force. The centerpiece of the Air Force's weaponry at that time was the B-36, a six-propeller, four-jet heavy bomber carrying atomic weapons. The Air Force claimed that, cruising at an altitude of 40,000 feet, this airplane could readily penetrate enemy airspace, where it would be both invisible to radar and invincible to enemy fighters.[1]

The new secretary of defense, Louis A. Johnson, and senior defense officials, including the Secretary of the Navy and the chief of naval operations, sided with the Air Force to convince Congress and the president to cut back naval aviation appropriations. Early in 1949, Johnson had canceled a new aircraft carrier under construction, and further deep cuts in naval aviation were planned by midyear. If the Air Force got its way, it would become the nation's first line of defense, and naval aviation would be subordinated and perhaps wholly subsumed into the fledgling Air Force. For the leaders of naval aviation, this was a matter of life or death.

The subsequent struggle between senior naval officers and the Washington establishment smoldered throughout the summer. Then on October 8 and 9, the House Armed Services Committee gave the Navy brass its hearing. Arthur Radford, by then a four-star admiral commanding the Second Fleet, returned to Washington as the chief spokesman for the Navy. The subject was the invincibility and effectiveness of the B-36, and Radford flatly disputed Air Force claims. "Today . . . American airplanes, by day or by night and all speeds and altitudes which the B-36 can operate on military missions, can locate . . . intercept . . . and destroy the bomber. . . . It is folly to assume that a potential enemy cannot do this as well." He also chided the Air Force for neglecting development of their own fighter aircraft, which he inferred might be why they placed such confidence in their B-36.[2]

To buttress Radford's arguments, Trap took the stand the following day before the committee on one of the rare occasions in which a test pilot had testified before Congress in a professional capacity. The following excerpts from his testimony are grounded in his intimate knowledge of the jet airplanes he had personally tested:

> During the past three years the Navy has acquired considerable experience in the operation of a series of jet fighters culminating in the so-called Banshee. This airplane gives us altitude performance superior to any other United States airplane presently in service. But it is not an interceptor fighter; it is a general purpose fighter carrying a rather large fuel load and having comparatively great range. Nevertheless, the Banshee flies at speeds and altitudes far greater than those of which the B 36 is capable.
>
> There is every reason to believe that the enemy will have fighters as good as ours. The British do. And the Russians have publicly demonstrated numbers of very advanced designs.
>
> At the Naval Air Test Center we get good results in detecting, tracking, and controlling jet fighters at altitudes well above 40,000 feet with radar equipment that is four years old and without any special electronic aids in the airplanes. Because the B-36 is a vastly more favorable target than these jet fighters, we expect better results against it. From our experience we see no grounds for the statement that the B-36 can go undetected in enemy territory simply because it is flying at 40,000 feet.
>
> You have already received testimony that we may not expect for [another] five years any night fighter capable of intercepting the B-36. This evidence has to be reconsidered [because] the Corsair night fighter now in service has performance adequate to intercept the B-36 at 40,000 feet. It has a radar which is effective with ground control. [Moreover] the Douglas Skyknight, a two-seat jet night fighter that will soon go into service, has performance and radar adequate under all conditions to intercept the B-36 at 40,000

feet. It completed five successful night interceptions above 40,000 feet on its first radar test, [and] the target airplane was another small jet fighter—a poor radar target. The night fighter version of the Banshee, with overwhelmingly superior performance, will go into service very soon.

The experience of the Navy in the operation of fighters at high altitude may perhaps be unique . . . if so it is impossible to avoid criticism of the Air Force's design policy. . . . That is, a notable tendency in Air Force designs to concentrate on high-speed at considerable sacrifice of high altitude performance.[3]

Trap concluded his testimony by suggesting that the B-36 program seemed ill-advised.

The Navy lost the battle over the B-36, and although naval aviation was not absorbed into the U.S. Air Force, the Air Force's Strategic Air Command became the pre-eminent strategic defense arm of the United States. The introduction of jet bombers and ICBMs carrying nuclear weapons gave rise to the prospect of mutually assured annihilation and the troubled peace of the Cold War.

The hot conflicts that later enmeshed the United States, however, presented challenges that were distinct from those of the Cold War, and naval aviation was a force to be reckoned with in every one, providing a robust demonstration of the value and versatility of carrier-based aviation. Banshees, Panthers, Corsairs, and Skyknights played decisive roles in the Korean War, and their successors served well in subsequent fields of engagement.

A NOTABLE CONTRIBUTION

In 1949, the Institute of Aeronautical Sciences (now the American Institute of Aeronautics and Astronautics) elected Trap to be an associate fellow and presented him the Octave Chanute Award, which was given each year for "an outstanding contribution to the advancement of the art, science, and technology of aeronautics." The citation highlights "his outstanding ability not only in flying every type of aircraft but also in detecting critical defects in new airplanes and suggesting ways to deal with them," noting in addition his "contributions to flight testing of experimental aircraft, with particular reference to operating requirements for carrier-based jet propelled airplanes."[4]

In 1950, when Trap turned forty-eight years old, he felt physically fit, but a few of his close friends occasionally hinted that he might be getting a little too old for the rigors of test flying. Coincidentally, early that year, Trap got word of orders in the works that meant leaving Patuxent for a new post. Years before, Radford had promised him command of a big carrier when he finished his mission at NATC, and now that the jets were moving into active service in the fleet, it was time for his promised ship. In the usual chain of events, as a successful senior naval officer, his prospects for higher command would put him mostly on the ground or on a deck. Struggle though he might, it was time to admit that his test flying days were largely over.[5]

Under Trap's leadership, Patuxent had become a full-fledged, state-of-the-art test center with broad capabilities to develop and implement highly advanced flight test methodology. He had played a key role in founding the Naval Test Pilot School and inspired a cadre of first-rate officers who would provide leadership for the ongoing development of naval aviation. Upon his departure from Patuxent, Navy carriers still operated propeller-driven aircraft for attack and other special missions, but all of their fighters were jets. He had guided the evolution and testing of the first generation of carrier-based jet fighters, thereby ushering naval aviation into the jet era and setting standards that paved the way for the modern aviation Navy.

DOWN TO THE SEA AGAIN

On April 29, 1950, Trap was piped on board USS *Coral Sea* at Norfolk, Virginia, as her new commanding officer. She was a magnificent ship, one of the three largest carriers in the Navy. Although he would miss the flying at Patuxent, it felt good to return to his first love, the open sea that had drawn him to the Navy in the first place.[6] *Coral Sea* would be the first U.S. Navy carrier to deploy with jet fighters and the first to operate McDonnell F2H-2 Banshees, which pleased Trap greatly. Having guided this airplane through development, he believed it to be the best of the current Navy jets.

After a four-month workup, they were under way in September to join the Sixth Fleet in the Mediterranean. Her deployment was not to be a luxury cruise, for in June the North Koreans had invaded South Korea, and intelligence suggested that the Korean affair was possibly a feint by the communists to distract from the real threat that would come through Eastern Europe.

Trap's proclivity for innovation found its way on board *Coral Sea*, where he began to ponder again a question that had gnawed at him over the years: how to launch aircraft more efficiently. New jet fighters were launched by catapult, but propeller-driven attack planes formed up on the flight deck in a single line and launched one after the other, just as Trap had done more than twenty years earlier flying off *Lexington*. The inefficiency of this operation prompted him to observe that new wider-deck carriers like *Coral Sea* made it feasible to launch alternately from two side-by-side lines of aircraft, an arrangement that would expedite operations and conserve fuel. So under Trap's guidance, they perfected this technique and the double-line deck launch was born.[7]

Coral Sea remained on a high state of alert throughout her five-month cruise, but there was no need for live shooting. In January 1951 she departed the Mediterranean for Norfolk.[8]

In February 1951, Trap was promoted to rear admiral and transferred from *Coral Sea* to become deputy commander of Sandia Base and of Field Command, Armed Forces Special Weapons Project at Albuquerque, New Mexico, the military center for nuclear weapons development. During that year, he became active in planning a nuclear-weapon future for naval aviation. He continued to log nearly thirty hours of cross-country flying per month, virtually all of it in his beloved Tigercat. These trips took him to both coasts, and he often made the round trip from Albuquerque to California in a single day.

Then in January 1952, a routine medical checkup revealed a problem with his heart. The prescription was swift and harsh: his flight log shows that he was grounded on January 22. It was a stunning blow. He was forty-nine years old and unprepared for this hard landing. During Trap's career, he had logged 6,272 flight hours in 5,012 flights in 162 different types of airplanes.[9]

Three months later, he suffered a severe heart attack, and after extended hospitalization, he elected to retire from the Navy effective in September. He was promoted one rank to vice admiral, as was customary upon retirement for those who had received combat decorations in World War II. The three-star promotion marked a bittersweet milestone for a man who had left nothing on the table through his lifetime of service in the Navy.

Upon hearing of his heart attack, Alice immediately flew to Albuquerque to be at his side, nursing and caring for him until he was no longer bedridden. Once he was back on his feet, she returned to San Francisco. There is little doubt among those who knew Alice and Trap that despite their on-again, off-again relationship, he was the love of her life.

Grounded at fifty years of age, Trap found his life suddenly wrenched from his chosen career in the Navy; it was hard to imagine life as a civilian. But encouraged by his old friend Bob Hall, now engineering vice president at Grumman, he moved to Long Island, where he was retained as a consultant to Grumman. He rented a place in Oyster Bay, New York, an easy commute to his new office at the Grumman plant at Bethpage.

He drew solace from his proximity to the water and boats and from his work among a new generation of aviators and engineers who revered him and regularly sought his counsel on matters related to aviation, test flying, and the Navy. Their hospitality had a healing effect, and as the despair of his clipped wings ebbed, he began to embrace civilian life.

37. Trap as a vice admiral

Fabian Bachrach, personal files of Frederick Trapnell Jr.

However, Trap continued to suffer painful angina. Against doctor's orders—but what would today be standard practice—he began a moderate exercise regimen in spite of the pain. Within weeks the pain diminished, and after a few months it completely disappeared. Later he would say, "Those damned quacks didn't know what in the hell they were talking about."

Alice continued to live in San Francisco but traveled regularly to visit Trap in Oyster Bay. Despite her lack of interest in sailing or aviation, she was determined to make a life with this stubborn but irresistible man she could neither live with nor without. In 1955 they agreed to try living together again and settled into a beautiful home in Oyster Bay, New York, overlooking the water. She was a gracious and capable hostess, and with Trap's charm and affability, they developed a vibrant circle of friends. Trap busied himself with Grumman, sailing and working on boats, none of which held any allure for Alice. Over time, their differing interests drew them apart, until 1966, when Alice left him to return to her beloved San Francisco.

He became a member of the Seawanhaka Corinthian Yacht Club, where he began working on boats and supervising races. He also joined the crew on board Bob Hall's racing yacht, *Nimrod*, as navigator and strategist. Later he became a member of the New York Yacht Club and the Cruising Club of America, and in 1960 he purchased and sailed a cruising yawl of his own, in which he cruised Long Island Sound and the New England coastline as far north as Maine, often by himself, relishing the salty solitude of long voyages under sail.

He also began work on a sailboat design optimized for single-handed operation over long distances. This concept led to a radically different rig for the sails, which he called a staysail ketch. He and his close friend James McCurdy, senior partner in the naval architecture firm of McCurdy and Rhodes in New York, designed this eye-catching new type of sailboat.

Trap named her *Diomedia Exulans* after the great wandering albatross he had encountered on his first cruise to the southern oceans on board *Marblehead*, a creature he still regarded as the most beautiful flying specimen he had ever seen. In 1966, he put her in commission and spent the next several years cruising Long Island Sound and up the New England coast. She proved comfortable, easy to manage, and good to windward, everything Trap had hoped for. In 1972, when Trap moved to Coronado, California, a friend sailed her through the Panama Canal and up the coast to San Diego Bay.

Alice joined Trap in Coronado in a final effort to revive their marriage, but to no avail. In 1973 Trap fell in love with June Frye, an attractive widow from a prominent San Diego family whom he had known since his early days at North Island. Following a painful divorce from Alice, Trap married June in October of that year, and they moved into a Coronado house that fronted onto San Diego Bay. June encouraged his appetite for sailing, allowing him to spend his last years close to family, sharing his love of the open sea and sailing *Diomedia* with the relish of an old sea dog.

On January 30, 1975, Trap died of flu complications in the U.S. Naval Hospital in San Diego.

CHAPTER 17

★ ★ ★

LEGACY

Trap gave little heed to his own recognition, nor did he fathom the scope of his legacy to naval aviation, a legacy that would carry forward to the present day. He stepped into flight testing at a time when the practice was still in its infancy: when test pilots were more likely to be stunt men than engineers; when airplanes served an ancillary and undeveloped role in the fleet; and when the airplane had not yet come into its own as a weapon of war. His vision and leadership shaped the evolution of naval aviation through its formative years and beyond, giving rise to his recognition as the "godfather of current naval aviation" four decades after his retirement from the Navy.[1]

Over the course of Trap's ten years in flight test, he pioneered the philosophy and perfected many of the methods of the engineering test pilot, demonstrating skill, ingenuity, and integrity that galvanized those who would guide flight testing into the twenty-first century. He demanded aircraft that pushed the performance envelope to the limits of safe, stable, and controllable performance in all flight regimes. And he insisted on comprehensive testing of an airplane with all its equipment in all missions, conditions, and maneuvers it would face in wartime fleet operations.

THE ENGINEERING TEST PILOT

Trap's rare combination of skill as an aviator and "uncanny engineering instincts" paved the way for a new kind of aviator—the engineering test pilot—who explored uncharted regions of flight to bring back quantitative data describing an airplane's behavior that could be used by engineers to design, redesign, or modify an airplane.[2]

During his three-year tenure as chief of Flight Test at Anacostia at the onset of World War II and his subsequent four years as head of the Naval Air

Test Center, Patuxent River, Trap advanced a "get the numbers" philosophy that pioneered a quantitative and analytical approach to testing. Not only did this advance the art, science, and technology of flight test, but it enabled the Navy to carry out the more comprehensive testing needed to safely explore and characterize the behaviors of ever more complex aircraft.

To advance the capabilities of Navy engineering test pilots, Trap used his considerable personal influence to get BuAer and the Navy powers that be to establish the U.S. Naval Test Pilot School at Patuxent as a permanent fixture of the Test Center. His insistence on a curriculum emphasizing test flying and gathering flight test data established a sound technical foundation for future flight testing. Notably, most Navy and Marine NASA astronauts are graduates of the U.S. Naval Test Pilot School.

As a result of his innovation and leadership, Trap influenced an entire generation of naval aviators who were moving into key positions at the time of his retirement, ensuring the depth of leadership necessary to keep naval aviation in the vanguard of aeronautics well into the twenty-first century.

A BALANCED-DESIGN PHILOSOPHY

Trap advocated a balanced aircraft design philosophy that called for optimum airplane performance consistent with adequate stability and control in all flight regimes, what he called "whole airplanes." This approach proved critical to the development of the Corsair and the Hellcat, two indispensable World War II airplanes he guided through evolution and testing on accelerated schedules. These airplanes gave the U.S. Navy and Marine Corps superior fighters that contributed significantly to victory for U.S. forces.

As noted in his congressional testimony, Trap was critical of U.S. Air Force fighter-design policies that sought speed at the expense of high-altitude performance and safety. He called these airplanes "hot rods." His World War II experience convinced him that a properly balanced carrier fighter design could be at least as combat-effective as any hot rod, and even more so at high altitude where the carrier plane's stability and control effectiveness, as well as low wing loading, would give it superior performance.

Following the war, this balanced-design philosophy continued to guide Trap's drive to get the first generation of carrier-based jets into the fleet. Refusing to sacrifice safety and stability for performance, the Fury, Banshee, and Panther were the fruits of Trap's push for first-generation jet fighters to join the operational Navy. These airplanes were unable to match the top speed of the Air Force's then-current F-86 and F-100; however, by 1955 Vought had produced the F8U Crusader and Douglas the F4D, both of which performed comparably to counterpart USAF fighters. This evolution led to the McDonnell

F-4 Phantom, which went into naval service in 1960 and was adopted by the USAF as a first-line fighter in 1963. So in one decade, this balanced fighter design philosophy prevailed in both services, and it continued to guide Navy development well into the twenty-first century. This philosophy was reflected in the design of the Grumman F-14 Tomcat and Northrop F/A-18 Hornet and Super Hornet, carrier fighters that were comparable in performance to their land-based counterparts.

Trap's leadership during this pivotal transition forged a bold path for the monumental changes in design, testing, and operations ushered in by new jet airplanes.[3]

COMPREHENSIVE TESTING

Another mark of Trap's influence was the Navy's insistence on comprehensive testing of all aspects of airplane operation. Testing only performance, stability, and control was not enough. Too many gremlins lurked in the rigors of operational flying that, if not exposed and addressed in flight test, would endanger lives later in service.

Trap pressed this approach during his time at Anacostia at the outset of World War II when the effective integration of new airplanes into the fleet was a matter of survival; his subsequent experience in World War II combat reinforced his determination to extend testing beyond initial development to include the evaluation of fully integrated airplanes in operation on board carriers and under combat conditions. When Trap returned to Naval Air Test Center to oversee the Navy's transition to jets after the war, broad-spectrum testing of airplanes moved into full swing in an effort to ease the transition into the fleet of the new, more complex aircraft and to safeguard Navy pilots and airplanes.

These innovations advanced the aeronautical performance of America's naval air arm and kept it at the forefront of modern aviation. They stand as an enduring legacy to the man who is regarded as the foremost test pilot in a century of naval aviation.

★ ★ ★

THE NEW GUARD

Trap's colleagues and protégés went on to distinguished careers in the Navy, Marine Corps, and aviation.

Robert B. Pirie, Trap's colleague at Anacostia in the early 1930s, later served as the commandant of midshipmen at the U.S. Naval Academy and commanded two aircraft carriers, including USS *Coral Sea*, before assuming division and fleet commands. He rose to the rank of vice admiral and was deputy chief of naval operations for air. After leaving the Navy, he held management positions with the Aerojet General Corporation, and for his contributions to naval aviation as a test pilot, he was elected honorary fellow of the Society of Experimental Test Pilots.[1]

Tom Connolly rose to the rank of vice admiral and held the positions of commander of naval air forces, Pacific Fleet, and deputy chief of naval operations for air warfare, a position in which he was instrumental in launching the Navy's F-14 program in the early 1970s. This new Grumman fighter plane, Tomcat, was named in his honor. He was elected honorary fellow of the Society of Experimental Test Pilots.[2]

Syd Sherby left Patuxent to take over the fighter desk in BuAer, where he was promoted to captain prior to his retirement.[3]

Marion Carl went on to senior combat commands in the Vietnam War and eventually retired from the Marine Corps with the rank of major general. He became a fellow of the Society of Experimental Test Pilots.[4]

Bill Davis later commanded USS *Franklin D. Roosevelt*, a sister ship of *Coral Sea*, and rose to the rank of vice admiral upon retiring from the Navy in 1960. He was also elected honorary fellow of the Society of Experimental Test Pilots.[5]

John Hyland left Flight Test and Patuxent in mid-1949 and then returned in 1951 to command the Tactical Test Division. Later he was given command of the U.S. Pacific Fleet and attained the rank of full admiral before retiring from the Navy in 1971.[6]

Corky Meyer became a senior executive at Grumman before retiring to Florida. He was inducted into Carrier Aviation Test Pilot Hall of Honor, USS *Yorktown*, Patriots Point, Charleston, South Carolina. He was a founding member and fellow of the Society of Experimental Test Pilots and later received the SETP James H. Doolittle Award for Outstanding Professional Accomplishment in Aerospace Technical Management.[7]

Bob Elder continued his stellar Navy flying career through the 1950s before returning to Patuxent as director of Flight Test, where he headed up the Navy test team that selected the F4H-1 (later F-4) Phantom II as the future first-line Navy fighter plane. Following his command of USS *Coral Sea* in 1964, Elder retired from the Navy. For the next twenty-three years, he directed Northrop Aircraft's flying and flight test operations and was instrumental in bringing the F/A-18 Hornet and Super Hornet to fruition as the Navy's principal shipboard aircraft weapon. He became a fellow and president of the Society of Experimental Test Pilots.[8]

HONORS

In 1956 Trap was elected a member of the Golden Eagles, the Early and Pioneer Naval Aviator's Association. His membership certificate recognizes him as "Navy Jet Pilot No. 1."[9]

In October 1957, the Society of Experimental Test Pilots elected him one of its first honorary fellows, along with Gen. James Doolittle, Howard Hughes, and Maj. Gen. Albert Boyd. His thank-you letter to the society president shows how deeply touched he was by this recognition of his peers: "[T]he Society [of Experimental Test Pilots], from my point of view, is the most distinguished group on earth. . . . The honor conferred at the Awards Banquet is the most gratifying thing that has happened to me in my association with Flight Testing. Please accept . . . my deepest appreciation."[10]

At the society's request, Trap submitted the "autobiography" included in the introduction to this book. In two brief paragraphs, repeated here, it says nearly everything he thought anyone needed to know about his life:

> *I was born naked in 1902 in Elizabeth, New Jersey, and attended Pingry School in that town and the Naval Academy—from which I graduated without distinction in 1923. This led to serving 29 years in the United States Navy, 26 of which were in the semi-respectable status of a Naval Aviator. Practically all of my shore duty was in Flight Test where I became familiar with the lingo and some of the*

primitive procedures of the 30s and 40s. I commanded a couple of Patrol Squadrons and the carriers USS Breton *and USS* Coral Sea—*without going aground—noticeably. So in 1951 I became a Rear Admiral. In 1952 the medicos caught up with me and grounded and retired me.*

Since 1953 I have been loosely associated with Grumman Aircraft and have resided in Long Island. I am very happy in my status as an Honorary Fellow of SETP, where I can harmlessly indulge my opposition to any further progress in any direction.

Very sincerely,
Frederick M. Trapnell

Trap was inducted posthumously into the U.S. Naval Aviation Hall of Honor in Pensacola, Florida, on May 8, 1986. Considered the highest honor that can be bestowed upon a naval aviator, his citation acknowledges his accomplishment in testing experimental and jet aircraft, recognizing Trap's status as "one of the most outstanding test pilots of all time."[11]

The following year he was enshrined in the Carrier Aviation Test Pilots Hall of Honor on board USS *Yorktown* in the harbor of Charleston, South Carolina.

On April 1, 1976, the runway complex at Naval Air Station Patuxent River, Maryland, was renamed Trapnell Field in Trap's honor. The plaque citation reads:

An early test coordinator and second commander, Naval Air Test Center, he was a pioneer test pilot whose calculated daring and prophetic vision served to advance the science of Naval Aviation Test and Evaluation. His insistence on formal test pilot training and a systematic approach to flight testing was instrumental in the founding of the U.S. Naval Test Pilot School and the emergence of the engineering test pilot. He served his country with devotion and great distinction.

THE LIFE AND NAVAL SERVICE OF FREDERICK M. TRAPNELL

Frederick Mackay Trapnell served twenty-nine years in the U.S. Navy, twenty-six as a naval aviator. His shore duty was mostly in flight testing. He commanded carriers USS *Breton* and USS *Coral Sea* and retired as a vice admiral in 1952. He was born July 9, 1902, in Elizabeth, NJ. He earned a BS from the U.S. Naval Academy and was commissioned as an ensign on June 8, 1923. On January 30, 1975, he died in San Diego, CA. His ashes were scattered at sea off the coast of San Diego.

HONORS AND AWARDS

1934 Commendation from chief of the Bureau of Aeronautics for invention of aircraft-stabilizing mechanism on board airships.

1940 Designated Master Horizontal Bombing Pilot.

1943 Commendation from Secretary of the Navy for skill, courage, and leadership of the Flight Test Section in developing warfighting naval aircraft.

1945 Awarded Legion of Merit for his conduct as chief of staff for TG 38/58.4.

1946 Awarded Gold Star in lieu of second Legion of Merit for contribution as head of the Navy section on the Strategic Bombing Survey for the war on Japan.

1949 Elected Associate Fellow of the Institute of Aeronautical Sciences (now the American Institute of Aeronautics and Astronautics) and received from them the Octave Chanute Award for "an outstanding contribution to the advancement of the art, science, and technology of aeronautics."

1956 Elected a member of the Golden Eagles, the Early and Pioneer Naval Aviator's Association, which recognizes him as "Navy Jet Pilot No. 1."

1959 Elected Honorary Fellow of the Society of Experimental Test Pilots.

1976 The runway complex at NAS Patuxent River, MD, is named Trapnell Field by the U.S. Navy.

1986 Inducted (posthumously) into the U.S. Naval Aviation Hall of Honor in Pensacola, FL.

1987 Enshrined (posthumously) in the Carrier Aviation Test Pilots Hall of Honor on board the USS *Yorktown*, Charleston, SC.

MILITARY SERVICE

Ranks

July 1919	midshipman
June 1923	ensign
June 1926	lieutenant (jg)
June 1931	lieutenant
June 1938	lieutenant commander
Jan. 1942	commander (wartime temporary, made permanent June 1942)
July 1943	captain (wartime temporary, made permanent Aug. 1947)
Feb. 1951	rear admiral
Sept. 1952	vice admiral

Duties

July 1919–June 1923	student, USNA
June 1923–June 1924	line officer, USS *California*
June 1924–Jan. 1926	line officer, USS *Marblehead*
Jan. 1926–Mar. 1927	student, Navy flight school, Pensacola, FL
Mar. 1927–Dec. 1929	aviator, various squadrons on board USS *Lexington*
Jan. 1930–July 1932	aviator, Flight Test Section, NAS Anacostia, DC
July 1932–June 1934	aviator, Heavier-Than-Air Unit on board USS *Akron* and USS *Macon*
June 1934–July 1936	senior aviator, USS *San Francisco*
July 1936–Sept. 1938	executive officer, VP-10, Pearl Harbor, HI
Sept. 1938–Oct. 1939	commanding officer, VP-21, Seattle, WA
Oct. 1939–May 1940	commanding officer, VP-14, San Diego, CA
May 1940–May 1943	senior flight test officer, Flight Test Section, Anacostia, DC
June 1943–July 1943	commanding officer, Fleet Air Wing 4, Kodiak, AL
July 1943–Nov. 1943	commanding officer, Fleet Air Wing 14, San Diego, CA
Nov. 1943–Nov. 1944	commanding officer, USS *Breton*
Nov. 1944–Nov. 1945	chief of staff, TG 38/58.4 (Radford)
Nov. 1945–Apr. 1946	senior Navy officer, U.S. Strategic Bombing Survey (Japan)
Apr. 1946–June 1946	student, CAA instrument flight school, NAS Atlanta, GA
June 1946–Apr. 1950	commanding officer (or test coordinator) Naval Air Test Center, NAS Patuxent River, MD
Apr. 1950–Feb. 1951	commanding officer, USS *Coral Sea*
Feb. 1951–Apr. 1952	deputy commander, Sandia Base and Armed Forces Special Weapons Project, Albuquerque, NM
Apr. 1952–Sept. 1952	sick leave
Sept. 1952	retired

NOTES

Acronyms and Abbreviations Used in Notes

FMT Personal files of (author) Frederick Trapnell Jr.

HWT Personal files of Herbert W. Trapnell, Trap's second son

NARA W National Archives and Records Administration, Washington, D.C. Personnel records and early deck logs

NARA C National Archives and Records Administration (NARA), College Park, Md. Records of the Bureau of Aeronautics, record Group 72 (BuAer) and photographs

PAX Historical records at U.S. Naval Air Station, Patuxent River, Md.

NGHC Northrop Grumman History Center, Bethpage, N.Y.

NHHC Naval History and Heritage Command, Washington Navy Yard, Washington, D.C.

NNAM National Naval Aviation Museum, Pensacola, Fla.

SETP Society of Experimental Test Pilots, Lancaster, Calif.

USNTPS U.S. Naval Test Pilot School, Patuxent River, Md.

Statements about Trap's flights—number, hours, and aircraft types—are taken from analysis of his flight log books, which are in the authors' possession.

Chapter 1. Dark Storm Eastward

1. Edward S. Miller, *War Plan Orange* (Annapolis, Md.: Naval Institute Press, 1991), 306.

2. Ibid., 133, 271. The March 1941 Joint Plan Rainbow Five projected an M-Day of September 1, 1941. We infer that this date was under discussion even earlier.

3. Frederick Trapnell, flight log, November 15, 1941, FMT.

4. A remark Trapnell made about different airplanes on more than one occasion.

5. O. B. Hardison, commanding officer NAS Anacostia, D.C., to chief of the Bureau of Aeronautics, "Preliminary flight test report on Model XF4U-1," November 22, 1940, National Archives and Records Administration. Test conducted and report prepared by F. M. Trapnell (see the typist's ID in the upper RH corner).

6. The National Advisory Committee for Aeronautics (NACA) was the predecessor of today's NASA. A theodolite range is an air space defined by a pair of surveying instruments set on the ground at either end, allowing observers to accurately measure the time for an airplane to traverse its length.

7. Hardison, "Preliminary flight test report." The XF4U-1 actually achieved 402 miles per hour. This flight was also reported in the *Washington Daily News*, December 20, 1940.

8. David Reynolds, *From Munich to Pearl Harbor: Roosevelt's America and the Origins of the Second World War* (New York: Ivan R. Dee, 2001), gives a detailed description of the politics and related events of the time.

Chapter 2. The Launching, 1902–25

1. Trapnell, from a letter written at the time in his own hand, FMT.

2. An example can be found in "Charlestown Men Dine: Discussion Over Expansion: Words of Benjamin Trapnell Against the Principle Excite Protest," *New York Times*, January 27, 1899.

3. Trapnell, "A Day in the Brooklyn Navy Yard," handwritten report, FMT.

4. His skill is revealed in several pen-and-ink drawings of ships and sailing vessels from the time, FMT.

5. An auxiliary is a sailboat that also has a motor for use when the wind is flat or the boat is maneuvering in tight spaces.

6. His drawings and offset tables can be seen in Trapnell, "My Ideal Auxiliary," *Motor Boating*, March 1919, FMT.

7. Ibid. Editor, *Motor Boating*, to Frederick M. Trapnell, February 4, 1919, FMT.

8. *The Lucky Bag* (1923).

9. "Class 1923," Register of Alumni, USNA Alumni Association (1845–1991), 193. 245 members of the class of 1923 failed to graduate.

10. "Frederick Trapnell," Navy Bureau of Personnel (BuPers) record, RG-72 01, National Archives and Records Administration.

11. Even late in life, Trap would recount his participation with hammer and chisel in these chipping-and-scraping parties on the *California* and describe them as some of the most frightening experiences in his career.

12. *Dictionary of American Naval Fighting Ships*, s.v. "Marblehead-III," http://www.history.navy.mil/danfs/index.html, accessed September 26, 2014.

13. "Trapnell," BuPers record, RG-72 01.

14. Many years later ornithologists figured out how, in a strong, steady wind, the albatross extracts energy from the boundary layer of air near the ocean surface and is able to fly, even to windward, without ever flapping its wings.

15. Roy A. Grossnick, *United States Naval Aviation: 1910–1995*, 4th ed. (Washington, D.C.: Naval History Center, 1997), 61, under "17 November 1924," http://www.history.navy.mil/download/history/prelim.pdf; Thomas Wildenberg, *All the Factors of Victory* (Dulles, Va.: Potomac, 2003), 125.

16. A capital ship is the largest class of warship, such as a battleship or aircraft carrier.

Chapter 3. Naval Aviation 1911–26, Historical Interlude

1. Thomas Wildenberg, *Destined for Glory* (Annapolis, Md.: Naval Institute Press, 1998), 21.

2. Also, in the Pratt-MacArthur Agreement of January 1931, the Navy agreed with the Army not to operate large land planes.

3. Grossnick, *United States Naval Aviation*, 61, under "14 December 1924."

4. Ibid., 52, under "3 July 1922"; 61, under "17 November 1924."

5. Lt. Col. Mark P. Jelonek, USAF, *Toward an Air and Space Force: Naval Aviation and the Implications for Space Power* (Maxwell AFB, Ala.: Air University Press, 1999), 19–29; Wildenberg, *Destined for Glory*, 21.

6. Grossnick, *United States Naval Aviation*, 37, under "22 November 1918."

7. E. W. Jolie, *A Brief History of U.S. Navy Torpedo Development* (Newport, R.I.: Naval Underwater System Center, Newport Laboratory, 1978), 31–34, http://www.history.navy.mil/museums/keyport/html/part1.htm.

8. Grossnick, *United States Naval Aviation*, 49, under "21 July 1921."

9. Ibid., 49, under "12 July 1921"; Jelonek, *Toward an Air and Space Force*, 14.

10. Grossnick, *United States Naval Aviation*, 51, under "6 February 1922"; 52, under "1 July 1922"; Walter A. Musciano, *Warbirds of the Sea* (Atglen Pa.: Schiffer, 1994), 41–42.

11. Grossnick, *United States Naval Aviation*, 65–66, under "13 December 1926"; 67, under "27 May 1927" and "17 July 1927."

12. Wildenberg, *Destined for Glory*, 10, describes the attack from which this is paraphrased; Grossnick, *United States Naval Aviation*, 65, under "22 October 1926."

13. Wildenberg, *Destined for Glory*, 30–47, has a thorough discussion of this evolution.

Chapter 4. Fighter Pilot, 1926–29

1. Adm. Arleigh Burke, USN (Ret.), letter to the author, March 18, 1975, FMT.
2. In Navy designations, V stands for heavier than air, like an airplane, while L stands for lighter than air, like a blimp or dirigible. B stands for bomber, while F stands for fighter.
3. Ambiguity in the Navy about the mission of fighters has persisted. At times they were expected to dominate the air, at others they were to bomb surface targets. So it was not unusual that "bombing" squadrons flew fighter types and routinely practiced bombing. In recent times, this ambiguity has been standardized, and currently such aircraft and their units are designated FA or Fighter-Attack.
4. "Squadron's History," the Red Rippers, http://www.public.navy.mil/airfor/vfa11/Pages/SquadronHistory.aspx, accessed June 29, 2014.
5. Wildenberg, *Destined for Glory*, 11–19.
6. E. R. Johnson, *United States Naval Aviation, 1919–1941: Aircraft, Airships and Ships Between the Wars* (Jefferson, N.C.: McFarland, 2011), 21–22.
7. Wildenberg, *All the Factors of Victory*, 136–48.
8. This scenario is based on an account told to the author by Barner himself, who said that he had tested Trap soon after his arrival in VB-1 and found him to be a "damned good pilot." This passage describes a likely sequence of maneuvers that Barner would have used in testing new pilots.
9. Trapnell, conversation with author.
10. Wildenberg, *All the Factors of Victory*, 177.
11. Ibid., 186–87.
12. Trapnell, flight log, January 1929, FMT. All Trapnell's flight logs are in the author's files.
13. Wildenberg, *Destined for Glory*, 59.
14. Ibid., 61.
15. "A New 'Caterpillar' Club Member," news release, November 16, 1929, FMT.
16. Trapnell, conversation with author.

Chapter 5. Test Pilot

1. Bureau of Aeronautics letter Aer-M-15-FAM, 601-1-2, 15-0, VV, August 3, 1926, National Archives.
2. Bureau of Aeronautics letter Aer-M-152-SP, 10-0, NA6, 602-4, December 14, 1926, National Archives; Vice Adm. Robert B. Pirie, USN

(Ret.), "The Development and Impact of Early Flight Testing on Naval Aviation." *NNAM Foundation* 4, no. 2 (1983): 17.

3. Burke, letter to author, March 18, 1975.

4. Trapnell, conversation with author. Eddie Rounds was a lifelong professional friend of Trapnell, who respected Rounds as a mentor even twenty years later in the jet era at Patuxent.

5. Johnson, *United States Naval Aviation*, 28.

6. Lt. Cdr. Paul Mullane, "Editor's Corner," *Naval Aviation News*, January 1972, 2; Capt. John Lacouture, USN (Ret.), "When Fish Could Fly, The Life of VADM Frederick M. Trapnell, USN," *NNAM Foundation* 12, no. 2 (1991): 79.

7. "Navy Day Crowd to See Air Stunts," *Sunday Star* (Washington, D.C.), October 26, 1930, photo caption.

8. Ernie Pyle, "Aviation," *Washington Daily News*, October 28, 1930.

9. The authors' files contain two White House invitations from President and Mrs. Hoover requesting "the pleasure of the company of Lieut. and Mrs. Trapnell" for events on December 11, 1930, and January 21, 1932. FMT.

10. Ernie Pyle, "Aviation," *Washington Daily News*, February 26, 1932.

11. Ibid.

12. United States Navy, "Lieutenant Frederick M. Trapnell, attached to the Flight Test Section, Naval Air Station, Anacostia," news release, February 25, 1932, FMT.

13. Ernie Pyle, "Aviation," *Washington Daily News*, February 26, 1932.

14. Ernest Lee Jahncke, Assistant Secretary of the Navy, to Frederick Trapnell, February 27, 1932, FMT.

15. A stall occurs when the angle of the wing to the oncoming air (angle of attack) is too steep, causing the airflow to separate from the surface of the wing, dramatically reducing its lift. This usually happens when the pilot allows the airplane speed to get too low.

16. Wesley Price, "Jet Buggies are Tough to Test," *Saturday Evening Post*, November 13, 1948.

17. Pirie, "The Development and Impact," 22; Vice Adm. Robert B. Pirie, interview by John T. Mason, May 3, 1974, interview 8, transcript, U.S. Naval Institute Oral History Collection, U.S. Naval Institute, Annapolis, Md.

Chapter 6. Airship Carriers, 1932–33

1. Richard K. Smith, *The Airships Akron and Macon* (Annapolis, Md.: Naval Institute Press, 1965), provided much of the information in this chapter.

2. Lacouture, "When Fish Could Fly," 80.
3. Capt. Richard Hoffman, USN (Ret.), *Curtiss F9C Sparrowhawk Airship Fighters* (Simi Valley, Calif.: Steve Ginter Books, 2008), 10, 13.
4. Rear Adm. H. B. Miller, USN (Ret.) to Mr. William A. Riley Jr., Aero Historical Society, January 22, 1958, FMT. The HTA (Heavier-Than-Air) unit comprised the airplanes, pilots, and airplane support personnel on board the airship.
5. Rear Adm. H. B. Miller, USN (Ret.), "Skyborne Aircraft Carriers," *Shipmate*, March 1984, 16. This paragraph was paraphrased from referenced journal with permission from the U.S. Naval Academy Alumni Association.
6. Dan Grossman, "USS Akron and USS Macon," *Airships.net*, http://www.airships.net/us-navy-rigid-airships/uss-akron-macon/uss-akron, accessed September 26, 2014.
7. Smith, *The Airships*, 69–70.
8. Trap's third parachute jump was one of the few stories about his Navy life that Trap would tell with glee to his friends.
9. Smith, *The Airships*, 66–67. Reference to this commendation can be found in Trap's history doc at NNAM. It quotes a historical summary originally put out by the Naval History Command, Naval Office of Information, Internal Relations Division (OI-430), 12 Nov 1968, which states that he received this commendation.
10. Smith, *The Airships*, 77.
11. The actions of *Akron* and her aircraft (including Trap's) as well as the reconstruction of this storm condition are based on Smith, *The Airships*, chap. 6. The thoughts and actions of Trapnell and the aerologist are based on the author's discussions with Trapnell elaborated to reflect their likely behavior.
12. Smith, *The Airships*, 99.
13. Miller, "Skyborne Aircraft Carriers," 17.
14. Smith, *The Airships*, 126.
15. Miller, "Skyborne Aircraft Carriers," 17.
16. Grossnick, *United States Naval Aviation*, 85, under "12 October 1933," 86, under "10–11 January 1934"; Smith, *The Airships*, 175; John Rickard, "*Consolidated PBY Catalina—Introduction and Development*," History of War.org, August 27, 2008, http://www.historyofwar.org/articles/weapons_PBY_catalina_development.html.
17. Trapnell, LTA flight log, FMT. Microfilm: M1067, Roll #170, General correspondence of the Office of the Secretary of the Navy, Lt. Frederick M. Trapnell, August 7, 1934, NARA W.

Chapter 7. Scouting and Patrolling, 1934–40

1. There is no record of why these assignments of HTA pilots were made, but the fact that they all seem to have gone into scouting units makes this a strong surmise.
2. Deck log, USS *San Francisco*, June 11, 1934, NARA W.
3. At different periods in the time span of this book, Vought had two scout plane designs and a fighter that were called Corsair. We try to make clear which we are talking about as we go, but the reader should be alert.
4. Deck log, USS *San Francisco*, NARA W, gives the movements of the USS *San Francisco* during this period.
5. Ibid., June 21, 1934.
6. Pilots and gunners had to be scored in gunnery periodically, and their scores went into their personal record. This was called "shooting for record"; Wildenberg, *Destined for Glory*, 55.
7. Trapnell, flight log, October 3, 1934.
8. Ibid., December 1934.
9. Author overheard discussion among Trapnell and colleagues.
10. Trapnell, flight log, April–June 1936.
11. VP was the Navy designation for patrol plane squadron.
12. Location confirmed in personal conversation between the author and Herbert W. Trapnell.
13. Johnson, *United States Naval Aviation*, 156–57.
14. Trapnell, flight log. His logs for this period suggest that the VP-10 mission was to develop and validate a plan for patrolling this vast area.
15. Trapnell, flight log, March–April 1937.
16. "18 Naval Planes Land in Hawaii Setting Record," *New York Herald Tribune*, January 20, 1938.
17. "Trapnell," BuPers record, RG-72 01.
18. Trapnell, flight log. His logs for this period suggest that the VP-21 mission was to develop and validate a plan for patrolling this vast area.
19. Vice Adm. Robert B. Pirie, interview by John T. Mason, May 19, 1972, interview 1, transcript, U.S. Naval Institute Oral History Collection, U.S. Naval Institute, Annapolis, Md.
20. Trapnell, flight log, July and October 1939.
21. Location confirmed in personal conversation between the author and Herbert W. Trapnell.
22. Signed certificate, FMT.
23. General Correspondence of the Office of Secretary of the Navy, 1930–1942, subj Lt. Frederick M. Trapnell, Microfilm: M1067, Roll #170, NARA W; Adm. John S. Thach, USN (Ret.), "Williwas, Gig'ems,

and St. Elmo's Fire," in *The Golden Age Remembered, U.S. Naval Aviation*, *1919–1941*, ed. E. T. Woodbridge, 223 (Annapolis, Md.: Naval Institute Press, 1998).

Chapter 8. Naval Aviation 1930–40, Historical Interlude

1. Musciano, *Warbirds*, 78.
2. George W. Gray, *Frontiers of Flight* (New York: Alfred Knopf, 1948), 114–17: 221–22.
3. Musciano, *Warbirds*, 69.
4. Johnson, *United States Naval Aviation*, 79.
5. Gray, *Frontiers of Flight*, 237–44.
6. Ibid., 238. The laws of physics require that compressing a gas (air) generates heat. Likewise the laws of thermodynamics cause compression efficiency to drop as the gas being compressed heats up. Furthermore, hot air entering the engine carburetor reduces efficiency of the engine and induces detonation. Thus the intercooler helps maintain engine performance.
7. Musciano, *Warbirds*, 146; Wildenberg, *Destined for Glory*, 156.
8. Wildenberg, *Destined for Glory*, 70.
9. Steve Ginter, *Northrop BT-1* (Simi Valley, Calif.: Steve Ginter Books, 2011), 12–13; Wildenberg, *Destined for Glory*, 136–39; Johnson, *United States Naval Aviation*, 43–44.
10. Captain Eric Brown, Royal Navy, *Wings of the Navy—Flying Allied Carrier Aircraft of World War Two* (Annapolis, Md.: Naval Institute Press, 1987), 20–28; Johnson, *United States Naval Aviation*, 46–48.
11. Johnson, *United States Naval Aviation*, 35–36.
12. Grossnick, *United States Naval Aviation*, 95, under "8 September 1939."
13. Wildenberg, *Destined for Glory*, 138; Rear Adm. E. J. King, USN, Chief of the Bureau of Aeronautics, to Vice Adm. R. V. Butler, USN, Fleet Air Detachment, August 8, 1935, Navair Fixed Wing A/C, F4F box, NHHC. In this letter King talks of phasing out fighter types altogether.
14. Johnson, *United States Naval Aviation*, 97; Wildenberg, *Destined for Glory*, 147.
15. Johnson, *United States Naval Aviation*, 95–96.
16. Musciano, *Warbirds*, 148–53.
17. Johnson, *United States Naval Aviation*, 95–96.
18. Frank L. Greene, "The Wildcat Story," *American Aviation Historical Society Journal* 6, no. 3 (1961): 6–7, NGHC.
19. Johnson, *United States Naval Aviation*, 98; Wildenberg, *Destined for Glory*, 152.

20. "Monday August 19th – Saturday August 24th 1940," *Battle of Britain Historical Society*, http://battleofbritain1940.net/0029.html, accessed July 1, 2014. This relates: The German Luftwaffe high command realized that the "Stuka" Ju87 dive bomber, although inflicting considerable damage to the British defenses, was easy prey for the Spitfires and the Hurricanes of Fighter Command. Ju87 casualties were high, costing the Luftwaffe dearly. So regular missions by the Luftflotte 2 Ju87 squadrons were withdrawn.

21. Leonard Bridgman, ed., *Jane's All the World's Aircraft*, 1941 ed., (New York: Macmillan, 1942), 30c:41c–42c.

22. Anthony G. Williams and Dr. Emmanuel Gustin, *Flying Guns of World War II: Development of Aircraft Guns, Ammunition and Installations 1933–45* (Ramsbury, UK: Airlife Publishing, 2003), 268, 300, 331. The Bf 109 packs two MG 17s and two MG-FFs for a total gun power of 282; the F4F packs four .50-caliber M2s for a total gun power of 232. As explained in the referenced document, gun power is a measure, developed by Williams and Gustin, of the total destructive power of a gun or guns.

23. The service ceiling is the maximum altitude at which the airplane can still maintain a climb rate of one hundred feet per minute.

24. Leonard Bridgman, ed., *Jane's All the World's Aircraft*, 1945–46 ed. (London: Sampson Low, Marston & Co., 1946), 49c:263c.

25. Bill Gunston, *British Fighters of World War II* (New York: Crescent Books, 1982), 10.

26. *Jane's*, 1941 ed., 88c; *Jane's*, 1945–46 ed., 67c.

27. David A. Anderton, *American Fighters of World War II* (New York: Crescent Books, 1982), 18.

28. Ibid., 26.

29. Jeffrey L. Ethell, "P-38 Lightning," in *The Great Book of World War II Airplanes* (Tokyo: Zokaisha Publications, 1984), 5.

30. Frederick A. Johnsen, "F4U Corsair," in *The Great Book of World War II Airplanes* (Tokyo: Zokaisha Publications, 1984), 216–17; Wildenberg, *Destined for Glory*, 154.

Chapter 9. Chief of Flight Test, 1940–41

1. Miller, *War Plan Orange*, 133:271.

2. The much simpler Wildcat was already destined to take nearly two years from first flight to fleet readiness. Greene, "The Wildcat Story," 7:13.

3. Adm. Charles D. Griffin, USN (Ret.), "Flight Testing at Anacostia before WWII," *NNAM Foundation* 5, no. 1 (1984): 20.

4. The author learned this from later conversation among Trap and his colleagues.
5. Ibid.
6. Frederick Trapnell to Cdr. Nicholas J. Smith III, USN, director, U.S. Naval Test Pilots School, May 11, 1964, FMT.
7. Trapnell, conversation with author; Boone T. Guyton, *Whistling Death: The Test Pilot's Story of the F4U Corsair* (Atglen, Pa.: Schiffer Publishing, 1994), 83, discusses similar instrumentation.
8. Capt. Sydney S. Sherby, USN (Ret.), "Personal Narrative," 4, USNTPS.
9. Lacouture, "When Fish Could Fly," 80–81.
10. Seymour Johnson Air Force Base in Goldsboro, N.C., is named in his honor.
11. Pirie, "The Development and Impact," 17.
12. Adm. Charles Donald Griffin, USN (Ret.), interview by James T. Mason Jr., January 28, 1970, interview 2, transcript, U.S. Naval Institute Oral History Collection, U.S. Naval Institute, Annapolis, Md.
13. Lacouture, "When Fish Could Fly," 81.
14. William Safire, "On Language; Pushing the Envelope," *New York Times*, May 15, 1988. The envelope defines the boundary of flight characteristics (speed, altitude, maneuvers, maneuvering rates, etc.) that have been explored in testing or operation. Within "the envelope" the pilot knows what to expect; beyond the envelope, the airplane's response is unknown. Flight testing is largely the process of exploring unknown flight characteristics, and thereby expanding ("pushing") the envelope to include all the characteristics required of the operational airplane and dangerous situations that may arise from simple mistakes. Safire says he was told by Tom Wolfe that the term "envelope" may have originated at Naval Air Station Patuxent River in the 1940s.
15. The author learned this from later conversation among Trapnell and his colleagues.
16. Trapnell called them simply preliminary tests or preliminary evaluations, the terminology we use in this book. The NPE nomenclature, which naval test pilots will recognize, didn't come into use until after his time.
17. Johnson, *United States Naval Aviation*, 96; Wildenberg, *Destined for Glory*, 152.
18. Johnson, *United States Naval Aviation*, 97.
19. Trapnell's recollections of Wildcat testing results, discussed with the author.
20. Ibid.

21. Ginter, *Northrop BT-1*, discusses the BT-1 and its evolution into the SBD; Wildenberg, *Destined for Glory*, 160–61.

22. Wildenberg, *Destined for Glory*, 137; Johnson, *United States Naval Aviation*, 50–51; Musciano, *Warbirds*, 154–55.

23. *Jane's*, 1945–46 ed., 249c.

24. Johnson, *United States Naval Aviation*, 54–55.

25. David Lucabaugh and Bob Martin, *Grumman XF5F-1 & XP-50 Sky-rocket* (Simi Valley, Calif.: Steve Ginter Books, 1995), 20.

26. Guyton, *Whistling Death*, 45.

27. Trapnell, conversation with author.

28. Hardison, "Preliminary flight test report XF4U-1," 1–2.

Chapter 10. The Desperate Gamble, November 1940

1. Hardison, "Preliminary flight test report XF4U-1," 2.

2. Tommy Thomason, *Bell XFL-1 Airabonita* (Simi Valley, Calif.: Steve Ginter Books, 2008), 49.

3. Ibid, 28–29.

4. Trapnell, flight log, April 1941. Trapnell, "opinion memorandum," on Grumman note stationery, probably between 1953 and 1964, written in his own hand commenting on a paper/article written by a "Mr. Woodha." This memorandum gives Trap's brief opinions on various fighters that were tested during his tour as Flight Test Officer in 1940–1943. FMT and NNAM.

5. Trapnell, "opinion memorandum."

6. Lucabaugh and Martin, *Skyrocket*, 2–3.

7. Ibid., inside front cover; Rene Francillon, *Grumman Aircraft Since 1929* (New York: Putnam, 1989).

8. Lucabaugh and Martin, *Skyrocket*, 11.

9. Ibid., 19.

10. Ibid., 6.

11. Ibid., 13.

12. Trapnell, "opinion memorandum."

13. Board of Inspection and Survey to Secretary of the Navy, March 9, 1943, Subject: "Contract 61544 – Model XF4U-1 Airplane – Service Acceptance Trials – Final Report on," 11. NARA C.

14. Griffin, "Flight Testing," 69.

15. Hardison, "Preliminary flight test report XF4U-1," 1–2.

16. Johnsen, "F4U Corsair," 219.

17. Trapnell, "opinion memorandum."

18. Robin Higham, *Unflinching Zeal* (Annapolis, Md.: Naval Institute Press, 2012), chap. 1.

19. Precise figures for fuel consumption for the Pratt & Whitney R-2800 are not easy to pin down. Johnsen, "F4U Corsair," specifies the Corsair's range to be one thousand miles at a long-range cruising speed of 182 mph with a fuel capacity of 363 gallons, which suggests 66 gal/hour (with no reserve). This figure is consistent with those quoted by http://www.mnstarfire.com/ww2/history/air/USA/CorsairF4U.html (July 1, 2014) of 42 gal/hr minimum (probably too slow for maximum range), 83 gal/hr at maximum cruise at low altitude (too fast for maximum range), 240 gal/hr at full power, and 290 gal/hr at takeoff. The Flying Bulls, who operate a Corsair in Salzburg, Austria, say it requires an average of 100 gal/hr and three times that much at takeoff.

For comparison, *Jane's*, 1945–46 ed., 263c, gives the Wildcat's fuel capacity as 160 gallons and cruising range as 925 miles. Assuming this airplane had a long-range cruising speed of 160 mph, it would have a cruising fuel consumption rate of 26.6 gallons per hour; the Corsair required almost two-and-a-half times this amount. The ratio of cruise-to-full-speed (bigger for the Corsair) in each of these two airplanes (and hence the ratio of power required) has the effect of increasing the two-and-a-half-times difference in fuel consumption when each is at its full speed and suggests that the Corsair's consumption was nearly three times that of the Wildcat!

20. Trapnell, "opinion memorandum."

21. Ibid.

22. A comment Trapnell made about the Spitfire on more than one occasion.

23. Trapnell told the author he thought the Spitfire's Malcolm hood canopy was innovative and had recommended it for the Corsair.

24. This was learned from later conversation among Trap and his colleagues.

25. Thomason, *Bell XFL-1*, 49. This gives performance comparison data for F4F-3, XFL, XF5F, XF4U, and F4U-1.

26. Corwin H. Meyer, *Corky Meyer's Flight Journal* (North Branch, Minn.: Specialty Press, 2006), 176.

27. David A. Anderton, "F6F Hellcat," in *The Great Book of World War II Airplanes* (Tokyo: Zokaisha Publications, 1984), 173; Lucabaugh and Martin, *Skyrocket*, 29. Roy Grumman did not give up on the F5F Skyrocket concept, and near the end of World War II Grumman produced a follow on, the F7F Tigercat. This was a twin Pratt & Whitney R-2800 engine fighter with an extended nose, single vertical stabilizer, and tricycle landing gear that would become a favorite of Trapnell's and many Navy and Marine pilots, as described in chapter 15.

28. Many years later, Trapnell voiced to the author recollection of this conversation with Roy Grumman.

29. Johnsen, "F4U Corsair," 217.

30. Guyton, *Whistling Death*, 62.

31. Johnsen, "F4U Corsair," 217.

32. Griffin, Oral History interview 2. As a lieutenant, Griffin had been Trapnell's number two in Flight Test.

33. Guyton, *Whistling Death*, 72–74.

34. In discussions with the author, Trapnell more than once emphasized the effort he put in to get the Corsair to roll quickly and easily.

35. Trapnell, conversation with author.

36. Johnsen, "F4U Corsair," 218–19.

37. Guyton, *Whistling Death*, 82–86; Board of Inspection, "Final report, XF4U-1," paragraph 26.

38. Trapnell, conversation with author.

Chapter 11. Flight Test at War, 1941–43

1. Jim Reardon, *Koga's Zero* (Missoula, Mont.: Pictorial Histories Publishing Company, 1995), 3–6.

2. The German Luftwaffe also adopted a loose two-airplane section, or *rotte*, in 1939, during the Spanish Civil War. Thach himself called the Thach Weave the "beam defense maneuver." Robert L. Shaw, *Fighter Combat* (Annapolis, Md.: Naval Institute Press, 1985), 210–11.

3. *Jane's*, 1945–46 ed., gives the Zero's top speed as 340 mph and the Wildcat's as 318 mph. "The Zero was superior (to the Wildcat) at all altitudes above 1,000 feet in speed, climb, service ceiling and range." Meyer, *Flight Journal*, 141.

4. John B. Lundstrom, *The First Team and the Guadalcanal Campaign* (Annapolis, Md.: Naval Institute Press, 1994), 534–35.

5. Musciano, *Warbirds*, 150. On the other side of the world, the Finnish Air Force, flying a couple of squadrons of the U.S. Navy's discarded F2A-1 Buffaloes that had neither self-sealing fuel tanks nor armor, was racking up an unbelievable fifteen-to-one kill ratio over Soviet airplanes.

6. Wildenberg, *Destined for Glory*, 214–15.

7. *Jane's*, 1945–46 ed., 236c; Brown, *Wings of the Navy*, 90–98.

8. Trapnell, conversation with author.

9. Decades later, even after the Corsair had been a resounding success in service for more than eleven years, Trapnell still regarded the airplane as "dangerous."

10. Trapnell, conversation with author.

11. Johnsen, "F4U Corsair," 218–19.

12. Grossnick, *United States Naval Aviation*, 123, under "11 February 1943."

13. Ibid., 121, under "2 Nov 1942."

14. Lundstrom, *The First Team*, 293–95. Just six months earlier, in April 1942, on the Bataan Peninsula (enclosing Manila Bay), the U.S. Army suffered a stinging defeat and the surrender of nearly 75,000 U.S. and Philippine soldiers at the hands of the Japanese army.

15. Reardon, *Koga's Zero*, 58:63–72.

16. Lundstrom, *The First Team*, 534.

17. Ibid.

18. Reardon, *Koga's Zero*, 73.

19. Wildenberg, *Destined for Glory*, 178–79; Marion E. Carl and Barrett Tillman, *Pushing the Envelope* (Annapolis, Md.: Naval Institute Press, 1994), 24.

20. Francillon, *Grumman Aircraft*, 195.

21. Ibid., 196.

22. Allan M. Lazarus, "The Hellcat-Zero Myth," *Naval History*, Summer 1989, 49.

23. "Aviation: The Embattled Farmers," *Time*, September 11, 1944, http://www.time.com/time/magazine/article/0,9171,775256,00.html.

24. John Torkelsen, interview with the author, February 2010.

25. Price, "Jet Buggies," 129; Meyer, *Flight Journal*, 181.

26. Griffin, "Flight Testing," 72–73.

27. Grossnick, *United States Naval Aviation*, 129, under "30 August 1943."

28. Ibid., 126, under "21 April 1943."

29. David M. Carpenter, *Flame Powered: The Bell XP-59A Airacomet and the General Electric I-A Engine* (n.p.: Jet Pioneers of America, 1992), 47.

30. Trap's flight scenario here is an elaboration from discussion with him and his own description of it in Carpenter, *Flame Powered*, 42; ibid., 32

31. Takeoff performance of the XP-59A is from author's discussions with Trapnell and Robert M. Elder, introduced in chapter 15.

32. *Jane's*, 1945–46 ed., 205c, 275c. Gives service ceiling of over 40,000 feet for the P-59A and over 35,000 feet for the P-38.

33. Griffin, Oral History interview 2.

34. The Secretary of the Navy to Captain Frederick M. Trapnell, USN, Subject: Commendation, June 11, 1943, FMT.

Chapter 12. High Noon in the Pacific, 1943–45

1. Chronology of Fleet Air Wing 4 History, NHHC.
2. Fleet Air Wing 4 War Diary, RG-38, NARA C. Reading through these logs, one is struck by the persistent reports of bad weather that causes cancellation of patrols and other missions.
3. Based on Trapnell, flight logs, June 1943.
4. Chronology of Fleet Air Wing 4 History. Fleet Air Wing 4 War Diary, May 1943. The monthly report is signed by commanding officer Gehres as a captain; the June report is signed by Trap; and the July report is signed by Gehres as a commodore.
5. "Trapnell," BuPers record, RG-72 01.
6. The events of the three airplane crashes and Trap's summarily relieving the commanding officer were related many years ago to the author by an officer in Patrol Wing 14 at the time.
7. Carl and Tillman, *Pushing the Envelope*, 46.
8. Deck log, USS *Breton*, November 13, 1943, NARA C, shows the ship under way at thirteen knots from Espiritu Santo to Pearl Harbor.
9. This story was related to the author thirty years later by a dentist who had been an enlisted hospital corpsman on USS *Breton* at the time.
10. Trapnell, conversation with author.
11. Ibid.
12. F6F Pilot's Manual, Appendix 1, indicates that a Hellcat carrying only fifty gallons of fuel and no ammunition can take off into a twenty-knot headwind in 190 feet.
13. Grossnick, *United States Naval Aviation*, 140, under "11 June–10 August 1944."
14. Bryan Perrett and Ian Hogg, *Encyclopedia of the Second World War* (Novato, Calif.: Presidio Press, 1989), 326–27.
15. Board of Decoration and Medals Citation of Frederick M. Trapnell, Capt., USN, by ComAirForcePacificFleet, January 24, 1946: "For meritorious service in connection with operations against the enemy as Commanding Officer of the U.S.S. Breton during the period 1 June 1944 to 7 Oct 1944." FMT.
16. "Task Force 58," http://pacific.valka.cz/forces/tf58.htm, accessed September 5, 2014. Count derived from log of Task Force 58 operations, January 1945.
17. In order to confuse the Japanese (one assumes the Navy did not confuse itself), the battle fleet in the Western Pacific was called either the Third Fleet or the Fifth Fleet, depending on who was in command at the time. Under this shore-based fleet commander, his operating ships at sea

were designated as a task force and numbered either Task Force 38 or Task Force 58, depending on the current fleet number. Fleet and task force commands rotated at four- to five-month intervals, and the fleet number, task force number, and task group numbers changed accordingly.

18. A carrier's air group comprises its fighting aircraft—fighters, dive bombers, and torpedo bombers—led by an air group commander. These aircraft were further divided into squadrons of twelve to fifteen operational aircraft of a given type.

19. "Task Force 38," http://pacific.valka.cz/forces/tf38.htm, accessed September 5, 2014; "Task Force 58," http://pacific.valka.cz/forces/tf58.htm, accessed September 5, 2014. "Task Force 38" provides a log of Task Force 38 operations and "Task Force 58" provides a log of Task Force 58 operations used in constructing the following narrative. Grossnick, *United States Naval Aviation*, 144–46, under "10 October–30 November 1944."

20. Grossnick, *United States Naval Aviation*, 147, under "18 December 1944"; "Typhoons and Hurricanes: Pacific Typhoon, 18 December 1944," *Naval Historical Center*, http://www.history.navy.mil/faqs/faq102-4.htm, last modified April 10, 2001; Paul Frisco Collection (AFC/2001/001/62207), Veterans History Project, American Folklife Center, Library of Congress http://www-sbt.brookdalecc.edu/pages/738.asp, accessed December 5, 2014; interviews by the author with Seaman 1st Class Willie Lagarde, who served on board the USS *Yorktown* from December 1943 to January 1946, were used in preparing this section.

21. The description of the job of chief of staff is based on the citation referenced below dated December 15, 1945, discussions with Trap's colleagues, and the author's knowledge of air strike operations.

22. Grossnick, *United States Naval Aviation*, 147, under "28 December 1944"; Barrett Tillman, *Corsair: The F4U in World War II and Korea* (Annapolis, Md.: Naval Institute Press, 1979), 116–17.

23. The author overheard discussion among Trap and his colleagues.

24. Being sworn to secrecy about his test flight in the jet plane and the XP-59A Airacomet itself set Trapnell up for an interesting situation while on board *Yorktown*, which he recounted later: "I found myself in a group discussing rumors then emanating from Europe of a weird and wonderful means of [aircraft] propulsion—without a propeller. The discussion became quite intense and very inaccurate, to say the least. I was supposed to be the most knowledgeable of those present, but I had to sit silent and act dumb. I couldn't say that I not only knew about it, but I had flown one. I was forbidden to say a word." Carpenter, *Flame Powered*, 42.

25. Grossnick, *United States Naval Aviation*, 148–49, under "16 February–16 March 1945."

26. At this point, Task Group 58.4 comprised the big carriers *Yorktown*, *Enterprise*, and *Intrepid*, plus the light carriers *Langley* and *Independence*. These were supported by three battleships, five cruisers, and twenty-four destroyers. "Task Force 58," under "18 March 1945," http://pacific.valka.cz/forces/tf58.htm, accessed September 5, 2014.

27. From October 1944 to the end of the Okinawa campaign, the Japanese flew 2,550 kamikaze missions, of which 475, or 18.6 percent, were effective in securing hits or damaging near misses. *U.S. Strategic Bombing Survey, Summary Report (Pacific War)* (Washington: Government Printing Office, 1946), 10.

28. Musciano, *Warbirds*, 312–14, has a vivid description of the USS *Franklin* disaster.

29. Grossnick, *United States Naval Aviation*, 149–51, under "18 March–21 June 1945."

30. Award of the LEGION OF MERIT of CAPTAIN FREDERICK M. TRAPNELL, UNITED STATES NAVY, signed J. H. Towers, Vice Admiral, U.S. Navy, under cover letters dated December 15, 1945. The citation reads: "For exceptionally meritorious conduct in the performance of outstanding service as chief of staff to a Task Group Commander from November 1944 to the successful close of hostilities against the Japanese Empire on 15 August 1945. . . . From the beginning his tireless efforts in coordinating the work of all members of the staff to the end that it would function smoothly and effectively under any emergency were outstanding. His quiet but dynamic leadership was such that he inspired every member of the staff to exert his best efforts, with the result that the Task Group Commander was burdened with a minimum of operational and administrative matters. His outstanding professional abilities, keen judgment and exact technical knowledge of the capabilities and limitations of the types of aircraft available were of immeasurable help to the Task Group Commander in planning, and contributed materially to the success of widely varying types of all offensive operations which the group was called upon to carry out. Under enemy attack his calm, cool courage created a spirit of confidence in those under him which was a tribute to himself and the high standards he so consistently demonstrated in his own performance of duty. His courage, inspiring leadership and professional skill were at all times in keeping with the highest traditions of the United States Naval Service." FMT.

31. Award of GOLD STAR IN LIEU OF 2d LEGION OF MERIT of CAPTAIN FREDERICK M. TRAPNELL, UNITED STATES NAVY, approved SECNAV, July 8, 1946. The citation reads: "Capt. Frederick M. Trapnell, USN, for exceptionally meritorious conduct in the performance of outstanding service to the Government of the United States, as Member of the Naval Analysis Division of the United States Strategic Bombing Survey from 7 December 1945 to 1 May 1946. His thorough and precise knowledge of the wartime operations in which he participated, his profound insight into the complexities of the art of war together with the high degree of diligence and analytical skill displayed by Capt. Trapnell made him largely responsible for the success of the Naval Analysis Division in securing and preserving evidence of the utmost value to all future study of the war against Japan and in completing a brilliant and scholarly analysis of the nature and implications of this conflict. His outstanding ability and devotion to duty reflected great credit upon the Naval Service. By his outstanding performance, Capt. Trapnell has made a significant and fundamental contribution to all future planning for the national defense." FMT.

32. Trapnell, conversation with author.

Chapter 13. The Challenge, 1946

1. Grossnick, *United States Naval Aviation*, 127, under "29 June 1943" and "15 August 1943"; 152, under "16 June 1945."

2. NATC History file, NHHC, Washington, D.C., gives functional descriptions of NATC divisions, as do NAS Patuxent River test reports at NARA C. Other insights into divisional responsibilities come from oral histories, especially of Adm. John J. Hyland, U.S. Naval Institute.

3. Gray, *Frontiers of Flight*, 51–54, 177–78.

4. This was observed by the author at the Naval Air Test Center, 1948.

5. Gray, *Frontiers of Flight*, 275–76.

6. Leonard Bridgman, ed., *Jane's All the Worlds Aircraft*, 1947 ed. (New York: Macmillan, 1947), 57d; John D. Anderson Jr., *Introduction to Flight* (New York: McGraw-Hill, 2012), Section 6.7.

7. This paragraph is a composite of whole sentences taken from two different statements by Carl about the cited mock dogfight. They are combined here to clarify his reasoning. They come from two sources: (1) Carl and Tillman, *Pushing the Envelope*, 56–57; and (2) Robert J. Esposito, "The Navy's P-80 Shooting Stars," *The Hook – Journal of Carrier Aviation* (Spring 1991): 31.

8. John D. Anderson Jr., *A History of Aerodynamics* (New York: Cambridge University Press, 1997), 370–71, 404–10.

9. Meyer, *Flight Journal*, chap. 11; Gray, *Frontiers of Flight*, 96–97, 153–54. At the end of World War II, the German Me-163 rocket-propelled interceptor and the Me-262 jet fighter both routinely approached the speed of sound during combat operations.

10. Chapter 10, note 19 suggests that the Pratt & Whitney R-2800 propeller engine burned 290 gallons per hour at takeoff power. Bridgman, *Jane's*, 1947 ed., 57d, gives the specific fuel consumption of the General Electric J-33, which powered the Lockheed P-80, as 1.185 lb/lbt/hr. (pounds of fuel per pound of thrust per hour). This translates to 790 gal/hr at full (4,000-lb.) thrust.

11. Bill Gunston, ed., *The Illustrated History of Fighters* (London: Phoebus Publishing, 1981), 115, gives loaded weights of the F4U-4 Corsair (late model propeller-driven fighter) as 14,330 lbs., and on page 165, the F2H-2 Banshee (early jet fighter), as 22,312 lbs.

12. Grossnick, *United States Naval Aviation*, 167–68, under "4 June 1947."

13. Burke, letter to author, March 18, 1975, edited with permission for clarity.

14. Price, "Jet Buggies," 130.

15. James Barner, Chronological Reports of Naval Air Test Center Operations, June 1946–January 1947, NATC Box, NHHC, Washington, D.C.

16. Ibid.

17. Grossnick, *United States Naval Aviation*, 167–68, under "4 June 1947."

18. The description of Trap's thoughts in these last few paragraphs is based on the author's knowledge of the problems he faced and his likely appreciation of them.

Chapter 14. The Quest, 1946–50

1. Chronological history, Naval Air Test Center, December 1946–February 1947, NATC box, NHHC.

2. Ibid.

3. Vice Adm. Charles S. Minter Jr., interview by John T. Mason Jr., August 14, 1979, vol. 1, interview 4, transcript, U.S. Naval Institute Oral History Collection, U.S. Naval Institute, Annapolis, Md.

4. Vice Adm. Thomas F. Connolly, interview by John T. Mason Jr., July 21, 1977, interview 4, transcript, U.S. Naval Institute Oral History Collection, U.S. Naval Institute, Annapolis, Md.

5. Ibid., interviews 1–4.

6. Ibid., interview 5.

7. Carl and Tillman, *Pushing the Envelope*, 5–50. The one-half results when two pilots share a kill.

8. Ibid., 57–58. Grossnick, *United States Naval Aviation*, 166, under "11 November 1946."

9. Capt. Sydney S. Sherby, USN (Ret.), personal narrative on the creation of the U.S. Naval Test Pilot School, undated, USNTPS.

10. Connolly, Oral History interview 4; Adm. John J. Hyland Jr., interview by John T. Mason Jr., March 9, 1972, vol. 1, interview 3, transcript, U.S. Naval Institute Oral History Collection, U.S. Naval Institute, Annapolis, Md.

11. Cdr. S. S. Sherby, USN, and Lt. Cdr. E. P. Schuld, USN, "Test Pilot Training Division History, 1 March 1948–31 May 1948," report under Naval Air Test Center letterhead, Ref NA83(1)A12–1 TPT/EPS/has, NATC box, NHHC. Connolly, Oral History interview 4.

12. Sherby and Schuld, "Test Pilot Training Division History." This document gives a brief history of test pilot training at Patuxent starting in 1945. Sherby, personal narrative.

13. Cdr. C. E. Geise, USN, "Flight Test Memorandum No. 3–45," February 21, 1945, NATC box, NHHC.

14. Cdr. Sherby et al to Capt. Carl Giese, memo, February 23, 1945, NATC History Dec 1948–June 1949 folder, NHHC. Unfortunately, no copy has been found of Trapnell's document mentioned in this memo.

15. Connolly, Oral History interview 4; Sherby, personal narrative.

16. Chronological history, Naval Air Test Center, December 1946–February 1947, NATC box, NHHC.

17. Capt. J. D. Barner to chief of BuAer, memo, March 20, 1946, recommending an extended test pilot school. Response of June 26, 1946, NATC box, NHHC; Capt. J. D. Barner to chief of BuAer, memo, August 1, 1946, NATC box, NHHC; Historical Narrative, "Background of Test Pilot Training in the U.S. Navy," U.S. Navy Test Pilots School, 1946, and other reports held in the NATC box, NHHC.

18. Sherby, personal narrative, edited for clarity.

19. Trapnell to Cdr. Nicholas J. Smith III, director, U.S. Naval Test Pilots School, May 11, 1964, FMT.

20. Connolly, Oral History interview 5.

21. Author's recollections from watching and listening around hangars at NATC.

22. Connolly, Oral History interview 4.

23. Trapnell, conversation with author.

24. Daniel O. Dommasch, Sydney S. Sherby, and Thomas F. Connolly, *Airplane Aerodynamics* (New York: Pitman, 1951), foreword. Four editions of this text would be used in airplane design courses by twenty-seven

universities over several decades, and it continues to be referenced in modern aeronautical texts today. Anderson, *Introduction to Flight*, chap. 6 bibliography.

25. Trapnell, conversation with author.
26. Sherby, personal narrative.
27. Connolly, Oral History interview 5.
28. Trapnell to Smith.
29. Connolly, Oral History interview 4.
30. Hyland, Oral History interviews 1–2.
31. The author overheard this conversation between Trapnell and his colleagues.
32. G. W. Hyatt and W. V. Davis III, *Winners' Viewpoints, The Great 1927 Trans-Pacific Dole Race* (Oldairfield, LLC, 2009), 66–76.
33. Ibid., 76.
34. Hyland, Oral History interview 2.
35. Carl and Tillman, *Pushing the Envelope*, 61; Marion Carl to the author, handwritten note, March 10, 1975, FMT; conversation between Carl and Maj. Gen. Kenneth Weir, USMC (Ret.), as recounted to the author by Weir, FMT.
36. Trapnell to Smith.
37. Commander, Naval Air Test Center, to chief of naval operations (DCNO Air) via chief of the Bureau of Aeronautics, "Flight Test School; establishment of," memo, May 1, 1947, BuAer files, NARA C.
38. Connolly, Oral History interview 5.
39. Chief of BuAer to deputy chief of naval operations (air), "Flight Test Pilots' School; establishment of," 7-3-47. BuAer files, NARA C.
40. OP-50 to deputy chief of naval operations (air), "Subj: Flight Test Pilots' School: establishment of," memo January 19, 1948. BuAer files, NARA C.
41. NATC box, NHHC.
42. Trapnell to Smith.
43. Ibid.
44. The original order establishing the Test Pilot School referred to it as the Test Pilot Training Division of NATC. At a later date it became the U.S. Naval Test Pilot School. For consistency hereafter, we use the latter or simply the Test Pilot School.
45. Trapnell to Smith.
46. Richard M. Harris, CIV USNTPS, e-mail to author, March 4, 2012, FMT, states that there have been "4072 graduates of USNTPS since class 0"; Carl and Tillman, *Pushing the Envelope*, 53.

47. The story of John Hyland's tailless Banshee is taken from the following sources: Price, "Jet Buggies," 20–21; Hyland Oral History interview 5; Minter, Oral History interview 4; and Hyland, personal conversations with the author.
48. Hyland, Oral History interviews 3 and 5.
49. Connolly, Oral History interview 4.
50. Sherby, personal narrative.
51. Trapnell, conversation with author.
52. Carl and Tillman, *Pushing the Envelope*, 68–69.
53. Lacouture, "When Fish Could Fly," 82.

Chapter 15. Harnessing the Jets, 1946–49

1. Musciano, *Warbirds*, 335–36. Confirmed in personal conversation between the author and Rear Adm. Edward "Whitey" Feightner, USN (Ret.), who had been the project pilot on the AD at Patuxent. According to personal conversation between Edward H. Heinemann, chief engineer at Douglas Aircraft Corp, and the author, with the Skyraider, Heinemann finally got the Navy to go along with his long-standing wish held throughout World War II. He had consistently pushed for a single-seat attack bomber, but the Navy insisted on a rear gunner, as evidenced in the SBD Dauntless and SB2C Helldiver. Hindsight suggests that Heinemann was right.
2. Carl, *Pushing the Envelope*, 57; Chronological history, Naval Air Test Center, May 1946–August 1946, J. D. Barner, commander, NATC; NATC file, NHHC.
3. Trapnell to Piloted Aircraft Division (Bureau of Aeronautics), "XFJ-1, Brief Evaluation," memorandum, FMT.
4. Confirmed in personal conversation between Rear Adm. Edward L. Feightner, USN (Ret.), and the author.
5. Richard Hallion, *Test Pilots: The Frontiersmen of Flight* (New York: Doubleday, 1981).
6. Stephan Wilkinson, "Mach 1: Assaulting the Barrier," *Air & Space*, December 1990.
7. Price, "Jet Buggies," 21.
8. Carl and Tillman, *Pushing the Envelope*, 59, recalls that Carl and Trap jointly tested the FJ-1 and the F2H.
9. Trapnell to Piloted Aircraft Division (Bureau of Aeronautics), "XF6U-1, Informal Evaluation," memorandum, September 3, 1947, FMT.
10. Trapnell to chief, Bureau of Aeronautics (Piloted Aircraft Division), "XF7U-1 Preliminary Observations," memorandum, November 16, 1948, FMT.

11. Carl and Tillman, *Pushing the Envelope*, 69. Problems with the Cutlass were further elaborated and illuminated in extensive conversations between the author and Rear Adm. William L. Harris, USN, deceased, who flew the Cutlass in service.

12. Tommy H. Thomason, *U.S. Naval Air Superiority: Development of U.S. Shipborne Jet Fighters Phantom - Phantom 11·1943–1962* (North Branch, Minn.: Specialty Press, 2007).

13. Musciano, *Warbirds*, 399–404. The Crusader was redesignated F-8 in 1962.

14. This appears to refer to the plane's static longitudinal stability, its stability in the up-and-down pitching direction.

15. Directional stability: stability in the left and right yawing direction. Trapnell to Piloted Aircraft Division (Bureau of Aeronautics), "Brief Evaluation XFJ-1," memorandum, February 4, 1947, FMT.

16. Grossnick, *United States Naval Aviation*, 170, under "10 March 1948."

17. Barrett Tillman, "Where Are They Now: Bob Elder," *The Hook – Journal of Carrier Aviation*, Fall 1989, 12–17; Robert Elder, personal conversations with the author.

18. Ibid.

19. Charles Tilgner Jr. and Joseph Lippert Jr., "General Notes on German Wind Tunnels and High Speed Research," Grumman Report, October 23, 1945, NARA C. Trap told the author that North American representatives said to him more than once that the F-86 was intended as a "Navy airplane" all along. Navy straight-wing fighters operational at the outbreak of the Korean War in 1950 had excellent altitude and rate-of-climb performance. Two years later, the Navy introduced a swept-wing fighter with speeds approaching its land-based counterpart. And by the end of the decade, with the evolution of far more powerful jet engines, a Navy fighter, the McDonnell F-4 Phantom II, set world speed, time-to-climb, and altitude records.

20. "North American F-86 (Day-Fighter A, E And F Models)," National Museum of the U.S. Air Force, http://www.nationalmuseum.af.mil/factsheets/factsheet.asp?id=2297, accessed October 10, 2014; "North American F-100 (YF-100, A and C)," National Museum of the U.S. Air Force, http://www.nationalmuseum.af.mil/factsheets/factsheet.asp?id=2304, accessed October 10, 2014.

21. Meyer, *Flight Journal*, 116–17, recounts Col. Joe Renner's cross-country flight: 2,324 miles in six hours and thirty-three minutes with a 40 mph tail wind yields 315 mph speed through the air.

22. Carl and Tillman, *Pushing the Envelope*, 74.

23. Rear Adm. Edward L. Feightner, USN (Ret.), e-mail to author, FMT.
24. Ibid.
25. Minter, Oral History interview 4.
26. The Tigercat nose wheel incident is based on personal recollections of the author, who witnessed it.
27. The Phantom was originally called FD-1 and the F2H-1 was designated F2D-1, because the Navy had given the manufacturer designation D to McDonald. In August 1947 the D designation was returned to Douglas, and McDonnell was given H. To sidestep this confusion, this book uses H for McDonnell consistently.
28. Grossnick, *United States Naval Aviation*, 163–64, under "21 July 1946"; 171, under "5 May 1948."
29. Gunston, *History of Fighters*, F2H Banshee.
30. Carl and Tillman, *Pushing the Envelope*, 59.
31. Trapnell to Piloted Aircraft Division, Bureau of Aeronautics (VF Design), "Preliminary Evaluation of the Thin Wing Version of the Banshee," memorandum, April 20, 1948, FMT.
32. Official U.S. Navy Photographs, February 27, 1950, show an aerial view of greater New York City and are officially labeled: "Altitude over 40,000 feet." Handwritten notes made from a discussion with Trap indicate they were taken by a photo Banshee (F2H) from 50,000 feet, FMT.
33. McDonnell's F3H Demon immediately followed the Banshee. It had a single engine and, coincidentally, a problematic career. McDonnell Aircraft merged with Douglas Aircraft to form McDonnell Douglas, which was later taken over by Boeing.
34. Meyer, *Flight Journal*, 176.
35. Tilgner and Lippert, "German Wind Tunnels."
36. Meyer, *Flight Journal*, 192.
37. Trapnell to Bureau of Aeronautics (Piloted Aircraft Division), "Preliminary Evaluation flights on XF9F-1," memorandum, March 19, 1948, FMT. This and the following four paragraphs summarize this five-page report.
38. Price, "Jet Buggies," 129.
39. Meyer, *Flight Journal*, 182.
40. Ibid.
41. Ibid., 183.
42. This fly-off is recorded in photographs. FMT.
43. Grossnick, *United States Naval Aviation*, 162, under "3 April 1946."
44. Trap frequently made favorable comments about Ed Heinemann and his skill as a designer.

45. Musciano, *Warbirds*, 354–56.
46. Scott Libis, *Douglas D-558-1 Skystreak* (Simi Valley, Calif.: Steve Ginter Books, 2001); Scott Libis, *Douglas D-558-2 Skyrocket* (Simi Valley, Calif.: Steve Ginter Books, 2002).
47. Libis, *Skystreak*, 7.
48. Ibid., 1.
49. Ibid., 4; Carl and Tillman, *Pushing the Envelope*, 59.
50. Carl and Tillman, *Pushing the Envelope*, 60. Marion Carl made the same comment about his helmet interfering with the canopy. Trapnell to BuAer (Piloted Aircraft Division), "D558 Evaluation Flight," September 3, 1947, Douglas Aircraft Co. flight test report for flights 19 and 20 of D558-1, NARA, Pacific Region, Laguna Niguel Office. The speed of sound decreases with temperature, so the airspeeds of Mach 0.86 at 7,000 ft. altitude and of Mach 0.82 at the desert floor (3,000 ft.) are probably comparable under the same weather conditions. Tilgner and Lippert, "German Wind Tunnels," on speeds achieved in wartime Germany, summarized earlier in this chapter. Adam Makos and Larry Alexander, *A Higher Call* (New York: Berkley Publishing, 2013), chap. 21, relates the German ace Franz Stigler's experience diving an Me 262 to escape American fighters and then losing control to transonic aerodynamic forces when the airplane exceeded its red-lined speed limit of 625 miles per hour. He was able to recover control when the airplane reached lower altitude, where presumably the warmer air reduced the airplane's Mach number and the corresponding transonic forces.
51. Anderson, *A History*, 370.

Chapter 16. Turmoil, 1949–52

1. Lt. Cdr. Andrew L. Lewis, USN, *The Revolt of the Admirals* (Montgomery, Ala.: Air Command and Staff College, 1998), http://www.au.af.mil/au/awc/awcgate/acsc/98-166.pdf, is a research report that covers the background to this situation cogently and broadly.
2. "Revolt of the Admirals," *Time*, October 17, 1949.
3. Statement of Fred M. Trapnell, Captain, United States Navy, Commanding Officer, U.S. Naval Air Test Center, Patuxent River, Maryland, before the Armed Services Committee of the House of Representatives investigating the B-36 and related matters, Wednesday, October 8, 1949, FMT.
4. "Bane and Chanute Awards Presented to Air Force and Navy Pilots: The Octave Chanute Award for 1949," *IAS News*, July 1949. *IAS News* was the newsletter for the Institute of Aeronautical Science, now the American

Institute of Aeronautics and Astronautics. The full citation reads: "Capt. Frederick M. Trapnell . . . received The Octave Chanute Award for 1949 for his contributions to flight testing of experimental aircraft, with particular reference to operating requirements for carrier-based jet propelled airplanes.

Capt. Trapnell has been responsible for the prosecution of the aviation test program of the Bureau of Aeronautics and has reviewed all projects under study and test at Patuxent. He has demonstrated an outstanding ability not only in flying all types of aircraft but also in detecting critical deficiencies in new airplanes after only one or two brief flights and in suggesting improvements that will remove these deficiencies. Through him, a highly efficient test organization has evolved at Patuxent which is developing many new techniques and methods for the scientific analysis of flight test data.

The Navy was faced with an extremely serious problem of operating jet aircraft from aircraft carriers. Capt. Trapnell, on his own initiative, proposed and undertook an accelerated evaluation program in which he personally flew every available new aircraft. He also made positive technical recommendations so thorough and complete that the boundaries of this major problem were completely defined. By his individual effort he tremendously expedited the use of jet propelled aircraft on aircraft carriers."

5. Burke, letter to author, March 18, 1975, edited with permission for clarity: "Testing and analyzing new aircraft requires high skill, great sensitivity, great knowledge, superb flying ability, and understanding of the problems involved; but it also requires youth. Trap was 48 years old, but he still loved flying more than anything else and preferred to do the flying himself. Other jobs that he was assigned were interesting and he did them extremely well, but it was with great reluctance that he found his other duties would not permit him to fly as much as he wanted to or to experiment with new airplanes as he would like to do."

6. "USS *Coral Sea*," historical Report, Jan 1, 1950–June 30, 1950, NHHC.

7. Capt. J. S. Russell to commander Air Force, U.S. Atlantic Fleet, from commanding officer, USS *Coral Sea*, "Aircraft Operations with Air Group SEVENTEEN," memo, March 29, 1951, NHHC. In this memo, Russell, who succeeded Trap as skipper of that carrier, wrote describing a number of innovations implemented on board the ship under Trap's command, saying, "In this type of launch no time is wasted waiting for airplanes to taxi up to the takeoff spot. The time consumed plugging in rockets is

halved, because two airplanes can be plugged in at the same time. A mixed deck load is normally launched with a 10 to 12 second average intervals, but launch intervals as low as 7 seconds have been attained."

8. Robert L. Lawson, *Carrier Air Group Commanders: The Men And Their Machines* (Atglen, Pa.: Schiffer Military History, 2000), 73–74, under "CDR. William H. Leonard, Rear Adm., USN (Ret.)." CDR Pete Clayton, USN, with Tobert J. Cressman, "More Than Just a Ship . . . USS *Coral Sea* (CV-43), 1946–1990," *The Hook – Journal of Carrier Aviation*, Spring 1990, http://www.usscoralsea.net/pages/mtjas.php.

9. Trapnell's flight logs, consolidated counts by the author, FMT.

Chapter 17. Legacy

1. Vice Adm. Donald D. Engen, USN (Ret.), interview by Paul Stillwell, September 16, 1994, interview 3, transcript, U.S. Naval Institute Oral History, U.S. Naval Institute, Annapolis, Md. In September 1994, in his oral history, Engen called Trap the "godfather of current naval aviation." At the time, Engen had been chief of the Federal Aviation Administration and was designated to become director of the National Air and Space Museum (Smithsonian), but he was killed in a glider accident before he could assume that post.

2. Sherby, personal narrative.

3. Lacouture, "When Fish Could Fly," 81–83.

Epilogue

1. "Robert Pirie, 84, Dies—Retired Vice Admiral," *New York Times*, January 12, 1990, http://www.nytimes.com/1990/01/12/obituaries/robert-pirie-84-dies-retired-vice-admiral.html, accessed July 2, 2014.

2. "Thomas Connolly, 86, Top-Gun Admiral, Dies," *New York Times*, June 9, 1996, http://www.nytimes.com/1996/06/09/us/thomas-connolly-86-top-gun-admiral-dies.html, accessed July 2, 2014.

3. Sherby, personal narrative.

4. Carl and Tillman, *Pushing the Envelope*, 97, 110; Paula Smith (executive director, Society of Experimental Test Pilots, Lancaster, California), e-mail to author, July 29, 2011.

5. Hyatt and Davis, *Winners' Viewpoints*, chap. 3.

6. Hyland, Oral History, vol. 1, 2–4; "Highly decorated retired Adm. John J. Hyland dies," *Honolulu Star Bulletin*, October 28, 1998, http://archives.starbulletin.com/98/10/28/news/obits.html.

7. "Corwin H. 'Corky' Meyer 1920–2011," *Test & Research Pilots, Flight Test Engineers*, September 27, 2005, http://thetartanterror.blogspot.com/2005/09/corwin-h-corky-meyer-1920.html, accessed July 2, 2014.

8. Barrett Tillman, "Where Are They Now: Bob Elder," *The Hook – Journal of Carrier Aviation* (Fall 1989): 12–16; Robert Elder, personal conversation with the author.

9. Trapnell's Golden Eagles certificate, FMT.

10. Trapnell to Ray E. Tenhoff, executive advisor, SETP, October 23, 1957, FMT.

11. U.S. Naval Aviation Hall of Honor, enshrinement ceremony program, Pensacola, Fla., May 8, 1986, FMT.

INDEX

ABOUT THE AUTHORS

Frederick M. "Fritz" Trapnell Jr. had a fifty-year career in computer and software engineering and engineering management, starting with IBM and retiring in 2007 from Hewlett-Packard. He is a lifelong aviation enthusiast with a special affection for naval aviation. He lives with his wife in Los Altos, California.

Dana Trapnell Tibbitts began her career as a writer and media relations professional at UCLA in 1980 and continued to work in higher education, media, and the arts for much of the next three decades. The stories of ordinary and extraordinary people inspire much of her work as a writer and teacher of biography in Lake Tahoe, Nevada.